Entrepreneurship

Entrepreneurship:
An international perspective

Alison Morrison
Editor

OXFORD BOSTON JOHANNESBURG MELBOURNE NEW DELHI SINGAPORE

Butterworth-Heinemann
Linacre House, Jordan Hill, Oxford OX2 8DP
225 Wildwood Avenue, Woburn, MA 01801-2041
A division of Reed Educational and Professional Publishing Ltd

℞ A member of the Reed Elsevier plc group

First published 1998

British Library Cataloguing in Publication Data
Entrepreneurship: an international perspective
  1. Entrepreneurship   2. Entrepreneurship – Cross-cultural studies
  I. Morrison, Alison
  338'.04

ISBN 0 7506 3825 7

Typeset by Avocet Typeset, Brill, Aylesbury, Bucks
Printed and Bound in Great Britain by Martins the Printers, Berwick-upon-Tweed

Contents

Contents

Contents

Contributors

Editor

Alison Morrison is a Lecturer specializing in entrepreneurship within the tourism industry at the Strathclyde Business School, University of Strathclyde, Glasgow, Scotland. She has an MSc in Entrepreneurial Studies and her PhD thesis was based on small firm strategic alliances. In addition, she has been an entrepreneur in her own right for twenty years.

Contributing authors

Fatima Allie is the Deputy Head of the Centre for Entrepreneurship at the Graduate Business School of the University of Stellenbosch, South Africa.

Aleke Dondo is the Deputy Managing Director of the Microfinance Research and Innovation Division, Kenya Rural Enterprise Programme, Nairobi, Kenya.

Miroslav Glas is a Doctor of Economics within the Faculty of Economics, University of Ljubljana, Ljubljana, Slovenia.

Linda Human is the Professor of People Management at the Graduate School of Business, University of Stellenbosch, South Africa and a Visiting Fellow of Goree Institute, Senegal.

Antero Koskinen is the Director of the Small Business Center of the Helsinki School of Economics and Business Administration, Mikkeli, Finland.

Susan Laing is a Senior Lecturer and Director of the Centre for Entrepreneurship at Napier University, Edinburgh, Scotland.

Frank Martin is a Senior Teaching Fellow within the Department of Entrepreneurship at the University of Stirling, Stirling, Scotland.

Mwangi Ngumo is the Executive Director of the Kenya Institute of Management, Nairobi, Kenya.

Rafael Alcaraz Rodriguez is the Director of the Entrepreneurial Program at Monterrey Institute of Technology, Mexico.

Wee-Liang Tan is a Senior Lecturer in the Division of Marketing and Tourism Management within the Business School, Nanyang Technological University Singapore. He is also Director of the Entrepreneurship Development Centre at the University.

Markku Virtanen is the Development Director at the Small Business Center, Helsinki School of Economics and Business Administration, Mikkeli, Finland.

Harold Welsch holds the Coleman Foundation Professor of Entrepreneurship at DePaul University, Chicago, USA.

Dianne Wingham is Principal Researcher and founding entrepreneur of M.D. Wingham Consultants, Bicton, Australia.

Foreword

For over two decades I have had an almost daily involvement with entrepreneurship around the world. This involvement has included serving as the International President of the International Council for Small Business and as its Executive Director since 1987. These roles and other activities have enabled me to personally experience first-hand the roles of entrepreneurship in every one of the areas of the world presented in this book. It is this experience and passion for global entrepreneurship that caused me to eagerly read and then reread the manuscript of *Entrepreneurship: An international perspective*.

Alison Morrison's vision of such an undertaking is to be admired and the resulting book is outstanding. She and her distinguished group of contributors successfully capture the similarities and differences of the entrepreneurial role and processes of these countries. The attention provided to cultural issues and to economic development programmes designed to foster entrepreneurship in the various countries is thorough and interestingly presented. Furthermore, the case studies allow the concepts, issues and programmes described to become 'flesh and blood' and greatly enhance the understanding of the background material provided.

I believe that readers throughout the world with a wide variance in educational background, work experience and purpose for reading this book will all benefit greatly from the efforts of the authors. Indeed, I expect that many will, like me, finish reading the book and immediately read it a second time to gain an even greater appreciation of the complexities of the cultural and economic issues that impact on entrepreneurial endeavours around our ever shrinking world.

Robert H. Brockhaus, PhD
Coleman Foundation Chair in Entrepreneurship and
Director, Jefferson Smurfit Center for Entrepreneurial Studies
Saint Louis University, Missouri, USA.

Preface

Entrepreneurship: An International Perspective was born out of the IntEnt96 Conference in the Netherlands which brought together persons interested and involved in entrepreneurship education. From discussion, within this international forum, it was clear that there are distinct differences in the extent to which entrepreneurial behaviour in different societies and geographic regions is stimulated. Furthermore, while there has been considerable interest in entrepreneurship internationally, the relationship between the environment in a country, embodying the cultural, economic and regulatory factors, has not been the subject of extensive study.

I strongly believe that if the 'discipline' which has become entrepreneurship is to survive and flourish we need to know more about these differences, rather than concentrating on globalized, conglomerate, sanitized similarities. The pivotal question which must be asked is: what is more important, the consolidation of existing knowledge and understanding into an easy to understand 'academic' package, or the need for more knowledge of a richer, more intense variety which further illuminates and enhances understanding of the subject area? It is believed that *Entrepreneurship: An International Perspective* provides that beacon of illumination relative to entrepreneurship at a subgeographic region level, and enhances our understanding and knowledge of this extremely human and cultural phenomenon. However, it is acknowledged that even the particularistic approach adopted in this text is in danger of being overly generalistic.

Aims

The specific aims of the text are to:

- highlight issues generally associated with entrepreneurship internationally;
- illuminate the factors which contribute to the promotion and/or inhibition of entrepreneurship within specific societies and geographic subregions;
- combine and consolidate these illuminations through analysis to identify common themes and peculiarities;
- progress understanding of cultural issues related to the process of entrepreneurship internationally.

Structure of the text

Entrepreneurship: An international perspective has a structure which incorporates one introductory chapter, nine country-specific chapters, and a final consolidating chapter. Chapter 1 introduces the reader to the subject area, investigating the process of entrepreneurship, and the features and attributes which make or shape entrepreneurs. This serves to clearly contextualize the associated theoretical frameworks and research approaches prior to reading the country-specific chapters. Chapters 2 to 10 adopt a thematic approach in the provision of country-specific accounts of what promotes and/or inhibits entrepreneurial behaviour within their respective societies and geographic locations. Each chapter is prefaced by a summary of key features, and terminated with a case study which focuses upon the background, activities and environment of practising entrepreneurs. The case studies are reviewed using the approaches developed by Cooper (1966) and Timmons (1994) which are introduced in Chapter 1. The final chapter uses the metaphor of the '*tree of entrepreneurship*' to analyse, consolidate and illustrate the material presented in the foregoing chapters.

Readership

The text has been written for a wide international readership. It will appeal to students of entrepreneurship and academics involved in the educational process, and small business advisers and policy-makers in agencies charged with creating the conditions conducive to stimulating entrepreneurship. Furthermore, it has application to the understanding of cultural issues which would be of interest to practitioners in the field. The attraction to both academia and practitioners is further enhanced through the presentation of case studies which effectively marry the practical realities of entrepreneurial behaviour to theoretical, social and economic constructs.

Acknowledgement

Finally, I wish to express my sincere gratitude to the authors who have contributed to *Entrepreneurship: An international perspective*, all of whom were enthusiastic collaborators in this ambitious project. They put their faith in me and I am now delighted, and considerably relieved, to have turned my own 'entrepreneurial dream' into a reality on their behalf.

Dr Alison Morrison
Strathclyde Business School
University of Strathclyde
Glasgow

1

An introduction to entrepreneurship

Alison Morrison

Introduction

This chapter introduces the subject area of entrepreneurship and explores associated issues. It begins by considering the process of entrepreneurship, and features and attributes that transform ordinary people into entrepreneurial persons. This provides a summary of the current state of knowledge relating to entrepreneurship. In addition, it serves to clarify the associated theoretical frameworks and research approaches which will enable a greater depth of understanding of key issues which emerge from reading the following thematic country-specific chapters.

The process of entrepreneurship

According to Fass and Scothorne (1990) the process of entrepreneurship is recognized as being at the heart of an economic development task and driven by the motivations of individuals, who are seeking to satisfy their personal goals. As such, the ultimate aim of economic development is to create opportunities for personal fulfilment through economic activity. This implies a partnership between policy-makers and entrepreneurs in order to achieve economic renewal and prosperity. However, there is no universally accepted definition of what constitutes entrepreneurship, and traditionally attempts have been made to describe it relative to: an economic function; ownership structure; degrees of entrepreneurship; size and life-cycle of firm; and as a resource base.

It is not considered to be a productive pursuit to attempt to pigeonhole the process of entrepreneurship relative to any one specific perspective. The process is much more holistic and dynamic in nature. At the heart are entrepreneurs, their persistent search for opportunities, and their efforts to marshal the resources needed to realize them. The essence of entrepreneurship is the initiation of change, through creation and/or innovation. This is described by Drucker (1986) as the effort to create purposeful, focused change in a firm's *economic* or *social* potential, plus the application of distinct entrepreneurial strategies and entrepreneurial management. This perspective is significant in that it serves to emphasize the creation of both material and immaterial wealth.

Curran and Burrows (1986, p. 269) contribute to this clarification by describing the process of entrepreneurship as:

The innovatory process involved in the creation of an economic enterprise based on a new product or service which differs significantly from products or services in the way its production is organised, or in its marketing

The importance of this characterization is that it moves the discussion away from the confines of small, owner-managed businesses to that of concepts and theories that can be applied to any economic enterprise. It progresses our understanding to a more all-embracing concept of entrepreneurship which has no reverence for business size, stage in the life-cycle of the firm, or organizational ownership structure. Instead the focus is on innovation and the creation of economic enterprise.

Table 1.1 summarizes the different definition approaches and associated features which are generally identified with the process of entrepreneurship.

Table 1.1 Process of entrepreneurship: defenition approaches and features

Approaches	*Features*
Economic function	• Personal initiative of entrepreneur • Risk-bearing function • Harnessing of factors of production
Ownership structure	• Creation of business with entrepreneur as founder
Degrees of entrepreneurship	• Size of firm • Personal financial risk • Creativity and innovation • Growth realization
Resource base	• Primordial to potential production process
Size and life-cycle of firm	• Association with young start-up firm
Consolidation approach	• Conditions of uncertainty and competition • Entrepreneurial management and strategy • Initiation of change • Innovatory process • Ownership, structure and size of firm irrelevant • Personal initiative through the spirit of enterprise

Sources: Cantillon (1755); Say (1800); Gilder (1971); Kirzner (1979); Kirzner (1980), Curran and Burrows (1986); Drucker (1986); Dale (1991).

This leads the author to assert that the process of entrepreneurship has its foundations in both concept and theory, and person and intuition. Unquestionably, at the heart is a human creative act that initiates economic activity and applies the associated management practices. Without such action there is no entrepreneurship. In this respect Kirzner (1979), believes the source to be within the human spirit that will flourish in response to uncertainty and competition. This enterprising spirit is described in inspirational terms by Gilder (1971, p. 258) as:

The spirit of enterprise wells up from the wisdom of ages and the history (of the West) and infuses the most modern of technological adventures. It joins the old and new frontiers. It asserts a firm hierarchy of values and demands a hard discipline. It requires a life of labor and listening, aspiration and courage. But it is the source of all we are and can become, the saving grace of democratic politics and free men, the hope of the poor and the obligation of the fortunate, the redemption of an oppressed and desperate world.

Thus, it is concluded that entrepreneurship is about more than an economic function. The essence is the application of innovatory management processes, directed at bringing about change of both a social and economic nature. The key to unlocking the potential of entrepreneurship lies within the individual members of society, and the degree to which the spirit of enterprise exists or can be stimulated. Furthermore, without this personal initiative the process of entrepreneurship is a non-starter.

Entrepreneurship in perspective

It is important to recognize that such definitions present a somewhat biased, idealist vision of entrepreneurship, which assumes that all intentions of entrepreneurship are morally sound and socially responsible. Entrepreneurship is concerned with the initiation of change. As such, it challenges, and perhaps destroys, the established order and the complacency of traditional social and economic systems. Furthermore, Gilder (1971) emphasizes that one of the key principles of entrepreneurship is the absence of clear and fast rules. With no rulebook to control the *game* that is entrepreneurship it is inevitable that there will be winners, losers and unruly behaviour. Consequently, it would be delusory to accept that all outcomes from the process of entrepreneurship will be positive, even if it is hoped that any, in Schumpterian (1934) terms, 'destruction' will be creative.

In addition, we must question the reality of why persons enter into entrepreneurship. Such persons are in fact 'buying' personal independence and control through the process of new venture creation. In this respect, entrepreneurship may be seen as an aspect of the theory of choice (Reid and Jacobsen, 1988). The insinuation of the freedom of this choice must be queried. Frequently, the truth is that in a situation of high unemployment, and/or other deprivations of a social or economic nature, persons are frequently forced to *choose* entrepreneurship as the only alternative to no job and no income. In this scenario individuals may be *pushed* into entrepreneurship. This moves discussion of entrepreneurship into a choice between earning money or not earning – starving or eating. Thus, it is important to recognize that the routes towards entrepreneurship may be various – a response to a crisis situation, exploitation of a market opportunity, or both.

Entrepreneurs

While it is a historical fact that there have always been entrepreneurs in societies across the globe, what is different today is the high esteem in which they are generally held in most countries. Culturally, being an entrepreneur has gradually become socially and economically legitimate. Furthermore, entrepreneurs are frequently exhibited as role models worthy of emulation, and associated with positive connotations, such as spirit, zeal and creativity. Burns (1991) goes as far as commenting that it would appear that the whole of the Western world is in the middle of a *love affair* with entrepreneurs. Moreover, they are presented as *economic heroes* (Cannon, 1991), combining the ability to innovate and challenge the established equilibrium of economy and society while in the process of recreating it.

So what characteristics are generally taken to define such extraordinary human beings? Indeed, we must consider if they are indeed extraordinary. Certainly, internationally we can see that many of today's dominant corporations, have been spawned by individuals with vision and, importantly, the commitment to turn that vision into a reality. What they have in common is that they saw an opportunity, commercialized it, and in the process created wealth and jobs that, hopefully, benefit the rest of society. Such entrepreneurs are people who have the courage and self-belief to turn their dreams into realities. Furthermore, they permeate all levels of society and every walk of life.

As is the case with entrepreneurship, a universally acceptable definition of an entrepreneur has still to be invented. A general conclusion, from a review of entrepreneurship literature, is that there are as many definitions as there are entrepreneurs! For example, the word is defined by the Oxford English Dictionary as:

> … a person who attempts to profit by risk and initiative.

A descriptive approach towards definition is presented by Richard Branson, of Virgin Management Limited (Anderson, 1995, p. 3) as:

> I am often asked what it is to be an 'entrepreneur' and there is no simple answer. It is clear that successful entrepreneurs are vital for a healthy, vibrant and competitive economy. If you look around you, most of the largest companies have their foundations in one or two individuals who have the determination to turn a vision into reality.

Perhaps, Pearce (1980) is astute in utilizing a metaphor comparing entrepreneurs with bees to describe what they do. He believes that, in most respects, entrepreneurs are ordinary human beings, seeking to do good for themselves in terms of material gain and social status. In the process they are unwitting catalysts, as with bees whose strictly private activities are the first cause of almost everything else, as their honey-seeking serves to pollinate. Thus, entrepreneurs can be regarded as first among equals in the process of wealth creation. In creating their own wealth, entrepreneurs also 'pollinate', generating wealth creation opportunities for others, and with the potential to bring about positive social consequences in the wider society.

Typologies and categorization

The admission that there is no universally acceptable definition contributes to the elusive nature of an entrepreneur. Furthermore, the imagery in the popular press with the entrepreneur as a 'hero' tends to result in an eulogistic aura which often obscures our understanding. However, given the premium which society is placing on the role of the entrepreneur as the saviour of economic and social systems, it is understandable that researchers are consumed with the desire to identify what makes or moulds this precious resource. As a result, researchers are continuously seeking to explore the forces which shape the values, attitudes and approaches to life which lead certain people to take on the challenges of initiating, organizing or developing activities associated with the process of entrepreneurship.

In an attempt to clarify the phenomenon, a number of researchers have developed typologies aiming to distinguish entrepreneurs from the remainder of the population. This has generally been approached from the following seven stances:

1 Managerial orientation and vocational attachment, i.e. traditional, technocentric, marketeers, isolationist (Goss, 1991).
2 Business format, i.e. craftsperson, self-employed, small business, growth, corporate venture (Smith, 1967).
3 Management style behaviour, i.e. entrepreneur, quasi-entrepreneur, administrator, caretaker (Stevenson *et al.*, 1989).
4 Stage model relative to the development of the business, i.e. start-up, post-start-up, established, professionally managed (Chell *et al.*, 1991).
5 Growth orientation, i.e. declining, plateauing, rejuvenating, expanding (Chell *et al.*, 1991).
6 Social variables, i.e. first generation, descendant of founder, social class, minority group, female (Stanworth and Gray, 1991).
7 Degree of dependence on other firms, i.e. dependent, competitive dependent, old dependent, new independent, franchise (Rainnie, 1989).

These typologies represent a mixture of foci on the associated business, management and entrepreneurial characteristics. Such typologies are useful in that they draw attention to the essential heterogeneity of entrepreneurs. Different motives, aspirations, characteristics and activities co-exist underneath a common banner. This alerts us to the danger of being overly generalistic when debating who entrepreneurs are, what they do, and how they function. The risk is that the associated labelling and terminology may be misleading, or lead to attempts to pigeon-hole hypothetical stereotypical entrepreneurs who do not exist in reality.

Research debate

Further research debate tends to focus on four key questions, which over recent times have become embedded in entrepreneurship literature. They ask whether entrepreneurs are:

- Agents central to economic development?
- A breed of individuals that are born not made?
- Formed through exposure to social influence?
- A combination of economic agent, born and made?

Each of these questions is now addressed.

Economic agents?

Key contemporary economic writers who have contributed to the development of views on the role and concept of the entrepreneur have been identified by Deakins

(1996) as Say, Kirzner, Schumpeter, Knight, Shackle and Casson. Each approach the issue from different traditions, which results in inconsistent treatment of the role of the entrepreneur. Their initial preoccupation, which has since been questioned, was with risk-taking and decision-making in conditions of uncertainty, as being fundamental to entrepreneurial behaviour. From their work Chell *et al.* (1991) conclude that there has been a gradual increasing awareness of the role of the entrepreneur in economic growth, with various approaches being used to explain motivation. However, there is still no agreement as to whether entrepreneurs serve an economic equilibrium or disruptive function.

Born not made?

Are we to sit around powerless until some mother gives birth to the next Bill Gates, Conrad Hilton or Walt Disney? This was certainly the perspective adopted in early studies of the origins of the entrepreneur, which concentrated almost entirely upon the in-born personalities and motivations of the entrepreneur. This approach assumed that the entrepreneurial flair, the ability to take risks, and the desire to create a business were inherent in the individual – that he or she was born with these characteristics in place. This would be exhibited in the form of personality traits. Such a trait model of behaviour argues that there exists a single trait, or cluster of traits, in the personality of the entrepreneur that differentiates him or her from others. (A trait is a persisting dimension or characteristic of the personality.) Examples of genetically bound traits generally associated with entrepreneurs are presented by various authors as summarized in Table 1.2.

Table 1.2 Genetically bound entrepreneurial traits generally associated with entrepreneurs

Alert to opportunities
Anxiety/Neuroticism
Creativity
Decisive
Easily bored
Flair and vision
Independent nature
Inner locus of control
Innovatory tendency
Leadership aspiration
Need to achieve
Risk-taking propensity
Self-confidence
Self-motivation
Self-realization through action
Versatile

Sources: McClelland (1961); Baty (1990); Brockhaus and Horwitz (1986); Schumpeter (1934); Chell, Haworth and Brearley (1991).

Whether a clearly definable entrepreneurial personality actually exists remains the subject of controversy. Furthermore, many of the identified entrepreneurial characteristics are the same abilities and skills that could be applied to most successful people (Chell *et al.*, 1991), such as Olympic athletes, or leading politicians. It just so happens that the individual has chosen the arena of business as a means of self-satisfaction. McClelland (1961), a leading academic in this field, implicitly rejects the *born not made* model. Furthermore, Deakins (1996) identifies problems associated with attempting to measure personality characteristics as:

- they are not stable and change over time;
- judgements are generally subjective;
- measurement ignores cultural and environmental influences;
- the role of education, learning and training in the entrepreneurial process is overlooked;
- issues such as gender, age, social class and education which can have a bearing on the propensity of an individual to enter entrepreneurship are ignored.

Thus, while it is clear that a number of the identified traits can be associated with entrepreneurial behaviour, they do not explain why the individual chooses to apply them within an entrepreneurial context.

Formed through exposure to social influences?

This approach does not ignore the personality trait model, but advances discussion through linking it to the social context of the individual. This represents a social psychological perspective that is interested in relationships between the individual and society in general. Approaches adopted to research from this perspective focus on the formative role of social influence in developing entrepreneurial tendencies. Furthermore, it has been suggested (Carter and Cachon, 1988) that entrepreneurs often share common features and experiences of a social context, which distinguish them from other individuals. For instance, ethnic minority groups, family businesses, and female self-employed. These are termed as antecedent influences and this thinking contributes to the social development model of the entrepreneur.

Kets de Vries offers an extreme generalization regarding the social development of entrepreneurs. A persistently controversial author, he is quoted as follows (1977, p. 49):

> … due to the frustrations and perceived deprivations experienced in the early stages of life, a prominent pattern among entrepreneurs appears to be a sense of impulsivity, a persistent feeling of dissatisfaction, rejection and pointlessness, forces which contribute to an impairment and depreciation of his sense of self-esteem and affect cognitive processes. The entrepreneur is a man under great stress, continuously badgered by his past, a past which is experienced and re-experienced in fantasies, daydreams, and dreams. These dreams and fantasies often have a threatening content due to the recurrence of feelings of anxiety and guilt which mainly revolve around hostile wishes against parental figures, or more generally, all individuals in a position of authority …

So there we have it! According to de Vries it is the formative role of family background and other deprivations which shape, what he describes as, the somewhat deviant personality to be found in entrepreneurs! In his opinion, it is a personality that is insecure and unable to operate effectively in an imposed and structured environment.

Kets de Vries's perspective represents an extreme interpretation that is unlikely to fit entrepreneurs in general. Academics are generally uncomfortable with this model, as it reduces our understanding of the entrepreneur to a deviant, who is a misfit in conventional organizational life. Chell *et al.* (1991) emphasizes that deviant or marginal characters exist in the population at large in the form of, for example, pop stars, tramps, drop-outs. Thus, this certainly cannot be regarded as a necessary condition for becoming an entrepreneur. Furthermore, successful entrepreneurs have proven capable of succeeding within existing frameworks of society. This presupposes that their behaviour is innovative and constructive, rather than deviant and destructive. Viewed from this perspective, the entrepreneur can be a productive member of society, and according to Jennings *et al.* (1994, p. 144) they are:

> … truly well adjusted individuals, in harmony with the environment and community, do not need to achieve great things but simply their own ambitions.

Human nature is such that we can rarely remain untouched by daily exposure to a range of values, situations and experiences. Every day individuals are meeting people and dealing with experiences which will influence their behaviour, attitudes and values. People live in the real world, not in a vacuum. Each person has their own life story to tell, of the experiences that have shaped, inspired and deflated them at different points in time. What is important then, is not to generalize that entrepreneurs can be categorized as resulting from being processed through a specific social development model. Life is not that simple. It can be concluded that the factors identified in Table 1.3 will surely have had an influence in the development of entrepreneurial behaviour, as they will in having developed a whole range of other behaviours which human beings exhibit.

This model is considered to be useful in that it situates individuals within their social contexts, working through personal transitions to satisfy their changing goals, needs and ambitions at particular points in the life-cycle. In this way we seek to understand the persistence of entrepreneurial action over time in some people, and how such action may be triggered on or off as the entrepreneur moves in and out of their various societal and life-cycle transitions.

Table 1.3 summarizes the influences that are generally associated with the social development model of entrepreneurial behaviour.

Table 1.3 Social influences on entrepreneurial behaviour

Availability of appropriate role models
Career experience over life-cycle
Deprived social upbringing
Family background
Family position
Inheritance of entrepreneurial tradition
Level of educational attainment
Negative/positive peer influence
Social marginality
Uncomfortable with large bureaucratic organizations

Sources: Collins and Moore (1964); Kets de Vries (1977); Chell et al. (1991); Timmons (1994); Deakins (1996).

Economic agent, born and made?

From the foregoing it is clear that the entrepreneur as an economic agent, both born *and* made represents a enlightening perspective. Cooper (1966) assists in this consolidation bringing together the various factors which have been identified as contributory to entrepreneurial behaviour. He classifies them into three distinct groups:

- **Entrepreneur**: economically active, in possession of certain genetically bound traits, subjected to a continuous social development process including the many aspects of his or her background which affect motivations, perceptions, skills and knowledge.
- **Organization**: within which the entrepreneur has previously been working, whose characteristics influence the location and the nature of new firms, as well as the likelihood of spin-off effects. This represents the concept of apprenticeship (Timmons, 1994), and can be an integral part in the process of shaping an entrepreneurial career. Thus, the part played by incubator organizations, and entrepreneur role models is significant.
- **Various environmental factors**: external to the individual and his or her organization, which make the climate more or less favourable to the birth of a new venture. Clearly factors at work in the environment external to the firm, such as cultural values, educational opportunities, unemployment and the economy, will impact in terms of the available volume of opportunities and resources, and the nature of consumer demand. These combine to influence entrepreneurial activities and degrees of success achievable within certain markets and societies.

Cooper (1966) categorizes these three groups respectively as: antecedent influences; incubator organization; and environment factors (Table 1.4). In this way it is possible to investigate the range of influencing factors derived from the psychological make up of the entrepreneur, the social development process to which the entrepreneur has been party, and relevant environmental influences. Thus, it facilitates a more comprehensive understanding of the relationship between the internal, individual factors, and the external and social components.

The debate regarding the supremacy of these different research approaches continues, and each tends to have its individual champion. All contribute significantly in their own way, to enhancing understanding about who the entrepreneur is, what he or she does, and why they do it. Cooper's approach is in itself limiting. In particular it neglects to explicitly identify the role of culture and society in the stimulation or stifling of entrepreneurial behaviour. However, it does provide the insight that it is a range of complex factors impinging together which contribute to entrepreneurial behaviour. No one approach has the definite answer, but together they bring us close to some degree of understanding (Carson *et al.*, 1995). Thus, it is clear that any approach to defining what shapes an entrepreneur must work from a consolidation of understanding relative to a wide range of variables at work in society and the economy which influence entrepreneurial behaviour. In this way a more constructive, holistic perspective can be developed, rather than attempting to categorize according to one specific academic discipline.

Table 1.4 Factors contributing to entrepreneurial behaviour

Category	Factors
Antecedent influences	• Genetic • Family • Educational choices • Previous career experience
Incubator organization	• Geographic location • Nature of skills and knowledge acquired • Contact with possible fellow founders • Experience within a 'small business' setting
Environment factors	• Economic conditions • Accessibility and availability of venture capital • Examples of entrepreneurial action • Opportunities for interim consulting • Availability of personnel, supporting services, and accessibility of customers

Source: Cooper (1966).

Characteristics, features, attitudes and behaviours

Each of these research approaches has spawned the identification of a vast array of characteristics, features, attitudes and behaviours that are generally associated with defining entrepreneurs. Timmons (1994) assists our understanding in the production of a consensus around six dominant themes, which he calls *desirable and acquirable*. These are presented in Table 1.5. Timmons's approach represents an evolving view that variables might be more usefully studied in clusters or constellations. Moreover, it allows more people to be identified as potential entrepreneurs. Clearly, it would take a super-human being to excel across the full range of attitudes and behaviours associated with each theme. Some entrepreneurs will exhibit strengths in some dimensions that offset weaknesses in others.

Adopting Timmons's themes as a framework, each is discussed in a generalistic manner.

Commitment and determination

Entrepreneurs are generally committed and determined characters. They need these qualities to survive. This represents a positive approach to life, in part due to their high level of self-confidence. Commitment is demonstrated relative to intense dedication to the job. They work long hours and regard their firm as by far the most important element of their lives, with the possible exception of their families. Clearly, much of their personal fulfilment, and confirmation of their worth as successful individuals, comes from their dedication to the work ethic.

Table 1.5 Desirable and acquirable attitudes and behaviours

Theme	Attitude or behaviour
Commitment and determination	• Tenacity and decisiveness, able to decommit/commit quickly • Discipline • Persistence in solving problems • Willingness to undertake personal sacrifice • Total immersion
Leadership	• Self-starter; high standards but not perfectionist • Team builder and hero maker; inspires others • Treat others as you want to be treated • Share the wealth with all the people who helped to create it • Integrity and reliability; builder of trust; practices fairness • Not a lone wolf • Superior learner and teacher • Patience and urgency
Opportunity obsession	• Having intimate knowledge of customers' needs • Market driven • Obsessed with value creation and enhancement
Tolerance of risk, ambiguity, and uncertainty	• Calculated risk-taker • Risk minimizer • Risk sharer • Manages paradoxes and contradictions • Tolerance of uncertainty and lack of structure • Tolerance of stress and conflict • Ability to resolve problems and integrate solutions
Creativity, self-reliance and ability to adapt	• Non-conventional, open-minded, lateral thinker • Restlessness with status quo • Ability to adapt and change; creative problem-solver • Ability to learn quickly • Lack of fear of failure • Ability to conceptualize
Motivation to excel	• Goal-and-results orientation; high but realistic goals • Drive to achieve and grow • Low need for status and power • Interpersonally supporting • Aware of weakness and strengths • Having perspective and sense of humour

Source: Timmons (1994, p. 191).

Leadership

The leadership style will reflect the personality of the lead entrepreneur. Consequently, it can range from authoritarian to participative, however, the skills required are the same. These include the ability to select appropriate team members, communication, mediation, negotiation and persuasion skills. Furthermore, motivation and empowerment, and the sharing of credit for achievement with team members and/or employees is crucial. In this way, entrepreneurs appreciate their own strengths and weaknesses when it comes to managing the business. Moreover, they understand its future prospects depend on addressing existing skills and knowledge deficit through entrepreneurial teams and external networks. Building and developing such relationships to sustain an effective internal team requires strong leadership and vision.

Opportunity obsession

The entrepreneur is market driven, continuously seeking that one idea on which the window of opportunity is opening and which offers the prospects of a worthwhile return on effort and resources, for some time to come. The entrepreneur is steeped in the market and sensitive to the market challenges. They seek to grasp opportunities and have the innovative and creative skill to envision how it can be enhanced and value added. The outputs of this opportunity obsession are directed at self-actualization and the fulfilment of their ambitions.

Tolerance of risk, ambiguity, and uncertainty

The environment of the entrepreneur is characterized by ambiguity, inconsistencies and substantial knowledge. For many, such an environment would be unacceptable and debilitating. For the entrepreneur, in such dynamic change lies opportunity from which the potential degree of risk is evaluated. Potential risk takes the form of financial, and damage to personal standing and reputation. This is not only in the entrepreneur's own eyes but also in those of social peers. This results in a level of caution and measured calculation of the risk element involved in entrepreneurial decision making. Thus, it is helpful to regard entrepreneurs as risk-managers, rather than as risk-takers. In this role they deal with uncertainty by identifying, assessing, evaluating, managing and transferring risk. It is a systematic process, not a function left solely to chance, luck or the 'lottery' of life. This represents a critical entrepreneurial skill.

Creativity, self-reliance and ability to adapt

Entrepreneurs are creative and innovative. They are not constrained by existing systems, and challenge established procedures and assumptions. Thus, they often produce something new rather than just modifying what currently exists. Entrepreneurs combine these creative and innovative skills with the ability to analyse a problem and quickly reach an effective solution. Such problem solving is seen as a fundamental skill, often not highly intellectual or rational, but more intuitive in nature. Central to this theme is an entrepreneurial learning curve that involves an experiential iterative process. It is highly personal, established from observation and confirmation of both a positive and negative nature. Thus, the entrepreneur tends to act first and learn later from experiences of his or her actions. In this respect, Gilder (1971) asserts that entrepreneurs need a willingness to accept failure, learn from it, and act boldly in the shadows of doubt.

Motivation to excel

Entrepreneurs are ambitious individuals with a strong passion to achieve. They are highly proactive and respond to challenges with enthusiasm, self-confidence and the determination that they have the potential to excel – to win. This motivation is driven by a need to achieve a combination of personal and economic goals. Thus, in addition to business profitability, many measure their success by the degree to which an inner sense of achievement has been satisfied. As business persons, entrepreneurs are both goal and result oriented, setting ambitious but realistically *do-able* goals. While entrepreneurs seem to be motivated by a self-belief that they can succeed, that does not imply a complete lack of the *fear of failure*.

The foregoing discussion serves a purpose in that it provides a useful framework within which observers can search for key themes, attitude or behaviours which are generally accepted as depicting an entrepreneur and 'normal' entrepreneurial behaviour. However, four points have to be emphasized:

- the same framework could be used to identify high achievers in every sphere of life;
- for the six dominant themes and associated attitudes and behaviours specified here, there undoubtedly exists a whole set of the unspecified which entrepreneurs will exhibit over time to differing degrees;
- each entrepreneur will develop their own set in association with the particular influences which have shaped, and continues to shape, their social development;
- social development influences are not static, but are dynamic in nature as the human being continuously evolves and interacts with society.

Chapter summary

It has been established that the process of entrepreneurship is essentially a human creative act, to which the entrepreneur is central. Furthermore, to a significant extent, entrepreneurs are products of their society. Thus, responses to events that affect them will be influenced by the value system of the host society, earlier formative experiences, and the entrepreneur's personal characteristics. Moreover, individuals may enter into entrepreneurship due to factors at work within their social context, such as unemployment, family tradition, need for independence, and/or lack of personal or financial security.

Each of the following country-specific chapters brings alive the theories and approaches discussed in this chapter. They clearly and colourfully articulate the specific factors that make and shape entrepreneurs within their particular geographical and societal environment. As you would expect, each account and treatise is unique, reflecting the ethnicity and culture of their country, alongside the academic stance of the author. Every chapter commences with a summary of key features identified, and concludes with a case study which effectively illustrates the key issues raised the text. The case study is then reviewed using Cooper's and Timmons's approaches as presented in Tables 1.4 and 1.5, respectfully in this chapter.

Significant country specific peculiarities relative to the promotion and/or inhibition of entrepreneurial behaviour can be clearly identified. However, as will become obvious with reading, a number of common themes emerge which are central to the process of entrepreneurship across all the countries represented in this text. In Chapter 11 these factors are consolidated in the 'tree of entrepreneurship' which is used to symbolize the organic reality of the entrepreneurial process.

2

Africa: Kenya

Aleke Dondo and Mwangi Ngumo

Key feature summary

In general, Kenya does not have a culture that is strongly supportive of entrepreneurship. Key features affecting entrepreneurship are:

- Conformist behaviour is promoted through the formal education system and reinforced throughout family life.
- Communal and collective values in society do not promote individualistic wealth creation and resource deployment activities.
- Short-term planning horizons and an attitude of 'living for the moment' permeates, rather than considering long-term business investment and development.
- A society in which respect for seniority and authority dominates diminishing the capabilities for creativity, independent thought and action.
- A reluctance to accept responsibility for the negative outcomes of any endeavours which are generally explained away as caused by an 'act of God', evil spirits, or some other form of divine intervention.
- Strong tribal identification leads to inter-tribe trading, employment and decision-making procedures which diminish the potential of entrepreneurial businesses.

Introduction

Kenya is a country rich in a culture that spawns a significant range of values, attitudes and beliefs. Furthermore, while these are deeply rooted in tradition, their effect is just as pervasive and strong within today's world. Moreover, the durability of the culture is significant, as communities become more fragmented as kinsmen migrate away from ancestral homes to more economically fertile rural and urban locations. This chapter presents a sensitive and comprehensive insight into the contribution that the Kenyan culture makes to entrepreneurial behaviour. The case study is based on Ann David, who is remarkable as a female entrepreneur in a male-dominated industry sector. She represents the new generation of entrepreneurs who recognize the importance of life-long learning, specifically related to planning and financial control capabilities.

The authors of this chapter feel that it is important to emphasize at the outset that Kenya, like the rest of Africa, is composed of different ethnic groups and subethnic groups with the latter totalling 18. Each group would no doubt totally disagree that they shared anything in common with each other. The Maasai who are Prairie Nilotics would disagree vehemently that they have anything in common with the Luo who are Lake Nilotics, or the Kalenjin who are Highland Nilotics. On the other hand, the Embu would hate to be likened to the Kikuyu or the Kamba, although a number of their cultural practices are similar. In fact, each of tribe has something 'in common' with another tribe, and many other things 'not in common'. Attempting, therefore, to talk about Kenyans, or worse still Africans, as if they were one is a hazardous business. Thus, the perspective presented in this chapter is largely based on the authors' own observations and experiences within Kenya, rather than an exchange of literature and research findings.

Theory and reality debated

The entrepreneur has always been an enigma in theories of economic development. The entrepreneur is, to economists, the fourth factor of production and the person responsible for bringing land, labour and capital together for the purposes of generating economic wealth. The traditional Western economic view of the reward for this role is profit, or relative to many African communities, a surplus that is to be used for the benefit of the whole community.

Entrepreneurs innovate, manage labour forces, open up new markets, find new ways of combining inputs, and respond to market signals quickly. The modern literature, for example, Timmons (1994) on entrepreneurship lists among the essential character traits: a high need to achieve; a preponderance to take calculated risks; self-confidence; persistence; leadership; ability to influence people; and so on. Although it may be true that many of the most successful entrepreneurs do exhibit all these qualities, there is also a larger pool of more modest entrepreneurs starting and running businesses on the strength of only a few of these traits.

In recent years, the entrepreneur has moved to centre stage in the field of small enterprise development. To a certain extent, the pioneering work of McClelland in India in the 1960s and 1970s contributed to this. The main, simple, theory behind much of his work was that if economic development is more rapid in communities that have a higher proportion of entrepreneurs, then economic development can be increased by stimulating entrepreneurship. McClelland (1961) designed a series of structured learning experiences that were aimed at stimulating the need to use entrepreneurial behaviour. The result, it was postulated, was enhanced entrepreneurship. These findings led to the proliferation of thousands of Entrepreneurship Development Programmes (EDPs) throughout India and South East Asia.

While this was going on in Asia something different was happening in Africa. Private entrepreneurship was considered with suspicion. It was associated with repression and the dominance of the indigenous by the non-indigenous. At the same time in Europe and the USA, the post-war boom led to a rapid growth in their public sector organizations. Since Africa received almost all of its aid from these countries, it was natural that most of it was directed at building up its public sector. The African answer to entrepreneurship was parasitical. The few programmes that were directed at generating indigenous entrepreneurship smothered the would-be entrepreneur with so much free assistance that dependency relationships were established instead of the desired self-reliance.

The authors question what the entrepreneurship theoretical perspectives really have got to do with: the ability of Ethiopian refugees in Kenya to become more capable to help themselves; helping the Akamba wood carvers to achieve a richer life; assisting a Kikuyu trader to develop his or her business; finding more outlets for graduate talent in Africa so that the young become more directly involved in wealth generation; and supporting millions of small business people around the world?

Of all issues that have fascinated scholars and practitioners of small enterprise development, none seems to stand out more than the issue of whether entrepreneurs are born or made. What has not been an issue, however, is the fact that societies that are successful do seem to have a mass of people who exhibit certain entrepreneurial characteristics, and therefore are regarded as having an enterprise culture. For the purposes of this chapter, we define an enterprise culture as:

> … that combination of factors that make a people intuitively respond in a positive manner to entrepreneurial behaviour.

While entrepreneurial behaviour is defined as:

> … a sum of activities that can reasonably be construed as likely to lead to greater and/or better results in any human endeavour, from playing football, to courtship, to running a business or the economy of a nation. So, an element of risk-taking, an element of drive, vision and planning will constitute part and parcel of this entrepreneurial behaviour.

Specifically, the questions that will be addressed in this chapter are whether the average Kenyan, were such a person to exist, could be regarded as one who portrays high entrepreneurial behaviour or not? Indeed, whether the Kenyan people, as a whole, exhibit an enterprise culture or not, if they could be made to act as one person? We shall also attempt to offer some views on whether there are any culture-specific constraints to enterprise development in Kenya.

Entrepreneurship in Kenya

In the 1950s and 1960s, it was regarded in society as impolite to be rich or to flout your wealth, perhaps because the majority of the population appeared to be poor. The average Kenyan felt that a rich man could be equated with a corrupt man, someone whose wealth had been obtained through devious means. The churches did not help to change this belief, with their incessant condemnation of the rich and their assertion that: 'it is easier for a camel to go through the eye of a needle than for a rich man to enter heaven'. In a country where a huge majority of the population are serious church-going people, no one knows what harm these messages were causing to Kenya's efforts to create enterprise, innovate and achieve. Those people who exhibited some entrepreneurial spirit were often rebuked, particularly in public, social places, while those who remained poor and generally unsuccessful were consoled since 'it was not their fault'.

It is our proposal that, to date, this 'anti-entrepreneurial' culture has not changed much. Generally, the Kenyan society does not encourage entrepreneurial thought and behaviour, such as risk-taking, good planning, assumption of responsibility, decisiveness, drive and foresight. Instead, it largely tends to encourage conformist behaviour, respect for seniority and authority, communal life and living for today. Kenyans strongly believe in God, or some other extraterrestrial force. What could, in other societies, be attributed to lack of foresight and good planning would in Kenyan society be attributed to an 'act of God', or some divine intervention, or even to a malicious external enemy with 'evil eyes'.

Dominant attitudes and beliefs

It is these types of attitudes, beliefs and consequent behaviour that have tended to constrain the development of entrepreneurship in Kenya and, perhaps, in the rest of Africa. We now look more closely at these factors.

Respect for seniority and authority

Over the generations in Kenya, the method of bringing up children has remained largely the same. This is a process through which a child is expected to learn from those who are older. Initiating and inculcating the 'right' behaviour is often achieved through the use of force or fear. It is accompanied by several stages of 'initiation' into older, more mature, groups. To date, therefore, the average Kenyan accepts and lives in awe of their seniors. This is whether that seniority is rightfully there or not, or whether it is being demonstrated, or is only perceived. It can emerge from age, and this was and still remains the most respected form of seniority, or it can emerge from formal education. A combination of seniority emanating from both age and education can result in tyranny on the side of one having this seniority, or in reverence on the side of one less 'senior'.

It is this 'seniority' that makes our educational institutions, particularly primary schools, very weak breeding grounds for future entrepreneurs. In those institutions children are inculcated with conformist ideals, while their natural curiosity is suppressed. They are taught how to obey and respect senior people, and that the success of their future careers can only accrue from this type of respect. The parents, again due to seniority of age, consolidate and reinforce this type of conformist behaviour in the home.

The other type of seniority is derived from rank. This is mostly official rank, through which the senior expects to be respected by those junior, and his or her decisions are not intended to be questioned. It is this type of seniority that leads to 'power distance', which is the extent to which the governed is willing to accept that this distance exists (Hofstede, 1980). The fact that one feels 'powerless' or less powerful in relation to another results in a dependency syndrome, and such entrepreneurial traits such as self-confidence and decision-making ability are seriously eroded. Seniority could also accrue from an enhanced economic status. People who are generally more affluent are often held in respect by those who are less affluent. This is the case even if the more affluent are the subject of gossip and intrigue from those less well off.

Thus, in the Kenyan society, the person who is more educated is the same person who is likely to have a higher rank, is more affluent, and is certainly more senior in age. The combination of these factors creates, on the one hand 'seniors' with autocratic tendencies, and on the other hand 'juniors' who are not only incapable of taking responsibility but are also docile and obsequious when it comes to their relationship with their seniors. This combination of factors cannot be regarded as a fertile breeding group for entrepreneurs.

Short-term planning horizons

An entrepreneur is somebody who is able to identify a business opportunity, assess its viability (even if in broad undocumented terms), and marshal resources to exploit the opportunity. To do this, he or she will need to be someone who possesses certain drives or characteristics. Many studies have been done in this area, pioneered by the afore-mentioned research of McClelland (1961). Although terminologies change from literature to literature, it is now generally agreed that a successful entrepreneur needs to be creative, able to take risks, is hardworking, has confidence in his own abilities to make things happen, and is capable of leading or influencing others. He or she has a positive attitude to life and is persistent even when faced with serious difficulties. Because entrepreneurs rely on their own initiative and abilities, it is proposed that a successful entrepreneur needs to be exceptionally good at planning.

The essence of planning is to minimize the risks associated with future events. Without it, one will be going through life on a day-to-day basis, and not be able to react in a predetermined manner to unexpected happenings. Perhaps, because of living a very 'grass root' and down-to-earth life, African societies have never been adept at planning. Beyond the granary that stored food after the main harvest, very little work was done in the way of planning on how to mitigate disasters. Famines, floods, droughts, diseases and even earthquakes would devastate whole populations because of this lack of adequate planning. Even today, Kenyan society confronts common disasters as if they never happened before. Our policy planners produce very impressive plans, but really only as an academic and perfunctory exercise, rather than as a way of preparing for the future. These plans, including those of a national development nature, are never referred to again until it is time to prepare the next series. Only researchers and elite organizations, such as the World Bank, refer to these documents.

A modern society protects itself from the unknown by meticulous planning, followed by strictly enforced implementation schedules and deadlines. It projects itself by evolving a savings culture to take care of the proverbial 'rainy day'; and by taking out insurance against known, but uncontrollable risks. Kenyan society as a whole does not struggle to create enough savings, being content to enjoy life as it is now. It does not seek insurance cover for future risks, unless it is compulsory as in the case of motor vehicles and business premises. The Kenyan man and woman remain a village, communal and rural person in their mentality with short-term planning horizons.

The interaction of land and entrepreneurial activities

In Kenya, the biggest form of insurance against a difficult future is the acquisition of a piece of land, no matter how arid, unproductive or inaccessible, with a view to building a rural house where he or she will 'rest' during their old age. Consequently, engagement in a business venture is, more often than not, seen as a means to that end. As soon as a plot of land has been identified, the proprietor draws money from the business and pays for it. He or she then continues to siphon any fresh earnings to construct a retirement home on the plot. Frequently, the business suffers irreparably. It is therefore no wonder that a large number of small enterprises in Kenya are not only born small as a result of insufficient savings, but also live small, and die young.

There was a time when education appeared as a viable alternative security and insurance against the vicissitudes of old age. Certain communities even disposed of sections of their land to raise funds to be able to educate their young ones. But, in today's society, with grown-up sons and daughters seeming preoccupied with living their own lives and not taking care of their aged parents, the land still remains the only security for the average Kenyan. It is irrelevant that the land is unarable, or if the rains fail, or people's eating habits have changed – land remains the only reason the Kenyan will go to work, seek promotion, or enter into a business.

It is easy to observe the part played by the land, or its absence, in the development of an entrepreneurial spirit among Kenyans. The Kikuyu are regarded to be more entrepreneurial people than, for example, their cousins the Meru. The Maragoli of Western Kenya are similarly described when compared to their fellow Luyhia. The Kissii are regarded as more entrepreneurial than their Luo neighbours. If one factor could be identified as to the reason why certain communities appear to be more entrepreneurial than others, it is land. Those who have little of it have to identify other means of survival, and have often migrated from their ancestral lands in search of 'greener pastures' – green both literally and figuratively. The availability of ample arable land is an inhibitor of entrepreneurship, while its absence may lead to higher entrepreneurial activity. That is to say that in this scenario adversity promotes entrepreneurial activities.

Belief in God and other extraterrestrial forces

A study was conducted in Kenya in 1993 on culture and management. It examined the role which witchcraft plays in the lives of an average Kenyan, whether well educated and in senior professional, business or political leadership, or lowly educated and living in rural areas. The role appears to be very prominent. Although not many persons confessed that they practised witchcraft, many felt that others were practising it in order to advance their careers, or to remain in the position they held. This was not a startling revelation. It is generally known that, in many communities, cultural beliefs and superstition affect the relationship between men and women. There are many working people who believe that promotions, or opportunities for advancement, require the application of 'medicine' to influence their superiors in their favour. By extension, there are those persons who believe that the reason why they have not climbed substantially up the corporate ladder is a result of witchcraft being used by their competitors, rivals or enemies.

As a result of these beliefs, people have failed to build attractive homes for fear of being bewitched. Quality cars have been hidden away from neighbouring rural people so as not to encourage envy. If an entrepreneur starts a business which fails it is due to witchcraft or a 'bad hand'. Others will say that 'God wished it to happen'. It is generally accepted that an entrepreneur takes responsibility for what goes wrong, and does not attribute failure to God, external forces, or the hands of evil people. The entrepreneur uses the resources available to him or her to make a gain, and regards failure as a learning experience and a reason for better planning and more diligence. In the Kenyan situation, the tendency to refuse to accept responsibility, and to attribute adversity to external forces, is an inhibitor towards the cultivation of an entrepreneurial culture.

Community and ethnic influences on entrepreneurial life

From time immemorial, Africans in general and Kenyans in particular practised a policy of 'communism' or 'collectivism'. All activities, from tilling the land, to the building of living quarters, to disaster management, were approached collectively. Children, for instance, belonged to the collective society. The weak and destitute in society were expected to be helped first, by members of the immediate family, and subsequently by the extended family members and clan. As a general rule, the strong and able members of the society were required to help the less able members. To date, this practice continues, albeit by the various Kenyan communities in various levels of intensity.

Specifically, the communal approach impacts on entrepreneurial behaviour in five ways:

1 limited capital free for investment;
2 extended decision-making process;
3 corrupt business practices;
4 favouritism in employment practices; and
5 ethnicity and micro-business in the urban informal sector.

Limited capital for investment

In days gone by, when individuals did not have 'private' needs of their own worth talking about, this collectivistic and communal spirit was invaluable to the society. However, the nature of work and expectations have changed. People are now expected to become successful in their own right. A communal approach to development is no longer as feasible, but nevertheless endures to a certain degree.

In a country where fewer than 20 per cent of all persons are in gainful employment, it is common to find that, in a family of ten people, only one person has a regular source of income. As soon as that income is received, it has to be shared among all these members of the immediate family. This is to say nothing of the extended family. Thus, it is not possible to accumulate sufficient savings that could be used for investment in a new business. Without investments, there will be no jobs that can increase the working population and reduce the number of 'mouths' one person has to feed. The communal spirit, once regarded as a quality of the Kenyan culture, has now become a millstone around the necks of aspiring entrepreneurs and acts as an inhibitor of entrepreneurial development.

Extended decision-making process

The communal approach can also be credited with another vice. In an attempt to please close relatives and members of the clan/community, the Kenyan entrepreneur has to engage in extensive consultations. Important business decisions are taken on the basis of irrelevant considerations, at least to the business, or simply delayed as more and more people are consulted. Spouses and friends, both male and female, are known to decide the direction of huge companies without working there, or even having a position on the Board.

Corrupt business practices

The communal approach has also contributed to the unacceptably high level of corruption in Kenya. A tender or a contract can only go to 'our' person or 'our' people, meaning members of our family, clan or community. If it cannot go to any of these, then 'outsiders' have to buy their way in. Companies have collapsed, new ones have been built only to become 'white elephants', persons have been hired and fired, contracts have been awarded and withdrawn. This is all because of trying to decide who should 'eat' and who should be stopped from 'eating' – 'our' people have priority.

Favouritism in employment practices

To a large number of Kenyans, jobs are obtained on the basis of 'whom you know', rather than 'what you know' or 'what you can do'. The person you know is likely to be a relative at best, or a clan/community member at worst. No one will ever know the cost of this 'favouritism' to the nation in terms of diminished potential productivity. A number of Kenyan companies, particularly the public-owned state corporations have been known to deliberately pursue an employment policy that is based on the ethnic composition of the senior management. It is easy to guess the origin of the top person in a state corporation – just find out from which community the majority of the workers come from.

Ethnicity and micro-business in the urban informal sector

Prior to the rural–urban migration in search of employment, further education, and better income opportunities, most of Kenya's ethnic groups lived in their respective rural regions, such as the Kikuyu in the Central Province, the Luhya in the Western Province, and the Maasai in the Rift Valley Province. The rural areas, inhabited by specific ethnic groups, were characterized by homogeneity in cultural traditions, and more important in language. Tribal rituals, such as circumcision and harvest dances, strengthened the bond of belonging to one ethnic group that usually claimed the same ancestry. Rural–urban migration which began in the 1950s, with increasing numbers in the following decades, brought together different ethnic groups who shared very little in common. They had different cultural traditions and different languages.

'Tribal identification' of Africans in cities is one aspect in which tropical Africa differs markedly from most Asian and Latin American cities. Even in the latter areas 'tribes' are recognized, but only a very small proportion of the urban population is regarded as 'tribal'. Tropical Africa is exceptional in that in each city, virtually all members of the population who are not members of racial minorities, that is to say whites and Asians, can say without hesitation to which 'tribe' they belong. This is true of Nairobi where virtually everyone except for Asians and Europeans will quickly identify themselves as Kikuyu, Luhya or Kamba. Contrary to expectations by sociologists, separation from tribal life and entry into urban life, far from weakening the bonds between tribal members, strengthens them. These bonds are articulated by urban migrants entering into entrepreneurial activities, particularly in the form of food kiosks, operating in the informal urban economy. Furthermore, these kiosks tend to be patronized by co-ethnics who substantially boost trade, and to whom credit is readily granted.

Chapter summary

We have written at length about Kenyan cultural practices that we believe have acted as inhibitors to the evolution of an entrepreneurial culture in Kenya in particular, and in Africa in general. It has been stated that, although entrepreneurs can be found in abundance in any part of the world including Africa, they tend to portray certain characteristics that are culture-neutral such as foresight, initiative, drive, organization and leadership. These are characteristics which anyone in any human endeavour needs to succeed. Our observations are that the average Kenyan does not exhibit those qualities to the same level as, say, their Western counterpart. This could be explained by the type of culture that a Kenyan grows up in, a culture that discourages independent thought and behaviour, fosters conformity, and tends to explain bad happenings as acts of God or evil spirits.

It is the culture that needs changing, utilizing intensive awareness campaigns through literature and the mass media. We need to identify and document our role models, such as the subject of the following case study Ann David, people whose exemplary and wise behaviour our new generations can imitate. We need to train our kinsmen that business can be both enjoyable and ethical. Furthermore, as much as we can be mindful of the welfare of the less fortunate among our relatives and clans, we can demand and indeed expect our relatives and employees to engage in honest hard work. No society ever developed with only a handful of hard-working persons while the rest were content with begging.

Entrepreneurship is a way of life that enables people to take charge of their own destinies, and the realization that their success will only come through their own efforts. Entrepreneurship cannot therefore grow in a society fond of blaming others and looking for scapegoats. The sooner Kenyans collectively start believing that they are and ought to be in control of their lives, the faster the spirit of entrepreneurship will rise, and the sooner Kenya will join the proud list of new economically thriving nations.

Case study: Ann David – Winner of the 1992 Enterprise Award

This case study is presented in the female entrepreneur's own words. In this way, the important sense and emotion of the account is not lost. Through this simple, but effective, style of communication we can live through the challenges which faced Ann David, feel for her as a mother striving to make a basic living to feed her family, and experience the heat of the sun as she toiled without shelter. It is a profoundly human story, which shakes our thoughts and values relative to what is generally espoused as entrepreneurship. Fundamentally, it is a very basic human activity, practised by ordinary, but at the same time exceptional, human beings.

My name is Ann N. David. I am 27 years of age. I studied at Lugulu Girls High School where I did my 'A' levels in 1985. I passed with two principal and two subsidiary qualifications. I had always wished to pursue my education to university level and become either an economist, radio announcer or one of the TV crew. My life seemed to have come to a sudden end when I finished school and was not able to fulfil my dreams.

Nevertheless, I resolved to teach as an untrained teacher. I looked for a job tirelessly, since my parents could no longer support me, and in February 1986 I was employed by Reliance High School. Later in 1987, I moved to Ambe High School in Webuye. I worked very hard as a teacher, and in no time was able to adjudicate verse speaking and music up to the District level.

I got married in March 1986 and in December of that year I was blessed with twins, Kenny and Emma. As if this wasn't enough, in February 1988 I delivered yet another set of twins Denis and Sylvia. The responsibility of caring for the children drove me out of my teaching job. In late 1988, through my husband's Co-operative loan of Kshs: 35 000/= at his place of work, Nzoia Sugar Company Ltd, we started by buying maize from rural areas and selling it to the Cereals Board in Webuye town. We started well but since this was a seasonal business, by early in 1989 the business went down. I made a loss of Kshs: 15 000/= because of the high moisture content of the maize from Mount Elgon and transport problems. This brought the business to an end, leaving me with only Kshs: 18 000/= of our savings left.

Now keeping the money meant consuming it. Even putting it into a fixed deposit account meant nothing, since my husband had to service the Co-operative loan with deductions from his salary. One morning my husband left for town and spent the whole day there. He came up with an idea of subletting an open space, measuring 24 ft by 20 ft for selling timber. Although the plot had some posts and wire around the sides, there was no roof. I began operating the business on 2 March 1989, under the name of 'SANLAGA JOINERY WORKS', and also under the scorching sun of the Western Province. The initial capital was Kshs: 18 000/= with which I bought assorted timber, workshop tools and employed two carpenters. In no time two schools gave me orders. I did their work but they failed to pay me in good time. Once again the business collapsed leaving me worse off than ever. Since that time I learnt a lesson – never give credit. With the little money that remained, we started making stools and chairs to attract new customers. In this way the business, and I, slowly recovered.

In July 1989, I approached the Informal Sector Loans Programme of KIE in Bungoma, for a loan. I was considered, and after going through training to prepare my own business plan, they granted me a loan of Kshs: 18 000/=. With this I embarked on cutting my own wood and installed a lathe machine at a friend's metal workshop because his plot had access to electricity. By now, I had five employees. I gained more customers and did well, especially since the machine brought in an average Kshs: 3000/= worth of business every month.

This situation did not go on for long. After only three months, the owner of the metal shop was jealous of my success and discontinued our arrangement with the lathe machine. Mark you, in his shop the electricity had been disconnected because of an overdue bill of Kshs: 2000/= which I owed for the installation of a meter, as per our agreement for using his premises. This was yet another big blow because I didn't have electrical power at my plot, so it meant that the machine could no longer operate. Later, at the end of that year, a thought struck my mind on how I would install electricity in my shed. At this time, we were servicing two loans and I had to work very hard to maintain my five employees, in addition to my domestic needs. I worked tirelessly to install electricity which finally came into being after one and a half years of struggle on 23 September 1991. The total sum needed for this was Kshs: 23 000/=.

As a result of all these hardships, I came to know another financier – SEFCO. I applied for finance for another machine and working capital. After a long period of waiting, applying and re-applying, they replied positively and processed the loan. It took about two years, until October 1991, when I finally received the machine – on the 13th of that month. I have also assembled another homemade machine, a circular saw, and have now fully roofed my shed – I no longer work in the sun.

Up to now, I have two machines in operation. I have seven employees who are permanent. Sometimes, I hire others on piece rate, especially when I get big orders from schools, individuals and companies like the Nzoia Sugar Company. I have also successfully repaid the KIE loan, finishing in category 'A' and, to my credit, as one of their best and most promising clients.

The value of my business today is presented in Table 2.1.

Table 2.1 Ann David's assets

Asset	Kshs
Shed	15 000/=
3 machines	93 000/=
Total stock	50 000/=
Tools	8 000/=
Total	166 000/=

In conclusion, I give credit to KIE for taking me to a business plan seminar, together with SEFCO for starting me in the orientation of book-keeping and banking, and the Chamber of Commerce and Industry for what I learned in investment promotion. Very soon I am looking forward to taking a course on advanced book-keeping.

My future plans are to buy another plot, and put up a commercial building to pave the way for light industry in the field of woodwork. Through this, I will be able to absorb the many Kenyan youth from polytechnics and schools alike, to help them be self-reliant as I am now. I feel privileged to be the owner, and woman manager, of a business in an industry normally dominated by men.

Case study review

Ann David exhibits the full range of Timmons's themes in an implicit, rather than aggressively explicit manner which represents a 'low key' entrepreneurial approach. In addition to those of a monetary nature, her rewards from personal endeavour are reflected in the ability to sustain the life-style of the family and provide employment for the educated young in Kenya. Factors contributing to here entrepreneurial behaviour are presented in Table 2.2.

Table 2.2 Factors contributing to Ann David's entrepreneurial behaviour

Category	Factors
Antecedent influences	• Her entrepreneurial action has been triggered by the need, literally, to survive and provide for her family. • She is a deviant from the social norm within her country • She is committed to life-long learning through participation in government training programmes and from experience. • She exhibits strong moral, work and business ethics.
Incubator organization	• Her business has not developed from an incubator organization, and skills and knowledge have been acquired through experiential learning.
Environment factors	• She is a deviant from the social norms of her country. • Despite limited support from the environment she has persisted and survived extremely exacting challenges. • Business is developed on intuition rather than market research and formal management information. • A private and public sector support network has been developed to her advantage.

3
Africa: South

Fatima Allie and Linda Human

Key feature summary

South Africa is currently in a transitional period following the political changes of the early 1990s, which will have a significant effect for future entrepreneurial activity within 'Black' communities in particular. Key features affecting entrepreneurship are:

- The legacy of apartheid's systematic discrimination of 'Blacks', which was reinforced through the formal education system, promoted a conformist behaviour which did not support entrepreneurship.
- Individuals within the 'Black' population have responded inconsistently to apartheid. Some have been stimulated to act entrepreneurially as a result of adversity, others succumbed to the political dogma.
- Recent political intervention (1995) is aimed at addressing issues of inequalities and covert racialism, and to support business development of small, medium and micro-enterprises.
- In this turbulent transitional period for South Africa, it is difficult to gauge what the response of the 'Black' community will be to an increase in entrepreneurial activity by their members.

Introduction

According to Berger (1991), many academics from various disciplines have emphasized the importance of cultural factors in entrepreneurship, However, South Africa, with its many cultures and dynamic and transforming socio-political environment, represents a particularly problematic case study with respect to the application of cultural arguments. However, it can be surmised that specifically relative to the 'Black' community, under apartheid rule there evolved a strong anti-entrepreneurial culture as a result of the political policy of the time. The complexity of the cultural and socio-political milieu is addressed. The case study of Navavee Mathews, a 'Coloured' entrepreneur, is presented and vividly and clearly illustrates the marriage of theory to reality. His story is one of triumph through entrepreneurship over significant social and economic deprivation.

Definitional debate

It would appear that there remains little consensus about the definition of entrepreneurship among those academics and practitioners working in this field. However, many of the definitions appear to revolve around two central tenets (Berger, 1991):

- entrepreneurship is perceived as an activity central to small business activities;
- entrepreneurship is perceived as a cluster of behavioural and psychological propensities including risk-taking, innovation and the ability to make decisions.

The problems associated with the former definition include the fact that some large businesses may exhibit entrepreneurial tendencies whereas some small businesses may not. On the other hand, problems associated with the latter definition include the fact that such traits are not necessarily required for many modern economic activities. Moreover, they can also be found in activities which cannot be defined as economic.

For the purpose of this chapter, a pragmatic definition of entrepreneurship is presented. Entrepreneurship is defined as 'an innovative and value-adding economic activity' (Berger, 1991, p. 8). At the same time, however, in view of the nature of the case study offered, as well as the complications created by a broader definition, this definition of entrepreneurship is discussed within the framework of small business in South Africa.

Entrepreneurship and culture

Any discussion of entrepreneurship and culture in South Africa begs that the complexity and dynamism of cultural, political and sociological forces is encapsulated. Perhaps more so than in many other countries, both culture and entrepreneurship in South Africa have been impacted by socio-political forces which have changed dramatically since the first democratic elections in the early 1990s. This means that any discussion of entrepreneurship and culture must take into account these forces and attempt to assess their impact. Thus, this section begins with a discussion of culture and then progresses to consider the effects of the changing socio-political climate on entrepreneurship in relation to small business.

One of the current debates on culture surrounds its definition, measurement and the utility of such measurement with respect to activities such as entrepreneurship. Protagonists in this debate appear to fall onto a continuum ranging from what can be called a 'maximalist' position at the one extreme, and a 'minimalist' position at the other (Blommaert, 1988). Put simply, the maximalist approach to culture argues, with varying degrees of reservation or qualification, that a person's culture will tend to determine how that person interacts with others and the world around him or her. At the other extreme, the minimalist approach takes an interactional approach to culture and argues that culture constitutes a subconscious part of a person's identity as a communicator and is therefore constructed to a large extent by the perceptions of the other party in the interaction. On a general level, maximalists tend to work with ideal-typical cultural differences which can be both monolithic and deterministic, whereas minimalist perspectives tend to deny the relevance of culture as perceived stereotypically by many human beings (Human, 1996).

One of the classic definitions of culture is that of Hofstede (1994, p.4) who defines culture as the 'collective programming of the mind which distinguishes one group of people from another'. Cultures, according to Hofstede, vary across four main dimensions: individualism versus collectivism; power distance; uncertainty avoidance and masculinity versus femininity. Hofstede does not maintain that all members of a particular cultural group will hold precisely the same values. Rather, he argues that the values are typical of that culture. Moreover, although he acknowledges that cultures do change over time and are dynamic in nature, he nevertheless believes that most value changes are peripheral and would not really affect the major dimensions.

The maximalist perspective is also evident in the work of Trompenaars (1993) and Berger (1994) and has influenced the research of other authors working in the area of entrepreneurship, for example Berger (1991). It is also evident in the work of South African authors such as Coldwell and Moerdyk (1981) who discuss the extent to which 'African cultural paradigms' negatively impact the performance of 'black managers'. More recently, some authors writing about culture in South Africa have argued somewhat differently. For example, authors such as Lessem (1993), Koopman (1993), and Beck and Linscott (1993) suggest that certain 'African' values are important for the long term success of the capitalist enterprise.

This ideological contortionist approach among South African writers on culture is suggestive of one of the four main problems with maximalist perspectives; namely, that it is almost impossible not to employ maximalist stereotypes in a value-laden way. Other problems with the maximalist perspective include the fact that it can be unduly fixed and inflexible, and fails to take into account other social variables impacting on individual identity (Human, 1996). Finally, such perspectives tend to suggest a continuum with, for example, collectivism at one end of the spectrum and individualism at the other. Experience of African communities in rural areas, however, indicates that they may be both more collectivist and more individualistic than Western urbanites. Issues relating to the complexity of individual identity are particularly relevant in the South African environment where apartheid, at worst, systematically destroyed aspects of the cultural life of those deemed inferior and, at best, changed such cultural forms, perhaps irrevocably.

The consequences of the impact of political forces on culture have been such that it is particularly difficult in the South African environment to impose maximalist perspectives in anything but a tentative way. Thus, according to De Haas (1990), African linguistic groupings are crosscut by many other variables. These include education, occupation, wealth, religion and area of residence, which are far more important in everyday life than differences based on traditional culture. Furthermore, such differences not only deeply divide 'Black' society but also create important links with 'White' society.

Although she does not explicitly mention the concepts of 'class' and power relations, what De Haas (1990, p. 18) argues is that the 'naturalness of ethnic groups' is taken for granted by 'Whites' in particular. She goes on to contend that a brief overview of the historical development of these groups highlights, however, that real as they are now in some respects and to some people, there is nothing immutable about ethnic identities. While differences in 'traditional' culture do exist between different African linguistic groups, as they do also between, *inter alia,* Afrikaans, English, Jewish and Portuguese 'White' South Africans, such differences also occur within linguistic groups, with class being an important variable in terms of both within-group differences and between-group similarities. Thus, according to Adam and Moodley (1993), urban–rural tensions in African townships are marked by generation, cultural and political differences. The predominant South African urban 'Black' identity is a mixture of the:

- traditional elements and rural customs;
- 'street wisdom' of survival in the townships and in the workplace;
- materialistic aspirations of secular Western society.

According to these authors, this is a politicized, individualistic, urban culture that strongly contrasts with that of many migrants and rural folk who are considered illiterate, unsophisticated country bumpkins.

The argument presented here is not meant to suggest that maximalist perspectives on culture are 'wrong' or not useful. What is being suggested, however, is that within the South African environment, such perspectives are confounded by a complexity of other social variables that impact individual social identity. The relevance of maximalist perspectives would also appear to vary between ethnic groups. For example, Godsell (1991) argues that both South African urban 'Blacks' and Afrikaners are lacking in an entrepreneurial history; however, South African Indians have historically been rooted in a vibrant entrepreneurial tradition. Indian communities were successful in circumventing the inhibiting legal and political constraints created by apartheid, both in terms of retaining a strong cultural milieu and by pursuing entrepreneurial activity. Afrikaner entrepreneurs, on the other hand, have tended to act alone without the mediating structure of the community. 'Black' entrepreneurs are also seen as isolated individuals, impeded by both the lack of an entrepreneurial culture and a restrictive socio-political environment.

Although the arguments presented by Godsell (1991) in relation to both Afrikaners and Africans could be debated, most South Africans would probably agree on the entrepreneurial culture of South African Indians. This type of culture is also evident among certain sections of the small Chinese community of South Africa. Numbering no more than 10 000 in 1980, the South African Chinese community appeared to display two major characteristics:

- a dynamic, small business entrepreneurial orientation among some members;
- a strong value attached to the education and professional development of the young.

However, research (Human, 1984) identified that the attitudes of those Chinese tended to vary according to individual psychological responses to the socially marginal position in which they found themselves. Classified as 'non White' but not as restricted as some other ethnic groups, a number of Chinese people felt confident to exploit their marginal position and to trade in either, or both, 'Black' and 'White' areas. For others, such marginality had more negative psychological consequences and appeared to undermine levels of both self-confidence and self-esteem.

The 'Coloured', mixed-race and Malay, community of South Africa has also found itself in a marginal position, both during the days of apartheid and subsequent to the democratic election of a new government. This community has consistently found itself sandwiched between the 'Black' African ethnic groups on the one hand, and 'White' on the other. Although the African National Congress-dominated government now espouses a spirit of non-racialism, many 'Coloured' people still feel marginalized between 'Black' Africans and 'Whites'. As in the case of the Chinese community, the 'Coloured' group, which comprises about 2.5 million people, has not responded consistently to this marginalization. For some, marginality has been compounded by the negative stereotyping reinforced by the maximalist classificatory system of the apartheid government. In addition a host of other sociological variables, appears to have impacted negatively on characteristics such as initiative, self-confidence and entrepreneurship. For others, the impact of the tyranny of apartheid has been much less damaging.

Indeed, Morris (1996) attempts to dismiss the myths and misunderstandings relating to entrepreneurship in South Africa, and does not even mention the concept of culture. He argues, that it is a mistake to equate entrepreneurship simply with small business, and that many small businesses are not particularly entrepreneurial. He asserts that entrepreneurship involves a definite process of identifying an opportunity, developing a solid business concept and assessing and acquiring resources. Furthermore, it involves calculated risk taking and vision. From this stance, Morris believes that entrepreneurs are not unique and predisposed to be entrepreneurial; rather the entrepreneurial potential which most individuals possess is depressed, or developed and sustained, within one's environment. He also suggests that entrepreneurial individuals are opportunity-driven, rather than resource-driven, hard working, insightful, adaptable and well organized.

Timmons (1978), Hornaday (1982), Brockhaus and Horwitz (1986) and Hisrich (1986) also suggest that entrepreneurs are tenacious; can tolerate uncertainty and ambiguity; are willing to take moderate risks; make good use of resources; and are imaginative and results-oriented. Ranasinghe (1996) argues that successful Sri Lankan entrepreneurs began their businesses with virtually nothing, and had left rural areas at an early age to find jobs in the cities. These initial business experiences were important in their development. Furthermore, Ranasinghe proposes that an important personal feature common to all these entrepreneurs is intuition. It had enabled them to respond to market opportunities, take calculated risks and innovate new products. They also seem to have been driven to succeed for self as well as kin, an observation that supports experiences of entrepreneurs in Africa.

A further major theme emanating from the literature is that of action learning; that entrepreneurial behaviour is an outcome of both creation and reflection. Johannisson and Landström (1996) and Kolb et al. (1984) suggest that, with regard to managerial and entrepreneurial activity, learning theory over-estimates the time available for theorizing. Surprising events in the environment must be dealt with inventively, in the sense of mobilizing unconscious understanding of complex phenomena and associated action, or by reference to analogous situations. Entrepreneurship calls for an 'action capability', in the sense of bringing talent and experience together with resolution and action orientation.

From this brief and relatively superficial overview of the historical relationship between culture and entrepreneurship within South Africa, it is clear that the complexity of the cultural and socio-political milieu and its impact on the traits of individual entrepreneurs makes the eliciting of firm conclusions problematic. However, it would appear that where the characteristics of successful entrepreneurs have developed among many members of the 'Black' community, they have done so despite the tyrannical political and social forces that have worked against them. It is apparent that entrepreneurship in South Africa cannot simply be understood in terms of 'culture' but also requires us to look at both the impact of apartheid on South Africa's many cultures, and the varied psychological responses to systematic discrimination.

The small business sector

A brief introduction to the small business environment, and the changes which are about to be brought to bear on this environment, is now presented. As the case study concerns a small business in South Africa, it is appropriate to discuss the emerging small business climate in more detail. However, it is emphasized that this chapter should not be read as one which links entrepreneurship solely with small business. Entrepreneurship is as much of a central issue in large organizations as in small ones.

Although statistical data relating to small, medium and micro-enterprises (SMMEs) is inconsistent, it would appear that these kinds of enterprises play an important role in the South African economy. It is estimated that there are more than 800 000 SMMEs in South Africa, employing about 25 per cent of the labour force of 15 million people. In addition, approximately 3.5 million people are involved in various forms of survivalist enterprise activities. In view of its diversity the small business sector in South Africa is complex. This is a consequence not only of a variety of stages of growth of enterprises, but also relates to a range of economic factors. As a result, different sectors tend to exhibit varying structures, problems, growth potential and access to support. The White Paper on National Strategy for the Development and Promotion of Small Business in South Africa distinguishes four types of small businesses (SMMEs) which can be contrasted with big business: survivalist; micro-enterprises; small enterprises; and medium enterprises (*Government Gazette*, 1995) as presented in Table 3.1 on page 33.

It would appear that the capacity to absorb labour is high in the small business sector, and that the average capital cost per job is generally lower than in big business. Moreover, in view of the domination of big business, limited competition, and inequalities in the distribution of wealth and income, many proponents would argue that the small business sector constitutes an important potential generator of employment, greater equity, competition, increased productivity and technical change. From the other side of the spectrum, the micro-enterprise segment of the small business sector plays a crucial role in the meeting of basic human needs. This sector and the small enterprise sector have been the ones within which 'Black' people have been able to make the most progress (*Government Gazette*, 1995).

Constraints facing small businesses

It is proposed that small businesses all over the world face more constraints than big business. These include:

Table 3.1 *Typologies of small business enterprises*

Survivalist	Run by largely unemployed people. They often fail to produce even a minimum income; virtually no training takes place and opportunities for growth into a viable business are extremely limited. Poverty and survival strategies appear to characterize these enterprises which are often run by women.
Micro	Very small businesses, often employing family members and one or two employees and run by the owner. Many are 'informal' in the sense that they lack the appropriate licences, value-added tax registration, permits and accounting procedures. The capital base is frequently limited and technical and business skills generally rudimentary.
Small	Constitute the bulk of the established businesses and generally employ between 5 and 50 people. These enterprises are usually owner-managed; operate from business premises; are registered for tax and meet other formal registration requirements.
Medium	Compose a category of enterprise falling between 'big' and 'small'. They still tend to be owner/manager-controlled but would generally employ over 200 people and hold capital assets (excluding property) of R5 million at the upper limit.

Source: *Government Gazette* (1995).

- the legal and regulatory environment facing SMMEs;
- access to financing, premises and markets;
- the development of skills;
- access to technology;
- problems with the business infrastructure available, particularly in rural areas.

In South Africa, constraints have impeded entrepreneurial activity among over four-fifths of the population, and particularly among 'Black' women in rural areas. The legacy of apartheid is such that 'Black'-owned, or controlled, small enterprises continue to struggle against such constraints. For most of this century, the majority of South Africans have been deprived of viable business opportunities through:

- systematic discrimination at a variety of levels from education through to laws relating to land and settlement;
- racially segregated residential areas;
- property ownership rights;
- marriage laws and laws governing employment.

Such discrimination has exacerbated the general constraints impacting on small business to the extent that the challenges for many enterprises have proved insuperable.

Although a number of institutions have attempted to support small business development, they have tended to be both racially and gender-biased. Central government historically made few attempts to support 'Black' businesses in particular, and most government tenders were awarded to 'White' businesses. In recent years, a number of organizations, in both the public and private sectors, have been created. However, these organizations are often in competition with each other and are largely ineffective in their overall impact (*Government Gazette*, 1995). Support has also been received from some foreign agencies. However, until the very recent past, a holistic and effective strategy for the support of small business development has not been forthcoming.

In addition to the overarching constraints that have been imposed by the legacy of apartheid, problems and constraints affecting the various segments of SMMEs appear to differ widely. It would appear, for example, that micro- and survivalist enterprises are far less able to deal with constraints relating to skills, market access and finance while those of medium-sized enterprises include international competition, technology transfer and skills training (*Government Gazette*, 1995).

Recent government initiatives

In view of the context of small business development in South Africa, a democratically elected government has recognized the need for a coherent and integrated small-business strategy. The promotion of the small-enterprise sector of the South African economy comprised a critical issue raised in the Reconstruction and Development Programme. This concern has subsequently been translated into a White Paper on a national strategy for the development and promotion of small business (*Government Gazette*, 1995). The key objectives of the national small-business strategy include:

- the creation of an enabling environment;
- facilitation of greater equalization of income and wealth;
- addressing the legacy of apartheid;
- supporting the advancement of women;
- creating jobs;
- stimulating sector-focused economic growth;
- strengthening cohesion between enterprises;
- levelling the 'playing field' and preparing small business for participation in an international competitive economy.

These objectives are supported in the White Paper by: a set of principles; the description of a support framework; required institutional reform; an action programme; and recommendations for funding.

The ultimate goal of the White Paper is to make SMMEs equal partners in the economy, and to maximize their contribution to the South African Reconstruction and Development Programme. Even sceptics agree that the sector has never been better placed to make a real contribution (*Financial Mail*, 1996). However, fears have been expressed that subsequent proposed legislation will not achieve its stated objectives of facilitating an enabling environment for small businesses (Ryan, 1996). These recent developments suggest that the operating climate for small businesses may change significantly over the next decade. Only time will tell.

Chapter summary

The following case study Navavee Clothing epitomizes all that has been discussed in this chapter. The firm constitutes a small business enterprise, employing thirty people.

It is owner-managed; operates to a certain extent from business premises (and is likely to do so more in the future), is registered for tax and meets other formal registration requirements. It is a business that is growing according to the vision and articulated strategy of its owner; and in so doing it is adapting to a more varied customer and supplier base.

The pioneer of Navavee Clothing is a man who has grown up during the dying throes of apartheid and who is witnessing the proposed changes to the small business environment in South Africa. This environment has already shed some of the cruder forms of racism but still struggles against entrenched privilege, inequalities and covert racism. As a 'Coloured' man growing up in South Africa, Navavee Mathews appears to be one of perhaps a relatively small group of marginalized people whose self-confidence and self-esteem have not been unduly affected by discrimination and systematic attempts to disintegrate the strength of 'Black' ethnic groups.

According to this entrepreneur, he went into business because he likes a 'good' lifestyle and wanted a better life. He believes in a sense of dignity, goal-setting and goal achievement. He claims that his culture, moulded to some extent by apartheid, has played a large part in his decision to become an entrepreneur. His community has always believed in a better and dignified life. The people are very supportive and believe in helping one another, ensuring the welfare of others. He is also of the opinion that apartheid has helped him and others to some extent. It was like taking revenge on the law: proving to the rulers that their laws could be broken, that they would succeed in creating a better life for themselves and their communities.

Thus, in articulating opinions on culture, Navavee illustrates a resistance to oppression, rather than the 'traditional' cultural values of a particular ethnic group. Perhaps more so than in other societies, culture in South Africa has to be placed alongside many other variables impacting social identity. One of the most important is individual response to both discrimination and unequal access to resources. Navavee Mathews has responded positively to the challenges with which he has been faced, particularly apartheid laws and lack of access to finances. His expulsion from school also suggests non-conformity within an apartheid educational system.

Navavee Mathews appears to fulfil many of the aspects of entrepreneurship presented by Morris (1996). For example, he has gone through a process, perhaps partly intuitive, of identifying an opportunity, developing a business concept and assessing and acquiring resources. He has a vision and has taken calculated risks. He has also been opportunity-driven, hardworking, insightful, adaptable and well organized. Tenacity, tolerance of uncertainty and ambiguity and a results-orientation are also defining entrepreneurial characteristics. Like Ranasinghe's (1996) Sri Lankan entrepreneurs, Navavee Mathews began his business with virtually nothing and obtained business experience by moving to a larger city. He also appears to be as much, if not more, driven to succeed for himself as for his kin. Navavee has learnt most about business through action, and surprising events in the environment that may sometimes have been dealt with more intuitively than consciously. This supports Johannisson and Landström's (1996) assertion that the time available for theorizing is probably less than Kolb *et al.* (1984) suggest. Navavee Mathews has displayed a dynamic action capability in the sense of bringing innate intelligence, talent and experience together with resolution and action orientation.

The changing small business environment in South Africa offers exciting opportunities for entrepreneurs. If, through legislation and greater access to resources and capital, the government can create a more supportive environment in which entrepreneurs can prosper, role models such as Navavee Mathews may well inspire other 'Black' people to try and succeed. Navavee is extremely optimistic about the future of the country. According to him through entrepreneurship 'there is hope for South Africa'.

Case study: Navavee Clothing

This case study presents a 'Coloured' entrepreneur who has set up his business in the highly dynamic and changing period between the demise of the former regime and the birth of the new. It should be read within the context of the highly restrictive and psychologically assaulting conditions within which the entrepreneur grew up.

Navavee Mathews, founder of Navavee Clothing, is a 'Coloured' (Malay). He can often be found at a table with his guitar and his collection of photos taken with his Canon camera and special lenses. His house is a cacophony of sound and bustle; friends, relatives and colleagues come in and out the house, the rooms of which are full of rails of clothing and shelves of raw materials. Adjoining the house is the workplace itself where seamstresses work at their machines and hum to background music.

Navavee Mathews was born in Cape Town in 1960. Navavee's father, Mogamat Mathews, is a retired builder; he worked for Robert Katz Construction for 38 years. His mother is the daughter of a tailor and has never worked for an employer in her life. She assisted her father in a business where she learnt her sewing skills. The Mathews couple had seven children. Navavee is the fourth. Navavee says that his mother stayed at home and sewed for his sisters and her relations, but never charged them money. This is all part of the culture; helping each other.

When Navavee reflects on his childhood, he remembers that his mother spent a great deal of time at the hospital with his little sister who had polio and his elder brother (deceased) who had an eye problem. He states that his mother always left him in the care of his aunt on the days that she attended the hospital with the two children. He resented that, because he felt confused at the time; he could not understand the situation and he also did not like his aunt. He says that he did not have such a good feeling about it, but says that he cannot explain the feeling.

He was expelled from school in 1978, and took up blue-collar work as a boilermaker working on energy plants. Navavee says that his expulsion from school was precipitated by his frustration about the effects of apartheid. Life was gloomy; the system made him aggressive and he built up a hatred towards 'Whites'. He speaks affectionately of his grandfather and states that, 'although the old man was aware of all the unfairness around us, he encouraged us not to give up hope'. This was due to his cultural beliefs, Navavee claims. He also said that although they did not like 'Whites', they were never rude to them, they just kept them at a distance. After leaving his blue-collar employment, he then obtained work with a large corporation that increased his earnings from R160 per month to R1400 per month. Navavee is now aware that he managed this sudden increase in income poorly. He admits to not being able to handle the situation, sending some money home to his family and spending the rest.

Navavee sees himself as an outgoing person who loves mixing with people from all walks of life, as he puts it: 'from candlestick maker to butcher, to all kinds of professional people'. He believes that he learns a lot from his interaction with all these people. He likes challenges in life; his motto is 'play hard, work hard'. He also believes that 'beauty will save the world'. He claims that he has lots of perseverance, but limited patience. He is of the opinion that his character has grown in spite of the obstacles of the past. 'Apartheid taught us to become creative, to con the system in order to survive', he states.

When talking to his friends, they all say that they regard Navavee as a knowledgeable, kind and helpful person. His friends call him 'Mr Know-it all', but not in a derogatory sense. They come to him for information and advice. This explains the constant stream of visitors.

In 1982, his cousin offered him a share in a clothing shop. Navavee was responsible for buying and shop fitting. After seven months, the business went bankrupt. The downfall of the business he blames on his naiveté, and the fact that he thought he could trust implicitly a family member to deal with the finances. He discovered when it was too late that his cousin was 'wheeling and dealing' on the side. Navavee lost everything and for six months didn't earn anything. Navavee comments that with hindsight, he learnt not to think with his 'heart' but with his 'head'. He also learnt that you have to use one's intellect when running a business and to be more aloof from people, their greed and ulterior motives when it comes to money matters.

In 1983, he moved to Johannesburg to start a new life. He began work in the mines and then roamed around Johannesburg looking for work. He finally managed to obtain employment in a power station for the next two years. He then fell in love with 'a beautiful girl' from a conservative family who was about to study at the local university. The fact that her family disapproved of Navavee led him to make a decision to improve himself and so he enrolled at a private college for a three-month course in practical drafting. He enjoyed his studies and subsequently enrolled at the Peninsula Technicon to study mechanical engineering. He chose this subject due to the fact that he was exposed to the field when he worked as an artisan on the mines and liked it at the time. His relationship with his girlfriend had, by now, broken down. He decided to move back to Cape Town, which he regards as his home. However, while studying, Navavee began buying baby clothes and had four people selling them for him. At about the time he started facing financial difficulties with his studies, he also saw an opportunity in the market that he felt could be exploited. In 1987, Navavee met Ali who gave him bangles and incense sticks to sell at flea markets. Navavee travelled round the country selling these at markets, much to the dismay of his family who regretted that he had abandoned his studies for trading.

A little later, Navavee took R180 and went to Ivitex to buy a packet of cotton knit material with which to start making clothes. The people at Ivitex were rather disconcerted by his appearance (sunglasses and earrings) when he went to the company to sell and collect. Mathews decided to go into manufacturing clothing, purely because of the opportunities available. 'Cape Town is the "hub" for manu- facturing clothes. Most "Coloured" people living in Cape Town, live off making clothes', he states. The majority of the women in Cape Town have worked, or are still working, in the clothing factories. Therefore, there exists a large skills base in this sector. According to Navavee: 'due to the economic situation and hence the unemployment rate in the province, people are resorting to making and selling clothes on the streets. It is a means of survival'. Navavee acquired his skills from his mother, and some other family members. In fact, his uncle also runs a cloth- ing manufacturing business.

In 1990, disaster struck Navavee's company. A burglary led to him losing all his stock and R8000 in cash. At the height of the season, just before Christmas, he found himself with no money and no stock. However, he was not deterred. He obtained stock on consignment and survived December. In January, he told a close friend what had happened and the friend asked to see his accounts. All of his financial records were contained in one small book. However, his friend was impressed with what he saw and offered to become an investor. He also helped arrange an overdraft. From then on, Navavee clothing started growing and Navavee bought back the shares from his friend.

The Navavee brand is founded on T-shirts, women's blouses, women's skirts, men's shorts and other sportswear. The T-shirts are high quality with a particular finish to allow the shirts to wash well and retain their shape. They are designed in- house and an attempt is made to keep on top of recent trends. Navavee seeks to produce quality clothes with a designer appearance but at affordable prices. The clothes were sold initially at flea markets but over time began to sell increasingly through retail outlets that requested consignments. About a quarter of the total production is now sold through such stores.

The clientele buying Navavee's clothing are divided by him into three main groups: 'White' office employees who, although often feeling economically inse- cure in the post-apartheid job market, still want to look good while not spending too much; the upwardly mobile 'Black' African middle class who tend to buy US and European labels; and the upwardly mobile or middle class 'Coloureds'. The market also tends to be seasonal and recently Navavee has also looked to exploit the market created by increased tourism to Cape Town.

Navavee's vision is to be the Daniel Hechter of Cape Town and to clothe the nation in quality clothes at affordable prices. Production is still located partly at his home. Part of his line is produced in his shop located in the back yard. His garage is the cutting room. The bedrooms contain the final products awaiting sale or shipment. Navavee also has an extensive network of 'CMTs' or 'cut, make and trim' suppliers. These suppliers are generally women working from their homes or small workshops. These women produce his clothing in accordance with strict specifications.

Competition for his business is mainly from a nation-wide quality store, the equivalent of Marks and Spencer in the UK and Europe. Competition from a large but less expensive retail chain is declining. Navavee is critical of what he per- ceived as exploitation of the small CMTs. According to Navavee, big buyers used to make an arrangement with some CMTs to purchase all of their production. Having become the sole buyer, and having made the CMTs dependent on them, the output is then often rejected for quality reasons. After a few days, the large buyers then offer to continue purchasing the products but at a lower price. The CMTs had no alternative but to accept. Navavee suggests that the large companies were controlling the industry in that way, but he adds a racial twist. The CMTs are largely run by 'Coloureds' who, probably as a result of the psychological contamination of apartheid, do not stand their ground. Navavee bemoans what he sees as a lack of an entrepreneurial spirit, particularly as, in his view, 'Coloureds are the best seamstresses'. Navavee is of the opinion that this situation has improved somewhat, in that the small guys realized that they must 'get their act together'. They have started becoming more professional. They are now operating better, there is an understanding between the two parties, simply because they realized that they need each other.

Mathews believes that apartheid worked to the state's advantage in some instances; for example, it managed to split communities. 'Some even lost their cultures, and adopted "phoney" cultures from America. The system also caused splits among the rich and the poor. The rich aligned themselves with the ruling party and the poor with the opposition or activists fighting for the noble things in life'.

'The community is still split. People need education and other basic needs in life. These basic human needs will empower the community', Navavee states with some anger in his voice. He is also of the opinion that the 'Coloured' people are still marginalized, and that they are losing out once again. 'The fight for survival and recognition is still on for us, but I think we have a better chance now than before. We need to do something for ourselves', he says.

Navavee has not been alone in the recent development of his business. Azzad, who left his family with nothing but his clothes, joined Navavee as a salesperson. After spending three years studying computer science at a prestigious local university, Azzad had to abandon his studies after interpersonal problems with his father. His family's lack of faith in him, he says, gave him the determination to 'prove them wrong'. While working for Navavee, Azzad and a fellow salesperson earned extra income by selling swimwear. When he was offered a quarter share in the company, Azzad bought the shares with this additional income and with a loan from his grandmother. A year later, he bought a further 10 per cent share and was brought into the manufacturing side of the business. Under the supervision of Navavee, he started off in the cutting room and worked his way through the entire manufacturing process. Azzad proved himself adept in the business and was given a further five per cent share as a birthday present-come-reward for his service and loyalty. Azzad is fully committed to the business and has proved himself invaluable. He has been promoted from production manager to operations manager and is now a co-owner of Navavee Clothing.

Navavee's vision of the future is a team of designers, a one-stop factory, CMT suppliers and a chain of retail shops carrying his products. He would dearly like to rent space in the prestigious Waterfront or at the equally relatively upmarket Tygervalley Shopping Centre. However, according to Navavee this dream may prove elusive, especially for a 'Black' or a 'Coloured'. He hopes to open up a retail outlet and move into the formal market, while not abandoning the flea markets altogether. 'There is just one hurdle I have to cross before I can go into a shopping centre', Navavee said. 'I am looking for cheap money – where can I get it?'

According to Navavee, the flea market environment is an incubator for entrepreneurs. He believes that about one in ten of the entrepreneurs found there could develop viable businesses, given a little support and assistance. Navavee regards the flea market as an action-learning and open-learning system, inasmuch as business is conducted in the open where everyone can see what everyone else is doing. Learning can take place through observation, particularly through seeing the ups and downs of other businesses. Navavee also views the flea market as an excellent support system as traders form networking groups and help each other both physically and psychologically. The other side of the coin is the fact that it is a 'snakepit' in the sense that some people compete viciously against each other. However, this is also a valuable learning experience.

He describes two types of flea market stall-renters: the hangers-on who tend to be survivalist, unemployed and desperate for money; and the real entrepreneurs who are committed to their businesses and their reputations and who are willing to go to the suppliers to make proper deals. According to Navavee: 'The hangers-on are like scavengers, looking for bargains and trying to cut deals everywhere. They are not consistent in their product line, they chop and change their commodities all the time. People get fed up with them and don't respect them. On the other hand, the entrepreneurs are consistent with their suppliers and can supply their customers on a continuous basis'. One of the benefits for entrepreneurs in the flea markets is the fact that they can watch the chain stores, copy them and sometimes improve on their styles. This means not having to travel overseas for ideas, although this is something that Navavee would like to do. He also believes that entrepreneurs have an advantage in terms of overheads. Their expenses need not be so high and so they can sell at much lower prices.

In contemplating the growth and development of his business, Navavee does not regard a transfer to larger premises as problematic. 'In the apartheid days, yes, it was more of a problem, with all the discrimination and the laws. Now I think all the laws are in our favour. Even the new labour laws are in favour of both employers and employees'. Although he is not quite sure of all the rules and regulations he is confident that both parties will gain from changes in legislation. He is of the opinion that the current climate is certainly better than the former situation. However, he stresses that workers do seem to have a lot more privileges these days and employers must therefore be on their guard. He believes that the new labour laws will protect everyone and they could ensure that better work relationships are established. The employers will treat their workers better and this will ensure improved productivity and above all, people will start respecting each other.

Navavee is, however, critical of employee attitudes towards work. He feels that many workers have little respect for small businesses and their owners and thus believe that they do not have to give of their best. He is also concerned about the role and attitude of the small business manager/owner, who has to manage many aspects of the business rather than just one functional area. He believes that, as his business grows, he and his employees will have to make major mind-shifts in terms of their respective roles and attitudes.

In spite of these difficulties, he still believes that he will move into the new shopping mall on the Waterfront and be successful when he gets there.

Note: in 1998 Navavee realized his dream. He opened his first retail outlet at the shopping mall on the waterfront.

Case study review

Navavee Mathews exhibits the full range of Timmons's themes. Factors which have contributed to his entrepreneurial behaviour are presented in Table 3.2.

Table 3.2 Factors contributing to Navavee Mathews's entrepreneurial behaviour

Category	Factors
Antecedent influences	• There is a family background of self-employment which may have had a positive effect on his entrepreneurial behaviour. • Despite being expelled from the formal education system, he made another attempt in later years and he is committed to life-long learning albeit through observation and learning from others. • He exhibits a 'trader's' instinct and impressive selling and negotiation skills. • He has strong moral, social and business ethics.
Incubator organization	• His business has not developed from any incubator organization, and skills and knowledge have been acquired through experiential learning.
Environment factors	• He is a deviant from the social norms of his country. • He has a catalytic role within his community acting as a focus for support and advice. • He interacts intuitively with the marketplace, rather than basing business development on formal market research.

Acknowledgement

The authors would sincerely like to thank the technical support of the Black Entrepreneurship and Enterprise Support Facility (BEES) who made the writing of this case study possible.

4

America: Mexico

Rafael E. Alcaraz Rodríguez

Key feature summary

Mexico represents a country confronted by severe economic and social challenges. At a governmental level it has selected entrepreneurship as a priority strategy directed at addressing these challenges. Key features affecting entrepreneurship are:

- Mexican society is characterized by poverty, low levels of education and employment, and a population dominated by the young 19 years or younger (50 per cent) for whom there are insufficient employment opportunities.
- Enterprises which are classified as 'micro' and 'small' account for 97.3 per cent and 2.3 per cent respectively of all businesses. In addition, these enterprises are extremely vulnerable to changes in the environment.
- Innovation and entrepreneurship are recognized as priority areas for political intervention in response to the social and economic crisis in general, and specifically to support small firms, and to enable the young to become economically productive members of society.
- Political intervention has supported the provision of appropriate entrepreneurship education programmes delivered from high school through to graduate levels. A holistic approach is adopted balancing economic wealth creation with social responsibility to the community sensitive to its cultural, historical and social values.
- The key aim of the entrepreneurship education programmes is to create a critical mass of entrepreneurial professionals who will act as change agents, and enable a cascade effect to the betterment of economic and social well-being in Mexico and internationally.

Introduction

This chapter explores the manner in which education can be utilized effectively to reverse adverse trends in Mexico, through the stimulation of entrepreneurial behaviour designed to ameliorate society and the economy in general. Instigated at national government level, such an educational programme addresses, in a holistic manner, the development of the entrepreneurial person. This is aimed at the optimization of an inherent entrepreneurial attitude, alongside the enabling of the acquisition of relevant skills and values within a stimulating entrepreneurial environment. A case study is presented based on Hugo Esquinca and his company Chi-A Cards. He represents a sound example of the output of the entrepreneurial educational programme delivered at Monterrey Institute of Technology and Higher Learning.

Mexico: an overview

As a region confronted with poverty, low levels of education and unemployment, Latin America has embraced entrepreneurship, and its innovative potential, as a possible saviour. With approximately 110 million impoverished people in Central and South America, living on an average of one dollar a day, the reality is that the act of 'innovating' has turned into a necessity for governments and citizens alike, should they desire to survive – never mind prosper. Within this context, entrepreneurship represents more than a desirable characteristic to enable an individual to triumph in life. It has become a means by which the welfare of populations can be saved from yet further degeneration.

Mexico presents an extremely representative example of the economic and social situation that Latin America as a whole is experiencing. This is evident when we look at certain related indicators. Currently, Mexico has a population of 94 million, of whom 50 per cent are 19 years old or younger (INEGI, 1995), and there is a demand for approximately 1 million new jobs every year. The country has an official unemployment rate of six per cent, and close to 25 per cent of the people who are old enough to work, work in 'economically informal' conditions. In other words, without a steady job and with very low salaries, which causes around 15 million people to live excluded from society, in extreme poverty conditions. Furthermore, in excess of 50 per cent of the population is found in subsistence conditions. Of those who begin basic education three per cent finish college. However, it should be noted that only one out of every 200 children has the opportunity to attend college.

Additionally, the political and economic crises that have appeared in the region during the last few years, have resulted in the closure of approximately 15 500 businesses from 1994 to 1997. This has resulted in the worst social and economic crisis since the beginning of the twentieth century. According to 1995 statistics, 2 million businesses exist in the country, of which 97.3 per cent are micro-businesses (from 1 to 15 workers), 2.3 per cent are small businesses (16–100 workers), 0.3 per cent are medium businesses (101–250 workers), and only 0.1 per cent are large businesses (more than 250 workers). Of all these businesses, 56 per cent are found in the commercial sector, 32 per cent in the service sector and 12 per cent in the industrial sector. Currently, businesses in Mexico confront a peculiar situation, which makes them very susceptible to changes in their surroundings. This is making their eventual disappearance probable. For example, conditions conspiring against enterprise include:

- **Educational level**: more than 60 per cent of business people possess an education inferior than medium basic level and have never received training related to the beginning, operation and development of a business.
- **Family-type organization**: businesses are lacking in any formal and defined organizational structure, and tend to reflect an extended family-type organization.
- **Markets**: there are low levels of awareness and knowledge relative to the domestic and international market place.

- **Work force**: a high percentage of the work force is unqualified and low skilled.
- **Technology**: the majority of businesses are operating with obsolete technology.
- **Resources**: there is extreme difficulty in accessing financial, technical and administrative resources.
- **Controls**: limited administrative or financial control systems are in place.
- **Fiscal**: business operation is under conditions of fiscal control that are not current, or in conditions of informality evading fiscal control.

Recognizing the impact of these negative conditions, the local, regional (state or district) and national government in Mexico, have increased their support for business development. Specifically, their aim is to attempt to improve the integration of young people into the productive sector, and to make business operation more effective in existing companies. It is believed that this can be achieved through the promotion of an entrepreneurial and business spirit, so that potential young entrepreneurs and existing businesses can contribute positively towards the solution of the region's economic and social problems.

Consequently, in recent years, the authorities have begun to create actions such as:

- **Administrative simplification**: facilitation and incentives in negotiations for the incorporation of businesses into a formal structure.
- **Information services**: counselling, business links, support in legal, fiscal and labour negotiations, etc.
- **Fiscal facilities**: lowering of rates imposed, easy terms of tax payment, simplified regimens for the business's operation, etc.
- **Tax accrediting**: as an incentive to create new businesses.
- **Investment and support funds:** effect financial support schemes and the promotion of the bank in the development of business.
- **Social and educational promotion**: to encourage the stimulation of entrepreneurial behaviour and the development of new businesses.

Entrepreneurship and education

In addition to these actions, it has been proposed that in order to be economically productive and socially responsible in the current dynamic and competitive society, individuals require to combine a sound education with a series of skills, values and attitudes which will enable them to maximize their education. Furthermore, it is recognized as important for Mexico that this be translated into entrepreneurship. It could be suggested that entrepreneurship represents an attitude adopted towards life, but it is more than that. Persons may exhibit an entrepreneurial attitude, but they need to know how to use it to best advantage. Thus, our stance is that in order to innovate successfully, it is necessary to have an entrepreneurial attitude, complimented with certain additional skills and values. For example, these would include the:

- vision, to detect areas of opportunity;
- creativity, to take advantage of the opportunities that have been detected;
- ability to plan, to create goals and attain them;

- feeling of responsibility, to assume the commitment to reach these goals;
- work ethic, to persevere in reaching the goals.

Thus, following research into the process of entrepreneurship, the Republic of Mexico's Senate proposed that the development of the entrepreneurial spirit be incorporated into the law. This will result in entrepreneurship being incorporated into the educational system from a basic level. In addition, the universities have committed themselves to promoting and developing the entrepreneurial spirit within their students and graduates, and within society as a whole. This has become a fundamental part of their educational mission. An example of this action and commitment towards the entrepreneurship and the community is the Monterrey Institute of Technology and Higher Learning (ITESM), also known as the Monterrey Tec.

ITESM

In the 1940s, the Monterrey Institute of Technology began its operations offering college majors in the areas of administration and engineering. Its purpose was to form specialists that were necessary for the operation of Mexican businesses of that era. The goal was accomplished and the 'Tec' became one of the universities with the highest academic prestige in Mexico, and in Latin America as a whole. By the 1960s, the need to strengthen the development of its students in administrative areas was identified. This was as a result of many of the ITESM graduates being appointed to senior administrative positions in the companies or organizations where they were employed following graduation. They found that they had not been sufficiently prepared for these positions during their time at ITESM.

Consequently, in the 1980s, ITESM made the decision to instil an additional series of skills, attitudes, values, and characteristics in its graduates. One of them was to introduce the students to the concept of being an entrepreneur in their own right as a positive career opportunity. This required that the Institute adopt a specialized approach. It needed to deliver a process that would permit the development of professionals with an entrepreneurial attitude, able to act in a way that would generate new paths – new ideas. The output would be creators of a new society, actors and not spectators of life: in other words, 'agents of change'.

In this manner, the Entrepreneurial Program was created to give a distinctive quality to the ITESM graduate. This is considered particularly significant as a key part of the Tec's fundamental mission is to:

> … form professionals and post-graduates with levels of excellency in their field of speciality, inciting in its students the development of the entrepreneurial and innovative spirit, the vocation of leaders committed with the development of their communities, respect towards human dignity, and an appreciation towards the cultural, historical and social values of their community.

Driven by this mission, ITESM's Entrepreneurial Program became the first formally structured programme in Mexico and, in fact in the rest of Latin America, giving valuable support to the entrepreneurial development of its students.

Background

As an initial approach, and searching for a way to prepare students not only as professionals but also as entrepreneurs, in 1978 ITESM established a project known as the Business Program (the Entrepreneurial Program's initial name). It had a work force constituted of a few of the Institute's professors, and business people who worked in the community. This committee's main objective was to create a company that could be used as a classroom, and a laboratory, for the students. The aim was to marry an academic programme with the opportunity to elaborate upon it through practical student participation, and exposure to the realities of business development and operation.

Thus, the company required to be formulated as a small business that could comprehensively develop all of its relevant areas such as production, marketing, technology, finance and human resources. This was to make sure that the participating student would acquire a holistic experience in all of the business's basic areas. A number of alternative models offered by the members of the committee were studied. The one that most closely met the requirements for the criteria that had been established was chosen.

The academic programme was designed by the Business Program's committee, and its establishment and control were assigned to the Administration and Social Sciences Division of the Monterrey Campus. Finally, the programme was created and approved. At the end of 1978 the committee proceeded to design the buildings, select the machinery, and sell shares in the company. The shares were sold to business people willing to share their experience and enthusiasm to support the academic content of the programme.

The business classroom

In 1979, the business was legally constituted, under the social denomination 'Guidelines for Information, SA'. During 1979 and 1980 the construction of the business facilities was completed, the acquisition of machinery taken care of, and labour and administrative employees were hired to initiate productive operations in March of 1980. In August 1979 the first students were recruited to the Business Program. To participate the students had to have been studying the last, or the second last, semester in any of the majors that were offered by the Administration, Social Sciences, Engineering or Architecture Divisions. The students commenced participation in the programme by enrolling in the introductory class called 'Business Workshop'.

This class was structured based on: the professor's communication of relevant knowledge and experience; a business workshop; conference attendance; the study of particular case studies; and an investigation (project) in the student's field of interest. These efforts were guided by teachers who had practical experience, and by the involvement of business people. The business people's participation had the aim of sharing their experiences with the students in the creation and development of a company. During its first two semesters, the Business Program had the participation of a total of 300 students and involved 25 Mexican business people in collaboration. In general, feedback from students who had graduated from the Program indicated that, those who had had the ambition of graduating to work in a company before taking the Business Workshop course, were now seriously thinking of creating their own business.

The Entrepreneurial Program is born

In 1984, a move to develop more extensive force and realism within the Business Program began to emerge. This was mainly because the student's experience ended with the business idea and there was the need to provide the opportunity to take it forward, translating it into a reality. In this context, and with the desire to advance student development, the Entrepreneurial Program was created in January 1985, and the model and resources necessary for its administration and operation were established. The support and commitment given to the Entrepreneurial Program by the Monterrey Institute of Technology, resulted in its constitution as a programme with a wide and futurist vision in the creation and formation of professionals, with the potential of selecting a new career alternative – being entrepreneurs.

The Entrepreneurial Program seeks the development of highly capable people, with a clear awareness of the social and economic environment in which they will operate. In addition, there is a special emphasis on the development of their spirit and abilities as creative entrepreneurs. Furthermore, the focus is towards the creation of innovative ideas that contain a high degree of technology. It is believed that such a programme has the potential to produce a new generation of leaders of society. Thus, the emphasis of the programme is towards the formation of the entrepreneurial person, completing the traditional studies with a real experience where the students could learn to generate and develop their entrepreneurial ideas. In September 1985 formal approval was given to the Entrepreneurial Program and it was made available to all of the major areas of study within the ITESM system.

Today's Entrepreneurial Program

To fulfil its mission, the ITESM system gave the Entrepreneurial Program its fundamental goal:

> To promote and develop the entrepreneurial and innovative spirit in the ITESM students.

To reach this goal, in 1990 the Entrepreneurial Program gathered a group of experts, in charge of co-ordinating, establishing and implementing the Program in all of the ITESM system's campus. This same group was in charge of redesigning the educational model and organizational structure, under which the Program's operation is structured, in order to provide it with quality and stability. The result of the reconfigured organizational structure is presented in Figure 4.1. The base course of the Program is known as 'Entrepreneur Development', and it is offered to all of the students, from junior high school to graduate level, as a mandatory course. All students who are enrolled in the system must take it within the study plan that corresponds to them.

Currently, the Entrepreneurial Program is co-ordinated at system level by the Mission Support Program's (DPAM) Council, chaired by Rafael E. Alcaraz Rodríguez, director of the DPAM in the ITESM system. The Council is composed of a group of experts and co-ordinators of each Rectorate of the ITESM system. These work closely with the Program's directors in every one of the 26 campus that belong to the system. This is to guarantee that the Program is functioning correctly, and to make sure that the uniformity and quality is being respected in relation to the students.

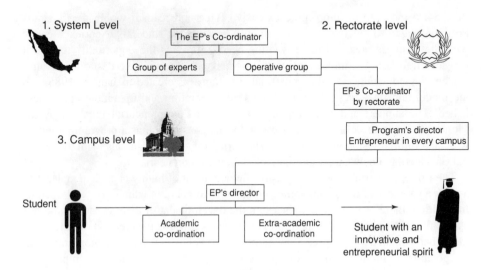

Figure 4.1 Organization of the ITESM Entrepreneurial Program

The Council meets every month to monitor the Program's progress, to design new teaching material and to identify further areas of opportunity. The Program's director, in each of the system's campus, liaises with their Program's professors and counsellors on a monthly basis. The Program's directors meet every semester with the Council, and all of the Program's professors and counsellors at system level gather annually at the International Congress of Entrepreneurs, organized by the ITESM system.

Three areas constitute the Program's educational model: academic, motivational and institutional support (Figure 4.2).

The practical tool that is used in this model is the gestation, development and implantation of a company or a student activity. This represents a task that, under certain guidelines, constitutes the key element needed to reach the development of the entrepreneurial spirit in everyone participating in the Program.

The Program's professors are aided by constant training for the delivery of their courses. This represents at least 40 hours per semester of training in instructional guides, in bibliographic actualization, etc. This results in the achievement of a standardization of the Program in all the campus of the ITESM system. The System's 'Professor's Training Program' runs every semester through the participation of experts from national and international levels, in the different areas that make up the Program. This enables the professor to develop an adequate management of the subjects which are represented in the Program's courses.

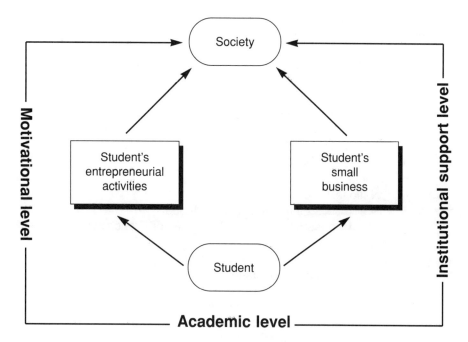

Figure 4.2 Basic educational model

The academic content of the educational model is supported by the Entrepreneurial Program's Educational Package. It is composed of more than 21 basic manuals and learning aids. In addition, more than 65 selected books that permit a deeper investigation of every subject of the Program's various courses support the learning process (Figure 4.3 on page 50).

Every semester new manuals are developed and integrated to the Program's Educational Package; eight of them have been published and two are in the process of publication. This extensive documentation means that any member of the population in the community can access the multiple content areas of the Program. Furthermore, the bibliography is enriched annually through the addition of conference papers and reports, which ensures the currency of the materials. Figure 4.4 on page 50 indicates the positioning of the different materials contained within the package relative to the level of study.

Further important aspects of the Program are found in the motivational area of the educational model. This involves student participation in the likes of the National and International Congresses, fairs and exhibitions that are held annually. These provide the opportunity to display the achievements of the Entrepreneurial Program to all of the student community, and also to give an occasion for stimulating academic exchange.

Technological developments are incorporated to improve the teaching programme in a number of ways, one of which being teleconferencing. Conferences for the Program involving professors and students are transmitted weekly via satellite, creating a virtual university. This programme is known as 'The Entrepreneur's Hour' and the subjects studied in this manner are illustrated in Figure 4.5 on page 51.

Entrepreneurial Program's
educational package has the
following books

1 Campus Manual
2 Student's Manual for each course (9)
3 Professor's Manual for each course (9)
4 Counsellor's Manual
5 Bibliography and Support Centre's Manual
6 Institutional Support Manual:
   • Local
   • National
7 PROITESM's Financial Support Manual
8 Manual Concerning the Legal Aspects for Franchises
9 Industrial Protection Manual
10 Manual on Fairs and Congresses
11 Manual on Legal Aspects for the Creation of a Business
12 Business Plan Prototype
13 Manual on the Entrepreneur's Abilities
14 Manual for the Societies of Entrepreneurship
15 Bibliography (60 selected books)

Figure 4.3 Educational package

1. High school level courses

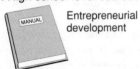
Entrepreneurial
development

2. Undergraduate level courses

Entrepreneurial
development

3. Undergraduate level optional courses

Figure 4.4 Levels of entrepreneurship study

Semestral Program
Subjects

- Training on the use of the Educational Package
- Innovation and Creativity
- Areas of Opportunity
- Development of a Business Plan
- Patents, Brands and Copyrights
- Legal Aspects for the Creation of a Business
- Financial Support
- Varied Subjects

Figure 4.5 The Entrepreneur's Hour via satellite conferences for teachers and students in the Entrepreneurial Program in all 26 campus that make up the ITESM system

Further technological support is provided in the form of the simulation of pilot plants, laboratories and experimental bases. These give students access to facilities which enable them to test out their projects in the company's 'virtual incubators', which, combined with the Institution's 'real and administrative incubators', provide an important additional dimension to the entrepreneur who wishes to establish his or her company in a commercial manner.

Financial support is also provided within the ITESM educational model. PROITESM, which is a venture capital company made up of the ITESM, BBV (private bank), NAFIN (a promoter of the government), and a group of private investors interested in supporting the development and modernization of the industrial sector and of community services. PROITESM offers interested students the possibility of financial services for their project. These are provided on the condition that the projects fulfil certain requirements, such as technological innovation, satisfaction of social needs, quality and respect towards the environment.

Benefits arising from the Program

To date, the Entrepreneurial Program has contributed in the personal and career development of more than 70,000 students, helping them to evolve their entrepreneurial spirit, and contributing socially to the creation of more than 3000 companies. Many of them have proved to be very successful. Today they are operating and generating a large volume of employment, sending forth a modern, dynamic and quality image into the different sectors of our economy.

Without doubt, the Entrepreneurial Program has had a significant impact in the ITESM's community. As can be seen in Figure 4.6, according to recent studies made by the Strategic Studies Group of the ITESM, it has been proved that 48 per cent of graduates establish their own companies five or ten years after ending their college studies. This means the creation of an average of 4000 companies and approximately 20 000 new jobs every year. In addition, approximately 34 per cent of the ITESM graduates become involved in a company in the form of either acquisition, inheritance, association or through offering their services as independent professional consultants.

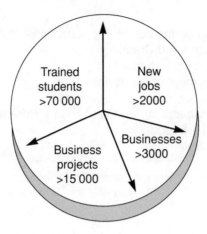

Figure 4.6 *The Entrepreneurial Program in numbers (statistics from August 1985 to December 1996).*

In the semester August–December 1996, the Entrepreneurial Program of the ITESM system gave tuition and support to more than 7000 students (full and part-time). Under the supervision of more than 100 professors, in excess of 150 internal counsellors and more than 100 external counsellors, they formulated around 2000 business projects. According to estimated projections, more than 200 commercial companies will develop in the following months, which will become part of the great family of ex-students of the Entrepreneurial Program.

Further 'creative' developments

Creation and Development of Business Program

The ITESM's existing Entrepreneurial Program has been complemented by the introduction of a new programme called the Creation and Development of Business Program (PCDE). It will enhance the students' educational experience, and has been designed with the goal of achieving a positive impact in the community. The PCDE aims to facilitate the creative processes that result in the development of innovative products and/or services. It consists of a series of steps leading to the construction of prototypes, and/or detailed plans or processes, which have the potential to be progressed to business creation through the Entrepreneurial Program. This enables these products/services to become commercial companies, with the start-up process facilitated through the provision of the Business Incubator unit. Alternatively, the output of the PCDE may result in a franchise or an exporting company, to be developed through the corresponding Franchise and Exporting Programs of the ITESM system. This model of creation and development is presented in Figure 4.7.

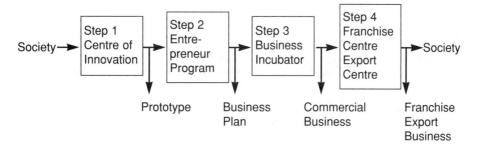

Figure 4.7 Model of creation and development of business

Transference Model

In the last years, ITESM has worked constantly towards the promotion of an entrepreneurial culture, not only within its student community, but also in the wider society. This is the reason why many of the Mexican and Latin American universities continuously seek support from the ITESM to initiate their own entrepreneurial programmes. Consequently, the Transference Model of the ITESM's Entrepreneurial Program was born.

It is based on basic training of 21-hour duration that is delivered to representatives of interested institutions. During this period the Program's philosophy is shared, the Educational and Operational Models are explained, and the participants are trained in the use of the Program's Educational Package. The process also includes the provision of the eight core manuals, and the three essential texts to enable them to initiate their own Entrepreneurial Program. This takes place using the resources of the university and through basic counselling and planning sessions.

The objective of the Transference Model is to train universities and organized groups within the community, in the national and international levels of the entrepreneurship education model. In this way, they can implant, develop and consolidate their own Entrepreneurial Program, with the goal of enabling an exciting cascade effect, extending the scope of promoting and developing the entrepreneurial spirit in students, academia, and the community as a whole.

With the Entrepreneurial Program's transfer, a legally binding contract is signed between the participating universities and ITESM. In this way, they are able to work in partnership in the promotion and development of the entrepreneurial culture in Mexico and Latin America. To date, the Transference Model has enabled ITESM's Entrepreneurial Program to support approximately 150 universities in five Latin American countries. This is the way in which the Entrepreneurial Program fulfils its mission, working within the ITESM system and with the society as a whole. In this valuable way, it is developing a greater mass of high calibre entrepreneurial professionals who positively contribute to the social and economic well being of Mexico and Latin America as a whole.

Chapter summary

Undoubtedly Mexico has faced, and continues to be challenged by, severe social and economic adversity. Entrepreneurship has been elevated to 'saviour' status as a means of improving the welfare of the mass of population from a base survival level, and to halt any further degeneration. Thus, at a national level, the government has recognized the wide range of potential benefits that can be achieved through members of the population being educated and developed to behave in an entrepreneurial manner. It is believed that through a partnership that involves government, educational institutes, the business community and society as a whole, negative social and economic trends can be halted, if not reversed.

Thus, a strategy has been adopted directed at improving the business environment through political intervention measures, and putting in place effective entrepreneurship educational programmes from high school level through to graduation. In this way it is hoped that future generations will emerge from the educational process, instilled with an entrepreneurial spirit and the skills necessary to succeed in business. They will then enter into a business environment that is supportive, enhancing business performance, survival and growth rates. In doing so these entrepreneurs are charged not only with being leading actors within the business arena, but also within society. Throughout this chapter, there has been a powerful message that emphasizes the importance of developing the future entrepreneurs who hold sets of values relative to both business ethics and social responsibility, sensitive to cultures, history and society.

ITESM provides a shining example of such a holistic entrepreneurial education programme, the success of which is evidenced by the statistics provided. Embodied in its programme is the ethos of wealth creation for the common benefit of society as a whole. There is no doubt that the vision which gave birth to ITESM's programmes was futuristic, and the success has been driven by the support and commitment at the highest level within the Institute along, with the enthusiasm and courage of its academic and business champions. This has now resulted in a cascade effect as it transfers its effective model from the centre outwards throughout Latin America, and no doubt in the future elsewhere world-wide.

In conclusion, we can see a real growth in the development of entrepreneurs in Latin America. It is the responsibility of public and private institutions, universities and the business community to work together in the promotion of the further development and stimulation of an entrepreneurial culture in their respective regions.

Being an Entrepreneur is a way of life based on the constant struggle to make our dreams into reality.

Case Study: Hugo Esquinca

For Hugo Esquinca, an ITESM student in his ninth semester of Architecture, the Entrepreneurial Program meant the beginning of a new way of life – aspiring to be an entrepreneur. This was a dream Hugo had held since his high school studies at Chiapas Campus. During the Program this extremely proud, young business-man generated the idea of 'Chi-A Cards', which necessitated him balancing his continuing studies at ITESM with the challenges of running a growing business. He is from Southeastern Mexico and tells us that the name for his business is derived from the concept Chiapas-Authentic. Hugo's original business idea evolved from an innovative concept of cards to say 'congratulations', or to give someone as a present. They are manufactured with exclusive paper, and made unique by having an indigenous embroidered square, characteristic of one of the many ethnic groups from the region of Chiapas, on the front.

Hugo's business development project matured when he entered Monterrey Campus to study. Here, he participated in the Entrepreneurial Program in an active and enthusiastic manner, persevering until he achieved his goal of establishing Chi-A Cards. For him, the Entrepreneurial Program has been the most important motivator of his entrepreneurial career. It has been the motor driving him forward, giving him counselling and motivational tools to go on with this project. Although very small in the beginning, with time and Hugo's hard work, in three years, it has become a solid, well-established business. Today, Chi-A Cards is self-sufficient, with two lines of products: craftsmanship cards; and jewellery made of amber mounted on silver. Currently, Hugo works with orders of approximately 3000 cards every month, which results in the generation of jobs for direct employees and the many craftsmen in Chiapas.

Hugo Esquinca is a prime example of the key business and personal develop-ment role which education can play in stimulating and supporting entrepreneurial behaviour. For example, he talks about the significance of one very real, funda-mental, learning experience. 'Once, when I participated in the Monterrey Campus Business Exhibition, there were many businesses exhibiting and therefore so much competition for the people's attention. It occurred to me to bring along some typical clothes from Chiapas that were very noticeable – embroidered with bright colours. I also brought an Indian mask that is used during the Indian festivities. Then what I did was to forget about what my classmates would think of me. I put on the mask and the suit, and I started walking around the area of the Exhibition. I walked through all the hallways and came back to my stand. By that time there was a line of people behind me who were very interested and curious to know about Chi-A. That is one of the most important lessons that I learned from the Entrepreneurial Programme – to be proactive, creative and always dynamic.'

'Counselling, training and vision have been the main support elements that the Entrepreneurial Programme has given me', says Hugo. He emphasizes the addi-tional power that being associated with ITESM has provided him, at both national and international business levels. For example, one of the most important activi-ties that Hugo has participated in has been entering various business competitions. As the founding entrepreneur of Chi-A Cards, Hugo has won in forums such as the 'Nuevo Leon Prize for Business Excellence', and the 'International Contest for Business Plans' in San Diego, California which he views as his greatest achievement to date.

This 21-year-old says that, 'these competitions help you to promote yourself, and evaluate the true potential of the business project within an independent forum. If you only developed it within the confines of the Entrepreneurial Program there is a danger that you become too conceited, and believe that no matter what your business will be a success. When you are in front of the judges of these competitions and people you don't know, and everything goes well, that gives you tremendous confidence that the project is going to work for real!' Indeed, the experience at the San Diego competition has been one of Hugo's greatest challenges. Nineteen universities from the USA, Australia and Latin America participated. Hugo, representing ITESM, obtained second place in the contest and with it $5000 prize money. However, Hugo considers that his greatest prize has been the promotion that these forums have given his business, which has translated into firm sales. For instance, he remembers that three years after winning the second prize in the 'Entrepreneurial Spirit' competition at ITESM, he sold the largest number of cards to that date – 13 000 Christmas cards!

Despite these successes, the business's financial aspects have represented the most important challenge for the owner of Chi-A. He explains that 1994 and 1995 were particularly difficult times for the business. This was, primarily, because of the economic recession crisis that Mexico was suffering during this period, which particularly affected micro-businesses in an extremely negative manner. However, Chi-A survived the recession and has recovered to be an economically self-sufficient company today. 'It is clear to me', explains Hugo, 'that the company needs an investment of both money and dedication. This is why I have had patience and energy to continue with the business, creating goals for the medium and long term'.

Hugo's greatest achievement has been to go on in spite of the many adversities that he has faced, being a student and a businessman at the same time. He has had to learn to co-ordinate both of these activities, which are equally important to him. In a few months, Hugo will finish his college studies. Then he will dedicate himself full-time to the development of his business. To achieve this he has been working on his new business plan since the beginning of 1997, with counselling from experts who work on the Entrepreneurial Program. His aim is to enter international markets by the beginning of 1998, taking a quality example of our Mexicanism, and the entrepreneurial spirit of our younger generation beyond the boundaries of our country.

Case study review

Hugo Esquinca exhibits the full range of Timmons's themes. The factors that contribute to his entrepreneurial behaviour are presented in Table 4.1.

Table 4.1 Factors contributing to Hugo Esquinca's entrepreneurial behaviour

Category	Factors
Antecedent influences	• He is committed to life-long learning through the formal education system and through informal means such as participation in international competitions and interaction with the business community.
	• He has strong moral, social and business ethics.
	• He exhibits a trader's instinct and impressive selling and negotiation skills.
Incubator organization	• His business has not emerged from a direct incubator industry organization, however, the educational institute has acted as a surrogate incubator.
Environment factors	• His entrepreneurial action has been mobilized as a consequence of support from the formal network relative to finance, examples of entrepreneurial action, and opportunities for interim advice and counselling.
	• He is determined to develop the capability to exploit international market potential.

Acknowledgements

The author would like to sincerely thank Mariano Gamboa Zuniga, Eugenia Aldana Farina, Jose Alsonso Cortes Jimenez and Leticia Lozano for their assistance in the preparation of this chapter.

5

America: North

Harold Welsch

Key feature summary

North America is unquestionably a country that has a culture in which potential entrepreneurs are nurtured, trained and supported. However, this statement is qualified in that entrepreneurship is not practised evenly throughout the population with certain racial and ethnic groups less prone to entrepreneurial behaviour as others. Key features affecting entrepreneurship are:

- Entrepreneurship is woven into the fabric of North American society and reinforced through media and social, political and economic institutions.
- It is an achievement-oriented society that has historically encouraged and honoured individual accomplishments and the attainment of material prosperity. Currently, this is resulting in entrepreneurs being depicted as modern day heroes.
- Emphasis is placed on the importance of entrepreneurial 'dreams' and visualization of entrepreneurial achievement as significant powers in igniting the spirit of North American entrepreneurship, materializing and shaping the yet unimagined.
- Individualism and a concept of 'self' is central to the North American character, and belief in individuals and individual rights are part of the heritage. This results in persons who seek a high degree of autonomy and independence which are central characteristics associated with entrepreneurship.
- Individuals are encouraged to rise above acceptance of, and conformity to, society's standards to reach an autonomous level.

Introduction

Two important roots have been thought to be associated with the history and origin of entrepreneurship. The first is agriculture, wherein the farmer sold the fruits of his labour for more than his cost. In most cases, family members contributed to the enterprise by carrying out chores and minding the home while others were toiling in the field. The other root, the Protestant Ethic based on Calvinism introduced new patterns of individualism, stressing diligence, reliability, fidelity and responsibility in all matters, which emerged, and was reinforced by the mechanism of peer pressure. Furthermore, Berger (1991) suggested that family agriculture and the Protestant Ethic led to new forms of production and emphasized hard work, frugality, individual accountability and reliability, as well as habits of self-regulation and personal drive. He asserted that:

> They fostered cognitive modes of rational calculation, of doing things for their instrumental utility, and of rationally balancing defensible risk against mere adventurism (p. 17).

Various authors have identified characteristics as being essential to entrepreneurship such as: open-mindedness; willingness to take risks; scepticism; motivation for profit; ability to innovate or combine familiar components in new ways rather than invent the components themselves; make purposeful decisions; influence the near environment; persevere in the face of adversity; and impacting the environment through individual initiative.

This autonomous sense of self stands in stark contrast to the Japanese, among other Asiatic groups. Social organization in Japan centres on the genealogical family and kinship group but also includes the neighbourhood and often by extension other groups such as the company by which one is employed, and the nation itself. Socialization involves the development of a strong identification by each individual with the group, and a continuing sense of mutual obligation among its members in which the desires of the individual are subordinated to the needs and expectations of the larger community.

Western individualism leads to a sense of self with a sharp boundary that stops at one's skin and clearly demarcates self from non-self. In dealings with outsiders or alien groups, the Japanese undoubtedly have an equally well-defined boundary between themselves and others. But within the context of groups with which the individual is identified, the Japanese sense of self is more permeable and more diffuse at its boundaries. The '*me*' becomes merged with the '*we*', and the reactions of others to one's behaviours gain priority over one's own evaluation. These contrasting senses of self in the two societies are produced by, and lead to, differing emphases on rights versus obligations, on autonomy versus interdependence, on the pursuit of happiness versus personal sacrifice, and on the priority of the individual versus that of the group differences that have broad ramifications for generating new businesses and nurturing entrepreneurship careers. This chapter investigates these differences, and the significant factors at work in North American society which have ramifications for entrepreneurship. The subject of the case study, Barry Potekin, is the personification of the North American entrepreneur, who is an intuitive arbitrageur, with a 'fire in his belly', driven to be 'number one'.

Entrepreneurship in North America

Entrepreneurship is ingrained in the very fabric of North American culture. It is discussed at the family dinner table among intergenerational members, practised by preschool children with their lemonade stands, and promoted every day through personal success human interest stories in the media. Furthermore, entrepreneurship is taught in school from kindergarten through to the twelfth grade, it has been integrated into college and university curricula, and is taught and promoted through various outreach and training programmes including government Small Business Development Centers (SBDCS) in every state of the nation. Consequently, throughout one's life as an American citizen, entrepreneurship as a career option is espoused early and reinforced regularly.

The advantages of a self-employment career are often described in glowing positive terms in US newspapers and magazines and the chance of success and the risks of failure are being considered daily in the minds of potential entrepreneurs who are planning their careers. Even though the actual rate of failure and termination of small business is relatively high, the self-employed person is often glamourized as a winner, folk hero, role model, cultural saviour, source of job creation and economic developer. The role of the entrepreneur is no longer one of a dull supplier of car parts or groceries, but was transformed during the 1980s into the *'courageous risk-taker'*. Popular culture has made heroes of entrepreneurs, transforming them into the equivalent status of 'rock stars' of the 1990s. Today it is acceptable to start an unknown company, to take risks and perhaps even fail! Indeed, it has become acceptable to *dare to be rich*.

It is socially legitimate to be an entrepreneur in America. In fact, millions of all ages and ethnic backgrounds are starting their own businesses, buying failing businesses, reinvigorating family businesses, inventing and innovating. In the past, the label of 'entrepreneur' used to imply something sleazy, such as a used car salesman or a snake oil promoter, a con artist, a manipulator or even a parasite. But today it is not only socially acceptable to be an entrepreneur, if you are successful you stand the chance of being elevated to the status of a *modern hero*.

Being a relatively recent country, America has assumed the mantle of an *'adolescent'* engaging in *'fire-ready-aim'* policies and rushing into action with a certain impetuousness. After the Revolutionary War (of Independence) Europe was no longer the *'father'* demanding obedience and exerting authority over an endangered civilization. Rebellion against tradition, and the struggle to counteract authoritarianism, was steeped into its society via various freedom and independence driven initiatives. In contrast France prides itself on reason; the UK exhibits reserve and caution not evident in the USA; Switzerland maintains its neutrality which is an attribute absent in most Americans; and Japan is patient, respectful of process, careful with time and dedicated to cautious, long-term planning. These cultures, by comparison, are more mature or *'adult'* than the US and tend to focus more on established, rather than start-up, businesses.

American cultural forces

Americans are not a contented people. They are restless, constantly on the move, always working on something new, or busy redefining themselves. They have a perpetual invention, or improvement, process based on the idea of 'let's fix it' so that they can go on to something new. In most other cultures, individual identity is fixed early in life as a result of family heritage, class, money or status, and once set it does not change easily or at all. This is not true in America, where mobility may be the highest in the industrialized world. Specific cultural forces at work in the country have been identified as: a frontier concept; preference for choice; subscription to the 'American Dream'; propensity to think 'big'; obsession with time; improvisation, mistake tolerance, and the 'dance' approach; and a fixation with all things 'new'. Each of these cultural forces is now discussed.

Frontier concept

If there is one concept that incorporates many of Americans' entrepreneurial characteristics, it is the word '*frontier*'. There was nothing but frontier when the nation started with vast and open spaces, and it is still being explored in the space frontier and in the current cyberspace frontier. The frontier theme runs from Plymouth Rock which was the landing point of the early Pilgrims, through Manifest Destiny, John F. Kennedy's New Frontier, cyberspace, and more recently in the platforms of its political parties. The frontier concept offers challenge, opportunity and a new start for individuals and businesses. Thus, by nature Americans generally seek unfamiliar territory and this characteristic has been termed the '*nation's narcotic*' by Hammond and Morrison (1996). It is a frontier in business, as companies constantly invent new products and services, expand customer relationships, and pilot new internal processes. There is a frontier in government which often represents counter forces, in the inner city in the form of bleak futures and job markets, and in the meaning of employment as the nature of work and jobs undergo their biggest transformation to date. America is fascinated and energized by the new frontiers, innovations and changes it is confronting.

Preference for choice

Americans have a strong preference for choice. Everyone who came to America in its formative years, and those who continue to come, came by choice. They arrived ready to start a new life in a land where they could choose what, where and who they wanted to be. Choice is the dominant force in America and in the pursuit of happiness, and drives American career selection and buying habits. It seems perfectly natural to Americans to encounter variety and choice in every part of their lives.

The 'American Dream'

Americans believe in the pursuit of impossible dreams. '*Impossible*' is perhaps a misnomer, because the genius of Americans is their ability to turn their personal, business and national dreams – the seemingly impossible – into the possible. America is the land where the potential exists that all dreams can come true. Of course, factors such as technology are great enablers, but the dreams must come first! Thus, America is the happening place for dreams, starting with the Pilgrims and not stopping for one day since. The place where the '*streets are paved with gold*', the American Dream has been the ageless magnet for immigrants. The endless choices enable people to dream the impossible and make them come true sooner or later. There are no limits to what Americans can become, try, fail to do and then try again.

Think big

Americans like to think in an expansive and grandiose manner. America is the land of wide-open spaces, rich in enormous natural resources and, reportedly, populated with Paul Bunyans (a mythical giant)! Because the country is so physically large, it comes naturally to its inhabitants to think big. However, in reality this force is concerned with America's obsession with being '*Number One*', which when taken to extremes has sometimes resulted in unfortunate international conflicts. America is now dotted with big stores – superstores. Stores such as Home Depot are up to five acres in floor space, stocking more than 50 000 separate items. On the way home one can stop by a Barnes and Noble, a super-bookstore chain, and choose from 60 000 titles in the smaller stores, and up to 175 000 in the bigger ones. Few people have any idea just how many toys there are stocked in the super Toys 'R' Us stores. Thus, it is clear that Americans tend to love '*big*' – it gives them more choice, and even enables their dreams to be big. However, it would be wrong to over generalise as 'big' is not always welcome. For example, there's the case of the city parents of Burlington, Vermont. Fearing the consequences for their (small) beloved downtown merchants, they made the entry of a big Wal-Mart store extremely unwelcome.

Time obsession

Americans may be the most time-obsessed culture in the world, intolerant of wasting time and are, in a word, impatient. For them, time is money, and they want it now, in case someone else gets it before them, beating them into second place that they do not like. Anthropologist Hall (1983) says that America is the most time-obsessed and time-compartmentalized culture in the world. They break it down into small formal units of time, such as one minute, five minutes, fifteen minutes, half an hour and an hour, which are meaningless in most other cultures. Even in speech they talk about split seconds, nanoseconds, and even say, 'Give me a second', or something took 'forever' when they really mean a few minutes or more. As a consequence, unlike other cultures, Americans live in the present/future, and tomorrow is too late and fast is not soon enough. All of these time dimensions have major implications for change management, public-policy expectations, all types of scheduling, child rearing, interpersonal communications, and compulsive entrepreneurs and their customers.

Improvisation, mistake tolerance, the 'dance'

Americans are tolerant of mistakes. Making mistakes is part of how they learn and achieve things. They unconsciously do not do things right the first time because they are not motivated by a desire for perfection. However, they 'learn' from their mistakes. This force triggers the emotional pay-off that comes through the urge to improvise. The script follows certain patterns and elements, habits of mind, and behavioural proclivities that Americans invariably follow and repeat over and over again. The basic sequence is that they:

- take on an impossible task;
- are unprepared to attain their goal immediately;
- discover they are underdogs;
- are goaded on by the odds against them;
- fail the first time but try again;
- get caught up in the process (no pain, no gain);

- triumph in the end and celebrate;
- move on to something else impossible (often to repeat the process).

Americans love to improvise and value fixing things more than doing things right the first time. This enables them to show how human they are and how good they can be at problem solving and innovation. The way they fix things, and create breakthroughs is through improvising. Once the situation is fixed (or almost fixed), they are free to move on to something else, and moving on is a major preoccupation in America. This approach to life corresponds to Americans' love to 'dance'. This is the force that they rely on day in and day out to get a stalled engine started, to save a flood victim, to talk their way out of a jam, to soothe an angry customer, to play basketball, to repair an emergency room patient and to make an audience laugh at the 'Comedy Center'.

Fixation with 'new'

Americans have a fixation on what is new and 'improved' and on innovations. As individuals, and even as a nation, they are in a perpetual search for new identities, new ideas, new strategies and new products, because they provide new choices. Not a day passes that something new is not being concocted, hatched or foisted on an eager audience. Evening television, newspapers and magazines battle to lay claim to the newest innovation. Every culture is interested to some degree in what is new, but in America it is an obsession. To keep up with the latest of anything, to be first to know something, or to have the latest gadget is conspicuously American.

Achievement drive and the impossible dream

America is an achievement-oriented society that has historically encouraged and honoured individual accomplishment and the attainment of material prosperity. In the past, Americans have spoken proudly of the American dream, which embodies the belief that this is a land not only of material prosperity, but also abundant in political and economic opportunity. With hard work and perseverance, it was believed, anyone with sufficient moral fibre could succeed. Furthermore, there was a buoyant self-confidence in the ability as a people to overcome all obstacles.

This need for achievement has been identified as an important dimension heading the list of entrepreneurial characteristics. Although Brockhaus (1982) concluded 'the causal between ownership of small business and high need for achievement is not proven', more recent evidence from McClelland (1987, p. 230) indicates that persons with high need for achievement:

> performed better when the task was challenging rather than routine or very difficult tasks; they insisted upon taking personal responsibility for the performance – they liked getting quantitative feedback on how good the performance had been and they were innovative in the sense of looking for new and better ways to improve their performance ... In fact, (these) people were more likely to go into business and to be successful.

McClelland concluded that 'a great deal of empirical evidence of various kinds supports the conclusion that the need to achieve ... is an important component in small business success.' More recently, Shaver and Scott (1991, p. 32) concluded: '... achievement motivation remains the personologist's best candidate in the attempt to account for new venture creation'.

However, it should be immediately acknowledged that despite the professed commitment to democracy and equality of opportunity, participation in the American dream has not been open to all. Women and blacks, members of ethnic and religious minorities, and often the poor have historically been excluded from the elect as purportedly being innately inferior or morally unworthy. These groups have had to fight, and many continue to fight, for legal and political equality and access into the social and economic mainstream.

Dr Martin Luther King had a dream and rose to greatness. Carl Sandberg said, 'nothing happens unless first a dream'. Dreams exert significant power in igniting the spirit of American entrepreneurship, materializing and shaping the yet unimagined. Dreams rocketed astronauts to the moon and have made millionaires. We must always be reminded that behind every entrepreneurial company, there is a dreamer who will build, or have built a powerful economic system and continue to fuel the engines of change. Recently, three dreamers/entrepreneurs formed a new company called 'Dreamworks'. Their dreams are so creative that Paul Allen, the co-founder of Microsoft, invested $500 million of his money to be part of whatever materializes.

Individualism and autonomy

At least since the time of de Tocqueville (1990), observers have recognized that individualism is central to the American character. As celebrated by transcendentalist writers such as Emerson and Thoreau, independence and self-reliance have historically been held up as virtues to be sought after and cultivated. In some contemporary critiques, individualism has been treated as if it were little more than selfishness. By focusing on its excesses, however, these critics have lost sight of the contribution of individualism to American concepts of 'self' and of its influence on many of the social and political institutions, which even the critics continue to cherish. The reason, perhaps, is that individualism is so central to the American character, and its positive aspects frequently taken for granted, that it is difficult to conceive of any alternative kind of self-conception.

As a major characteristic of an American entrepreneur this individualism is manifested in the unwillingness to be tied down, controlled, supervised or dictated to. Entrepreneurs tend to 'march to the beat of their own drummer'. This autonomy has long been thought of as a major characteristic of entrepreneurs. The person who did not 'fit into' the corporate environment, or who was resentful of the supervision and control of a possibly capricious boss, often longs for the day that he or she could start their own business. In this way they believe they will no longer be under the 'yoke' of someone else, or restrained in a bureaucratic 'straitjacket.' Shapero (1975) described the 'uncomfortable' entrepreneur as one who is dissatisfied with his or her job or position, waiting for the chance to become 'free' to start their own business. Collins and Moore (1964) suggested that the entrepreneurial personality is characterized by an unwillingness to submit to authority, an inability to work with it, and a consequent need to escape. Mescon *et al.* (1981) provided a list of adjectives that defined a person with a high need for autonomy including: tries to break away from restraints, confinement, or restrictions of any kind; enjoys being unattached, free, not tied to people, places, or obligations; and may be rebellious when faced with restraints.

Such behaviour is based on Maslow's need for autonomy which Collins and Moore defined as 'the condition of having full direction in one's life' (p. 251). Schwartz (1976) conducted one of the early studies identifying a high need for independence among women entrepreneurs. Other studies suggested similar levels of autonomy between women and men entrepreneurs (Goffee and Scase, 1985; Chaganti, 1986; Ginn and Sexton, 1990). More recently, Reynolds and Miller (1992) found 'autonomy/independence' to be the major personal objective (44 per cent) when comparing it to 'challenge/pursue idea' (22 per cent) and 'income/estate for family' (20 per cent) among white females. These data were quite similar for minorities and white males in Minnesota and Pennsylvania. Earlier Chaganti (1986) and Sexton and Bowman-Upton (1990) utilized autonomy in describing entrepreneurs in their research. Hills and Welsch (1996) found a strong relationship between independence and entrepreneurial intentions among 2000 university students. McGrath *et al.* (1992) conclude that throughout the psychological commentary in the literature on entrepreneurship, there is a common thread of 'autonomy' or 'desire to be independent'.

The essence of Protestantism, which the founders of the country brought to the American shores, is the direct relationship between persons and their Maker. People are both able to know God without the necessity of intermediaries, and are directly responsible to their Creator. These religious beliefs combined with the philosophy of the Enlightenment to produce the Declaration of Independence and the American Constitution. These documents were rooted in the assumption that the individual is paramount and that government exists to serve the governed, and not the governed to serve the government. In the words of the Declaration of Independence:

> We hold these truths to be self evident, that all men are created equal, that they are endowed by their Creator with certain inalienable rights. Among these are life, liberty and the pursuit of happiness.

Although realization of these goals has in practice been flawed, the national commitment to democracy and equality of opportunity remain. Although they need not have done so, these ideals initially flowed from, and continue to be sustained by, the concept of individualism. In other words, the belief that each person is an entity separate from every other and from the group, and as such is endowed with natural rights. These beliefs in individuals and individual rights are part of heritage, and are incorporated into a basic sense of self. For example, early on, children are expected to learn to be self-reliant and independent. At the same time, they are conceded to have rights and unique needs and capacities that should be respected.

The socialization of entrepreneurs

In his book, *The Lemonade Stand*, Emmanuel Modu writes about how to encourage the entrepreneur in a child. Modu is a senior treasury analyst at Merrill Lynch and founder of the Center for Teen Entrepreneurs in Newark, New Jersey. 'Children who feel they are able to control their destiny and their lives, or at least affect the outcome, are the ones who tend to become entrepreneurs', says Modu. How do you give children that sense? It helps, he says, to forgo allowances and make children work for the money they want. That teaches them that their efforts can and do make a difference.

Illustration

Thirteen-year-old Stephen Lovett of Reston, VA loved cars and needed pocket money. So, with his parents' blessing, he started a car cleaning service. After school and on weekends, Lovett, now 18, still washes, waxes, polishes and shampoos cars. He charges up to $80 a car, depending on the service, and now has five youngsters working for him. He won't say how much he makes, but he recently bought himself a Chrysler Le Baron. 'The way my parents encouraged me was by not giving me an allowance,' he says. Anyone can wash and wax cars, but as is typical of successful young entrepreneurs, Lovett realized early on that he'd have to be creative to get and keep customers. He distributed business cards and fliers in his neighbourhood and placed pieces of candy and thank-you notes in the cars he serviced. He then called customers a month after servicing their cars to make sure they were satisfied, and to see whether their cars needed another servicing. Then there's Lovett's rain-date guarantee – if it rains within three days, he offers to re-wash the car free!

Is entrepreneurial skill an inherited trait? Usually not, say the experts, nor is it something that can be taught. But it certainly can be nurtured. Modu suggests getting entrepreneurial hopefuls involved in programmes such as Junior Achievement, Future Business Leaders of America, Entrecon at Wharton, or Camp Entrepreneur at DePaul University, Chicago. Furthermore, a programme at Cornell University will repay student loans up to $25 000 ($5000 a year for five years) for graduates who become entrepreneurs. The year-old programme is designed to make it easier for cash-strapped graduates to start their own businesses sooner. In 1997 the school was repaying 16 loans. Books also provide nurturing and guidance, such as *Capitalism for Kids* by Karl Hess and *The Teenage Entrepreneur's Guide* by Sarah Riehm. Modu also suggests that it is a good idea to expose kids to the workings of the stock market at a young age by having them set up and track dummy portfolios of stocks and funds they themselves pick. This is easily accomplished these days through media such as Prodigy, CompuServe or America On-line.

The values of achievement and autonomy find full expression within contemporary American psychology. For example, it is taken for granted by child psychologists that independence training is one of the major tasks demanded of parents. Another particularly revealing illustration is found in contemporary theories of ego and moral development that postulate that the highest stage is one in which the individual rises above acceptance of, and conformity to, society's standards to an autonomous level.

Illustration

Brad Boisvert, 16, who has always loved to cook, often takes cooking classes at a school near his Rhode Island home. 'I'd like to own my own restaurant,' he says. But he's not just waiting for that to happen. After attending a one-day vegetable-carving seminar, Boisvert started a catering company. Word of mouth and posters advertise his delicately crafted, edible centrepieces, which Boisvert makes for $20 to $80.

Illustration

Even before he was a teenager, Geoff Allen of McLean, VA was a whiz at the computer. He learned how to write his own programs but was a little young to start selling those services. So for a few years, as soon as he was able to work legally, he flipped hamburgers. 'When my friends were going to the beach on the weekends, I was waking up at 5 a.m. to open McDonald's', he recalls. The work habit stayed with Allen. By the age of 16 he was working part time as a systems analyst, and by 18 he had launched his own consulting firm. At 19, he started Digital Systems, which does video editing, produces animation and creates video kiosks for point-of-sale purchases. Sales in 1994 were $8.5 million. 'My parents told me that anything I wanted to do was possible. They never told me I couldn't do anything', Allen says.

In America, children are socialized into believing that they can have an impact on their environment and can accomplish their goals if they set their mind to it. This phenomenon is best explained by the concept of '*instilled*' internal locus of control. These young people described in the illustrations are early evidence that entrepreneurs tend to believe that they are in control of their own destiny. '*Internal*' control suggests that entrepreneurs can master their environment and their success is not determined by luck, fate and 'powerful others'. Entrepreneurs seem to be characterized by internal locus of control rather than an 'external' one, the latter being shown to be positively associated with 'powerlessness' (Maddi, Kabasa and Hoover, 1979). Begley and Boyd (1987) reviewed studies that substantiate the tie between locus of control and a variety of performance indicators. These include effective group leaders (Anderson and Schneider, 1978), and resilience in the face of environmental stressors (Anderson, 1977). Brockhaus (1982) has suggested that 'this internal belief and the associated greater effort ... hold promise for distinguishing successful entrepreneurs from the unsuccessful.' Shaver and Scott (1991, p. 30) have concluded that Rotter's (1966) Internal-External scale has 'successfully predicted behaviour in a variety of interpersonal and health-related settings'.

Illustration

Larry Villella, 11, was in charge of watering the lawn at his home. He hated having to move the sprinkler around the bases of the trees to saturate their roots. So he went to the basement of the family home in Fargo, ND and cut a circular sprinkler into a C-shape that fit around tree trunks and shrubs. A company was born! Villella's ConServ Products Co.'s sprinklers are sold nation-wide through hardware stores and catalogues. Villella, now 15, has grossed about $70 000 since the company was launched four years ago.

Illustration

At age 12, Ben Narasin of Manhattan was an avid collector of comic books. One day he asked his father for a $65 entrance fee to work as a dealer at a regional comic book convention. His father balked at first, but gave in 'to teach Ben a lesson'. It was the father who learned the lesson. At the convention he watched in awe as his son bought a comic book from one dealer and walked across the floor and sold it to another dealer for a higher price. 'It was a shocker to see how effective he was', recalls the senior Narasin. Young Ben's total take-home that day: $2500! Narasin, now 28, doesn't arbitrage comics anymore. Several years ago he founded Boston Prepatory, a men's sportswear manufacturer (1993 sales, $8 million).

Young entrepreneurs

What is the nature or form of the initial thought processes of potential entrepreneurs? At an early, or adolescent, state young people are often influenced by role models and mentors which plant the seed in their impressionistic minds as children move from 'firemen', 'astronaut', and 'rock star' types of career aspirations to those of a more realistic nature. Later, as self-employment possibilities are considered, the 'entrepreneur' image becomes a dream that may be reinforced by dozens of books, talk shows, seminars, lectures, courses in schools and even corporate slogans stressing the 'entrepreneurial approach'. This dream or vision has been identified (Frank *et al.*, 1989) where 'strategic vision' was an important component of the entrepreneur in recent start-up firms. This visualization has also been identified in a study of over 50 entrepreneurs that utilized 'visualization' in the process of starting a business. Further, interviews yielded insight into how visual imagery resulted in keeping the challenge and excitement alive, clarifying the business activity, developing the business plan, and projecting oneself into an aggressively growing business. One entrepreneur pictured himself as the owner of a number of companies: 'I envisioned my staff, various business opportunities and, of course, financial rewards.' Another entrepreneur reports visualizing an event as a learning experience. 'It's as if I've been there and I've got it in my head permanently. In fact, I can vividly recall visualizations I had years ago, including some I had as a teenager'.

Entrepreneurial intensity

This visualization, combined with parental and spousal support in addition to the right circumstances such as life stage, education, in a nutrient rich environment, can cause a young individual to generate a great 'fire in the belly', termed high 'entrepreneurial intensity'. This level of commitment to the entrepreneurial endeavour can be characterized as the passion required for entrepreneurial success. It is further characterized by a single-minded focus to start a business and work towards its survival and growth, often at the expense of other worthy and important goals. The Entrepreneurial Intensity (EI) scale developed by the author has been administered in the USA, Mexico, Russia, Poland, Romania, Hungary and several Baltic countries with significant success. Entrepreneurs in various stages of development and various industries in these countries have responded to the following items on a five-point Likert scale.

1 My business is the most important activity in my life.
2 I will do whatever it takes to make my business a success.
3 There is no limit as to how long I would give a maximum effort to establish my business.
4 I would be willing to make significant personal sacrifices in order to stay in business.
5 I would go to work somewhere else only long enough to make another attempt to establish my own firm.
6 My personal philosophy is to do 'whatever it takes' to establish my own business.
7 I plan to eventually sell my business.
8 I would like to make a significant contribution to the community by developing a successful business.
9 I would rather own my own business than earn a higher salary employed by someone else.
10 Owning my own business is more important than spending more time with my family.
11 I would rather own my own business than pursue another promising career.

Preliminary alphas of scale reliability range in the high seventies to low eighties. The theoretical base and rationale actually arose from an argument generated from Central/Eastern Europe regarding entrepreneurial intentions and behaviour. The first argument contends that Eastern Europeans 'unlearned' the work ethic by being provided for, and having secure jobs and social benefits from their socialistic governments. Therefore, entrepreneurial intensity should be weak or non-existent. The counter argument posits that the Protestant Work Ethic originated in Europe and is inherent and permeates the Central/Eastern European culture. The individuals are hard workers exhibiting sacrifice, determination, diligence, with a focused commitment to entrepreneurship and it was only temporarily suppressed by the Communist regimes. Therefore, entrepreneurial intensity should be high. Thus, it is a question of what caused entrepreneurial intensity. Was it the environment or was it inherent in individuals? While comparative analysis across countries has not yet been completed, preliminary results show EI to be related to entrepreneurial motivations, willingness to make sacrifices and incur opportunity costs, intentions to grow the business and various demographic variables. The EI variable holds promise to show how culture and history has impacted on this distinguishing factor.

Ethnic entrepreneurs

Americans like to think of themselves as self-starters. Just how entrepreneurial is the American culture? According to economists Fairlie and Meyer (1996), in 1990 11 per cent of men and 6 per cent of women in the USA were self-employed,[1] however, entrepreneurship is spread unevenly among ethnic and racial groups. Even after allowing for controlling factors, such as age and education, Fairlie and Meyer found widely varying self-employment rates for 61 ethnic categories. On the high side for men are Israelis and Koreans, both of whom have self-employment rates near 30 per cent. Among women, Koreans top the list at 19 per cent followed by Russians, with 12 per cent. The groups with the lowest rates of self-employment are Laotian and Puerto Rican men, at fewer than 4 per cent. African Americans and black Central Americans have the lowest female rates, at 2 per cent.

The differences are striking even within broad racial groups. For example, among Asians, Korean men are almost nine times as likely to be self-employed as Laotian men. National Federation of Independent Business economist William Dennis says the primary impediment to entrepreneurship for ethnic groups on the low end of the scale is a lack of community role models. 'It's history perpetuating itself', he says. 'We need to make people aware that this (entrepreneurship) is an avenue available to everyone, not just someone else'.

Because of the lack of a well-established economic and social network, many immigrants go into business for themselves, rather than enter the salaried labour market. Immigrant business owners in the USA are admired for their enterprising spirit, but they may also be the target of envy and hostility, as was evident in the attacks on Korean businesses during riots in Los Angeles in 1992. Recent research shows that Koreans are more likely than members of many other US immigrant groups to go into business.

Chapter summary

The North American society is extremely individualistic with a clear sense of the concept of 'self'. It is a country that has been compared to that of an adolescent who is impetuous, rebellious, non-conformist and tends to be passionate about whatever the focus of attention at a particular time. Driven by cultural forces including a frontier

---

1 It should be noted that self-employment is not the only term that signifies entrepreneurship. There are also corporations, sub-chapter S corporations, partnerships, joint ventures, franchises, etc. that characterize the American scene. Small business in fact generates 43 per cent of GNP, creates most of the new jobs in recent years and provides a significant proportion of the innovations in the market. About 800 000 new small businesses are initiated annually in the US and many more entrepreneurs work at home or in the underground community.

mentality, achievement orientation, and the 'American dream' that the impossible is just waiting to become a reality, it represents a society that is open and exceptionally supportive of entrepreneurship. However, despite these positive characteristics some ethnic and racial groups are excluded from entrepreneurship, purportedly for being innately inferior or morally unworthy.

Of particular significance is the socialization process to which American children are subject. It explicitly nurtures, educates and trains them as to the values of achievement, self-reliance and entrepreneurship. From an early age the young are instilled with the need to develop an internal locus of control in order to become powerful in mastering their environment, as opposed to being powerless. This has the potential to develop a rich pool of future entrepreneurs contributing to the material wealth and moral fibre of the nation.

The following case study illustrates many of the characteristics identified and issues raised in the chapter. In particular, Barry Potekin exhibits a strong need to achieve in the present/future. He is an expert at the 'American dance' continuously moving on to the next business challenge. Potekin's entrepreneurial learning is through improvisation and mistakes. He has a strong internal locus of control and is driven to be 'number one'. However, we are left with one question to answer. Is his undoubtedly strong entrepreneurial intensity caused by the environment in which he is located, or is it inherent to him?

Case study: The Hot Dog Entrepreneur

Barry Potekin had been a star baseball athlete during his youth and had acquired the nickname 'golden boy' because of his success and endeavours. The athletic experience had fine-tuned his competitive spirit. Earlier he had worked as a 'hawker' on Maxwell Street pulling in customers and honing his selling skills. Barry also played the role of a 'puller', the person who literally drags you into the store when you really don't want to go. That, and subsequent life experiences, taught him the value of persistence, heavy promotion, well-conceived marketing and public relations strategies. The entrepreneurial instinct was evident early in Barry's life. He taught himself to play the stock market while still in high school, subscribing to the *Wall Street Journal* and trading stocks through an account he opened in his mother's name. He skipped college and travelled in California for several years. Beginning in 1973, he started dealing in silver and gold.

'I read a book in the early 1970s about the coming explosion in silver, and all of a sudden I got interested in money again', he said. He was in his late twenties when he took some of his own money and that of his father's. Silver was at $5 an ounce, gold at $100. The metals were later to peak at $50 and $850, respectively. 'I just caught the elevator when it was about to take off', Barry recalls, noting that soon he was making what he calls 'serious money'. Emboldened by his success, he started trading foreign currencies, then got his broker's license and began converting 8- and 10-appartment buildings into condominiums. His parents, seeing him doing so well, made the near-fatal decision to give him their entire 'nest egg' to invest. 'To them, I was like a golden boy', Barry says. 'Everything I touched turned to gold. All this time, I was thinking I'm such a savvy guy, that I'm better than anyone else, when the truth is, from 1972 to 1980 a chimpanzee could have made money in these markets'.

As an entrepreneur he was 'unstoppable'. He had acquired a mansion, a new Cadillac every year, a fat bank account, real estate holdings as well as precious metals. He recounted, 'If I wanted to, I could have retired. I really thought it would last forever'. In his arrogance, Barry did not see the recession developing. 'I took my eye off the ball', he says simply. The results were devastating. 'In 1979 I was caught in a squeeze by the recession. I was converting apartment buildings into condominiums. I couldn't sell them and I couldn't borrow any money. At the same time, I was investing in gold and silver. When the condo and precious metals' market collapsed at the same time I was bankrupt and so were my parents due to their 'nest egg' investment. My car was repossessed. I was sleeping on a friend's couch. My net worth was the change in my pocket'. Over the span of two black months in 1981, he lost everything. 'I learned a tremendous lesson in humility', he says. 'People I had known since grammar school turned their backs on me. When you're making money everyone wants to be your friend. But no one wants to be in a loser's corner – especially when he wants to borrow money. I lost all my self-confidence. I felt like I knew nothing'.

What happened to his parents was worse. Both his mother and his father had to go back to work, she as a secretary, he as a $300-a-week assistant to his older brother. 'And you can imagine how much my Dad loved that', Barry says ruefully. However, his Dad never lost faith in him. 'I was meeting my father off and on for breakfast to try and figure out what to do. One day I met him and neither of us had one dollar. Between us we had eighty cents. We split an order of toast and coffee. Over it my father started to cry. Our future looked bleak'.

That afternoon Barry overheard someone at a real estate office boasting about how fast food is the quickest way to make a lot of money by putting up the least amount of collateral. The idea of a hot dog stand began to take shape in his mind. 'I had always wanted to be in the restaurant business. Although I knew absolutely nothing about it, I decided on fast food, but I knew I didn't want to compete with 10 000 other places. I didn't want to run with the herd. I saw a spot in the market that nobody was in – upscale high quality fast food. My burgers would be fresh and ground daily. I would hand cut fresh potatoes and serve fresh, not frozen, swordfish and chicken sandwiches. I would ship cheese from Wisconsin, use white albacore tuna in the tuna salad, and serve authentic Chicago-style hot dogs! I noticed that most fast food restaurants were dirty so I decided to keep mine very clean. I also noticed that good service and a good attitude towards customers were hard to find. I decided to treat customers like they had never been treated, as if they were spending $30 on a meal'.

The problem was that neither son nor father Potekin had any notion of how to open a restaurant. 'The joke is we were following a false premise,' Barry said. 'The statement that it's the fastest way to make money with the least investment was all wrong. But then God takes care of babies and fools'. Like post-Second World War Russians trying to figure out how to build an atom bomb, they set out to learn everything they could about the hot dog business. They consulted Chicago's Vienna Sausage Manufacturing Co. They spied upon local hot dog establishments until the managers went home, then paid the grill kids $10 to show them the ropes. They picked the brain of brother Fred, who in addition to having managed various restaurants, had run a Franksville when he was a teenager. Barry also came up with some ideas of his own. Recognizing that the city has more than a thousand hot dog stands, most of them clones of one another, he struggled for a way to make the Potekin enterprise stand out from the pack. 'I noticed no one was running an upscale stand', he says. 'I figured, why not serve healthier fast food with all-fresh ingredients and appeal to health-conscious young people who were affluent?'

For a location, they settled on a low-rent ex-florist shop on State Street in the shadow of several office buildings that they thought would provide a steady clientele. Then they focused on raising the $25 000 they naively assumed would be enough to remodel the shop and start the business. The banks laughed at them. The Potekins had no assets and no credit. Barry and Irv turned to offering acquaintances a piece of the place for some ready cash, but everyone turned them down except for two old friends, Don and Bernie Schneider, who gave them a big chunk of working capital in return for 25 per cent of the business. They engaged a contractor to work on a delayed-payment schedule, but still they fell far short of what it took to open their doors.

'In one day the deal collapsed. The investors changed their minds, the landlord changed his, and the contractor wanted cash. Within one week I talked them all back'. 'Gold Coast Dogs' was built and about to open when I ran out of money. I made a list of people to tap for $200 each. Eighteen people gave me the money. Then I ran out again. On 13 January 1985, the day before the grand opening, the Potekins had $9 in the bank. There was no money to buy food. In desperation, Barry started going door to door, begging people he knew for $10 and $20. Some of them treated him like a bum. 'Here, take this. Don't pay it back and don't come back', they told him.

The morning 'Gold Coast Dogs' opened, the place was like an iceberg. Barry and Irv couldn't afford to pay for heat, so the customers who drifted in to eat raised steam clouds with each breath. But there was food, and when it ran out Barry made an emergency run to the Vienna headquarters for refills. 'That first week, I was buying food twice a day', he says. 'We just missed going broke'. They survived hand to mouth like that for several weeks until Barry began to call on his self-promotional skills. The old 'puller' from Maxwell Street began walking around the neighbourhood introducing himself to strangers, telling them to stop in his place, mention his name and have a hot dog 'on the house'. 'You won't taste anything better in the city', he bragged. Around lunchtime he would telephone nearby businesses and ask how many employees they had, then he would send over enough free hot dogs, hamburgers and chicken sandwiches to feed everyone. Also, there were the cabbies. 'Cabs are little information centres', Barry says. 'Out-of-towners get in and ask where's a good place to eat. So for two months I would take cab rides to places like Washington and Clinton, bending the driver's ear about Gold Coast Dogs. Then I'd tip the guy $5 and tell him to come in and try a sandwich on me. It worked. Cab drivers started pouring in, and even today you can find cabs triple-parked outside at lunchtime. Today cab drivers are a large part of the business. I just wanted people to come in and see that we treat customers better than any other crew'.

'After six months the unbelievable happened. The *Chicago Sun Times* wrote us up for Best Hot Dog in Chicago. *Crain's*, the *Chicago Tribune*, and the WTTW TV continued to write up our story and about our service and food. My brother became my partner and we opened Gold Coast Dogs II. The publicity and hype meant that we had to hire new employees and figure out new systems'. While out driving he saw the driver next to him talking into a car phone. This casual observation suddenly triggered an idea. Why not encourage people to call their orders into Gold Coast on their car phones and then meet them at the curb with their food? Within days, the chain had put the idea into practice, and in the first week nearly 60 cars pulled up outside to partake of the new service. Not bashful, Barry sent out a press release announcing the carryout breakthrough, and it ran in *Crain's Chicago Business* journal.

Re-energized by his creativity, Barry designed several additional public relations campaigns. In one, he picked a fight with a competitor from New York. Barry learned that Nathan's, a venerable New York city hot dog chain, was about to move into the Chicago market, opening an outlet on Rush Street for its famous Coney Island dogs. Barry zoomed into action, composing a press release that framed the event in terms of a duel between New York and Chicago with hot dogs as the weapons. Included in the release was a list of the 'Ten Commandments' of hot dog making that set Chicago-style dogs apart from the rest, as well as a quote from Mayor Richard M. Daley contending that Chicagoans, as discerning frankophiles, would be able to distinguish between quality and mere pretenders. Then Barry issued a challenge to Nathan's through a top-rated disc jockey on New York's WOR radio station, on whose show he complained that, 'Chicagoans are tired of people from the East Coast coming here to tell us how to eat our food. We're not farmers. We're trend-setters'. To reinforce his boast, Barry agreed to 'Federal Express' the disc jockey two One Magnificent Dogs in dry ice for a taste-off with Nathan's.

The result was a tie. 'A draw is pretty good when you're on the enemy's turf', philosophized Barry, who is obviously fond of such antics. 'The hype makes me a little squeamish', he says, not terribly convincingly. 'I don't like to talk about myself. I've learned humility. But it's a necessary evil. If you don't toot your own horn, no one else will!' he concludes.

Case study review

Barry Potekin exhibits all of Timmons's entrepreneurial themes. The factors contributing to his entrepreneurial behaviour are presented in Table 5.1.

Table 5.1 Factors contributing to Barry Potekin's entrepreneurial behaviour

Category	Factors
Antecedent influences	• Family support and influence has had an important positive effect. • While he rejected the formal education system, he is committed to life-long learning through reading, observation and learning from others. • He is a 'trader' who is not afraid to operate across industry sectors without any prior knowledge or expertise.
Incubator organization	• His business has not developed from any incubator organization, and skills and knowledge have been acquired through experiential learning.
Environmental factors	• He is deviant from the social norm and places importance on the symbolism of material possessions. • His level of business success has risen and fallen with economic conditions, which suggests limited strategic management capabilities. • The existence and/or influence of role models, other than his father, does not appear to have played an important part in developing his entrepreneurial behaviour. • He sources business advice through informal networks. • Business is developed on intuition rather than market research and formal management information.

6

Asia: Singapore

Wee-Liang Tan

Key feature summary

Currently, Singapore is a country that enjoys a situation of full employment, coupled with a strong economy. It has embraced entrepreneurship as a means of strengthening the intensity and business performance of indigenous firms. Key features affecting entrepreneurship are:

- The importance of entrepreneurs and local enterprises was realized and redis-covered by the politicians at the time of the 1985 economic recession. As a consequence political intervention has been directed towards the development of a strong indigenous population of firms to provide a necessary counterbal-ance to volatile multinational company (MNC) activity. This has resulted in a partnership between entrepreneurs and local enterprises, MNCs and govern-ment-linked companies.
- Job creation is not an imperative in the stimulation of entrepreneurship as the unemployment rate is extremely low (1.9 per cent in 1994). Wealth creation is the priority through the development of strong, vibrant enterprises, and partic-ularly those based on innovative technology with global growth potential.
- Due to the 'full-employment' position and currently buoyant economy in Singapore, factors 'pushing' persons into entrepreneurship are relatively non-existent. The development of a critical mass of entrepreneurs is therefore dependent on potentials being 'pulled' voluntarily into the process of entrepre-neurship.
- The government controlled Provident Fund saving scheme operates for those in employment. It provides a 'safety net' or 'nest egg' for old age. This scheme may act as a deterrent relative to persons entering into self-employment. Alternatively, it could provide the necessary funds for business investment fol-lowing several years in employment.
- Singaporean society has a low tolerance to failure with perceptions that it will result in castigation and ruin. This conditioning commences in school, shaping persons who are generally ultra-cautious which is not conducive to entrepre-neurial risk taking.

Introduction

Singapore has been singled out for attention in recent years partly because of the World Bank Report, *The East Asian Miracle* (World Bank, 1993). This report recognized eight economies, including Singapore, which accounted for East Asia's high and sustained economic growth from 1965 to 1990, and identified the reasons for their high growth. While focusing on the role of astute government and public policy, the report noted that small and medium-size enterprises played a key role, with the economies benefiting from a profusion of such enterprises (World Bank, 1993). Singapore is no exception, and entrepreneurship has played an important role in economic development.

The factors influencing entrepreneurship have varied over the different periods of Singapore's economic development. It has also manifested itself in a variety of ways, forms and individuals. Thus far, the term entrepreneurship has been used in its traditional definition of 'starting a business venture'. This chapter addresses the factors that have influenced this phenomenon. However, it is recognized that entrepreneurship has other wider definitions, such as the one advanced by Kao (1994) which characterizes Singapore well. According to Kao, entrepreneurship is the process of doing something new, or something different, to create wealth for oneself and to add value to society. The reason why this definition characterizes entrepreneurship in Singapore lies in the fact that, at the national level, entrepreneurship has made a significant contribution. This is because the country has little land and resources, apart from its inhabitants and its geographic location. Elements of this wider definition of entrepreneurship will be addressed in the concluding section of this chapter. Thus, the chapter is structured to outline the various factors that have impinged on entrepreneurship in the traditional sense, in the period before Singapore's independence in 1965, and from 1965 to the present. The observations made are drawn from secondary sources, anecdotal evidence, and a section on empirical research from a study involving the author into the social, cultural and economic factors and entrepreneurship. The case study of Mr Tan the stationery entrepreneur is representative of entrepreneurial behaviour and attitudes in Singapore. It clearly illustrates the societal and wider environmental influences at work.

Entrepreneurship in the early days before independence in 1965

Sir Stamford Raffles founded Singapore in 1819 on behalf of the English East India Company, and it became a British trading port along with Penang and Malacca. The indigenous people were the Malays. It is the early immigrants we turn to for our understanding of entrepreneurship in those days prior to 1965. They came to Singapore from mainland China, India and from the Arab region, with the majority being represented by the Chinese. In general, they saw themselves as being transient visitors to the island. Hence, one of their main objectives was to send their earnings home, and they had a short time horizon on their activities. These early immigrant entrepreneurs could be characterized as opportunistic entrepreneurs in the same vein as those described by Kirzner (1979) as 'arbitrageurs', seeking out the opportunities, provided by their presence in Singapore.

These early entrepreneurs and their opportunistic ventures are typical of most Asian economies that were once colonies. For example, Hong Kong's economic development and growth was contributed to by opportunistic entrepreneurship rather than Schumpeterian-type entrepreneurs, who bring about new combinations and inventions.

The opportunities were those that existed in the environment created by the colonial governments, which did not apparently have agendas for economic development. They sought to harvest the crops when spices such as pepper and gambier were in demand, and to reap the wealth from, and through, the colonies. Further, they were keen to use the cheap labour that existed then for their own ends. The early entrepreneurs had opportunities in the areas where the colonial powers were not engaged. Most of them were traders primarily in import and export with Singapore's 'entrepot' port providing the opportunities for re-export of goods to the neighbouring countries, and for the export of products from the Malay Peninsula. Others engaged in commerce meeting the needs of the domestic markets.

There is a difference in the immigrants to each of the former colonies. Hong Kong, for instance, is noted as having received entrepreneurs from Shanghai after the Communist take-over who had not just business experience and expertise, but also capital and technical knowledge when they fled the communists (Sit *et al.*, 1991). In Singapore's case, over the years, the Chinese immigrants came because: there was a scarcity of employment in the coastal regions; in the period prior to 1920 there were wars and economic uncertainty; and prior to the Second World War, there was the Sino–Japanese War in China. These constituted the push factors for their emigration. The age range of the Chinese immigrants was from 16 to 26 (Chan and Chiang, 1994), leaving their homelands to seek their fortunes, and motivated to earn a decent living (Lee, 1988; Chan and Chiang, 1994). They came with little capital and few business skills and network alliances, which are not exactly considered to be the best conditions for business start-ups. The Indians were initially brought to Singapore by the British as convict slaves, then as workers for farms, plantations and construction workers. In Singapore's economic development they have been conspicuous as textile and piece-goods wholesalers and retailers, money-lenders, civil servants and labourers (Sandhu, 1993). They also had almost a monopoly of the laundry business in early Singapore (Mani, 1993).

The early entrepreneurs used their ethnic resources in their entrepreneurial efforts (Chan and Chiang, 1994). For example, the Chinese entrepreneurs sought their markets and customers among their clansmen and Chinese immigrants, and relied on the networks and contacts in the Chinese community. In the early days of immigration, each group of immigrants, Chinese, Arab, Indian and the rest would form groups for mutual help. Hence, it is no surprise that the clan connections and the mutual help associations also became centres of business discussion. In addition, it was their ethnic groups whose needs they aimed to meet when they sought out opportunities for business.

The social backgrounds of the immigrants was a factor in the nature of their activities when they landed on Singapore's shores. Those who were familiar with the process of doing business, and having family backgrounds in commerce, were likely to engage in the same trade or industry sectors. Other avenues of exposure to business may have also contributed to the immigrants' involvement in commerce, such as being clerks, administrators or employees while in China. Some moved from working for others into starting businesses for themselves, as was the case of Chew Choo Keng, who later established a business which is presently a success – Khong Guan Biscuits.

Another key feature of the early entrepreneurs in Singapore was the tendency to establish businesses that were family owned and controlled. In a few instances, the early enterprises were extensions of original businesses from the country of origin, providing the initial head starts. However, the Japanese occupation made it difficult for most businesses to be transferred to the next generation, and the war also led to the loss of wealth and capital which meant that many had to rebuild their enterprises. Despite these setbacks, family businesses have thrived, and a number of them have grown into dynamic large companies well into their second generation of successors (Fock, 1995). For example, some of them are represented in the hospitality industry as hoteliers, in the finance industry as bankers and owners of finance companies, in the real estate and construction industry as property developers, and in the pharmaceutical industry as manufacturers of Chinese medical products.

As Singapore is a port and a centre of commerce, it is not surprising that early entrepreneurs were involved in commerce. Most of them engaged in the import and export of spices, rubber and other produce. A few pioneers did engage in manufacturing, for example, Tan Kah Kee who experimented with early automation at his factories that manufactured, among other things, shoes. Others in manufacturing were involved in the processing of the products from the hinterland in the Malay Peninsula, such as, processing rubber and canning pineapples. In addition to these arenas, entrepreneurs ventured into the retail, finance, building and construction, and property development industry sectors. Examples of present day enterprises that had early beginnings include Tangs Department Store founded by a retailer C. K. Tang, and Hong Leong Finance Ltd. which is involved in the finance, hotel and property development sectors.

1965 to the present: the role of government

After independence in 1965, Singapore saw two decades of continuous high economic growth, which took place despite what happened in the rest of the world. It was as if Singapore was independent from the business cycles that affected the rest of the globe, such as global economic recession and oil crises. It was achieving 5 per cent Gross Domestic Product (GDP) growth in a bad year and 15 per cent in a boom year (Singapore Ministry of Trade and Industry, 1986). Then recession struck in 1985, which led to the appointment of the Economic Committee by the government to review the progress of Singapore's economy, and to identify new directions for its future growth. Among the recommendations in its report are those on entrepreneurship and local business. It was then that the importance of entrepreneurs in the economy was realized and rediscovered as Kent (1984) observed has been the case in many rapidly developing economies.

Prior to this, there had been little direct emphasis on local enterprises (Doh, 1996), with the focus being on multinational companies (MNCs) and the development of state enterprises in the area of manufacturing, shipping, air transport, international trade, long-term finance, marine-related services and technology and defence-related industries. However, it was realized then that there was a need for a buffer to the MNCs, especially when they 'fled' Singapore during the recession for greener pastures. At that time, the local enterprises accounted for 30 per cent of Singapore's domestic exports. Further, an emphasis on local enterprises reflected the desire to seek out innovative opportunities and to embark on new ventures. It was decided that local companies must be a healthy and self-reliant component of the economy, contributing their fair share to GDP.

The Economic Committee recommended that the government take steps to remove impediments and actively encourage the growth of enterprise (Singapore Ministry of Trade and Industry, 1986). In May 1989, the *SME Master Plan* was published which embodied the efforts of a national level SME Development Workshop held in May 1988. This report revealed the SME Initiative for Singapore. It was decided that instead of the creation of a separate SME agency, the existing agencies in the public sector would be employed, together with private sector organizations. The strategy enunciated is that of stimulating local enterprises through:

- the creation of a more pro-enterprise environment;
- providing help for self-help;
- accelerating the pace of growth with incentives.

The government's role is to guide and assist enterprises by setting the direction, improving the business environment and building up a supportive infrastructure (SME Committee, 1989). The reason for this policy was the realization that in Singapore's future economy SMEs must increasingly play an important role for the following reasons:

- SMEs have the potential to represent a source of entrepreneurship and innovation, and result in a stock of future successful indigenous companies that may even grow into companies of a global stature.
- MNCs are more footloose in their operations and have the habit of relocating to other countries with cheaper resources. While they contribute to the economy, MNCs only employ 34.7 per cent of the working population.
- A vibrant indigenous SME sector would be a counterbalance to any pullout by MNCs. Moreover, the MNCs need a strong SME base to supply their needs.
- There are now opportunities in areas of technology and services for SMEs to develop niches.

Hence, entrepreneurs and local enterprises are integral partners in economic development in Singapore together with MNCs and government-linked companies. The tripartite partnership can be depicted in Figure 6.1.

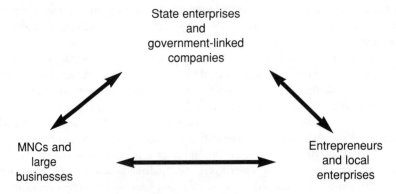

Figure 6.1 *Partners in Singapore's economic development*

Singapore's strategy involves SMEs having a global perspective and encouraging their participation in regional and global business (Doh, 1996), with the government issuing a call for Singapore businesses to go regional, and establish the external wing of Singapore's economy. The key elements of the strategy are as follows:

- **Enable capitalization on MNCs' presence**: MNCs are encouraged to serve as mentors to local enterprises through the Local Enterprise Upgrading Programme (LIUP), and through SMEs providing the support industries and services to MNCs. Under the LIUP, the Economic Development Board (EDB) brings local companies and MNCs together for the purpose of improving the operating efficiency of participating SMEs, widening the product ranges and introducing new processes to the MNCs' local suppliers (Maddox, 1992).
- **Improve international competitiveness**: SMEs are provided with the necessary technical expertise and skills through the Local Enterprise Technical Assistance Scheme, which involves their employees being sent for training, with the employers being able to recover part of the costs through the Skills Development Fund. In addition, the Trade Development Board (TDB) offers international marketing assistance to SMEs through their participation in trade missions organized by the TDB, and in international trade fairs in established and new markets, and assists SMEs who have established franchises and wish to take them overseas.
- **Computerization:** There is assistance available from the National Computer Board which is given the task of making Singapore an intelligent island by the year 2000 under its IT2000 plan. This automation is linked to the improvement of international competitiveness.

The various assistance schemes, and the multi-agency network involved, can be considered as an infrastructure put in place to support entrepreneurship relative to private and non-profit organizations. The various elements could be classified into assistance, information, resources and knowledge (Tan *et al.*, 1995).

However, there is a characteristic that underpins the various activities of the government in SME development. Although the assistance is available to all SMEs who qualify under the specific schemes, there is an emphasis on winners (Doh, 1996). The various government agencies are on the lookout for start-ups and local enterprises that have the critical mass, capacity, capability and commitment to innovate and grow. Consequently, a new statutory organization, the Productivity and Standards Board (PSB), was launched in April 1996 with a responsibility for developing SMEs in Singapore. The emphasis is on promising SMEs, with winning potential in terms of products and services. The strategic focus is now on upgrading all SMEs so that they will be efficient and effective users of resources. This is in line with Singapore's future economic development policy that growth is to be propelled by total factor productivity, rather than by inputs and investment. As such, the government has done much to promote entrepreneurship in the form of growing local enterprises. However, there may be a lack of awareness on the part of Singapore's entrepreneurs and SMEs of the existence of numerous programmes (Teo and Lee, 1994).

The recent rediscovery of entrepreneurship, and the involvement of government, has resulted in a greater social recognition of entrepreneurship. Role models have been presented to the public and to the younger generation still in the education system. There are numerous awards and media communication that recognize entrepreneurs. For example:

- The Nanyang Technological University's Entrepreneurship Development Centre presents an annual award for Entrepreneurship Excellence.
- The *Business Times* and DHL had a special award for the Enterprise of the Year.
- A television programme was aired in 1996 that profiled various high profile entrepreneurs, and there are at least three television programmes that offer interviews and stories of successful entrepreneurs including those who have regionalized their businesses.
- A television series, entitled *Singapore Entrepreneurs* aired in 1995 was followed up by a CD-ROM designed to stimulate entrepreneurial behaviour.
- Various publications have appeared detailing the success stories of entrepreneurs, large and small.
- A number of technopreneurs have gained publicity providing examples of how to meet the challenges of entrepreneurship through effectively employing technology.

Economic factors

Employment

Unlike most other economies, where job creation is the chief rationale for encouraging entrepreneurship and enterprise development, Singapore is an exception. Job creation is not the imperative, developing vibrant and growing enterprises is. The reason is simple – there is no unemployment and a labour shortage, a situation that has prevailed since the economic recovery following the 1984 recession. While one cannot call it 'over-employment', it is more than full employment, and a more correct term would be to observe that there is a 'tight' labour market. For example, in 1994 the unemployment rate was approximately 1.9 per cent. A large part of Singapore's labour needs, especially at the lower end of the skill spectrum, continue to be met through the importation of labour and the increased participation in the workforce of women and older members of the population (Asian Development Bank, 1995). In fact, there is a concerted effort to recruit professionals from overseas to reside and work in Singapore.

As such, there has been no 'push' factor for graduates and professionals to venture forth into their own businesses, which would appear to be riskier than being in secure employment. Further, the growing demand for graduates especially in the technical disciplines has not been fully met by the output from the tertiary institutions. It has recently been reported that Singapore requires another 7000 graduates.

The 'safety net' or 'nest egg' integrated with employment

Apart from the appeal of employment, there are other social factors that make entrepreneurship less appealing. With employment, there is a compulsory savings scheme for retirement called the Central Provident Fund. Under the scheme, an employee contributes a fixed amount to an account in their name and the government statutory board is charged with managing the funds. Their employer is required by law to make a monthly contribution, pegged to a portion of the salary paid to the employee. The current combined savings each month for most employees is 40 per cent of their salaries up to a maximum of $2600 a month. Most of the Provident Fund savings can be utilized by employees under the regulations for residential property and designated investments, save for sums that must be set aside for medical uses and minimum sums for old age.

This safety net can be an inhibitor to entrepreneurship, a fact that was acknowledged by the Economic Committee (Singapore Ministry of Trade and Industry, 1986). However, it has been argued conversely that the savings enable those embarking on entrepreneurship, after some years of work, to start a venture knowing that they had a safety net for old age (Chew, 1996).

Competitive domestic market

Local enterprises and new ventures face a highly competitive domestic market where the market opportunities, while still in existence, require careful consideration relative to strategic fit and the developed nature of some industrial segments. The days when one could start another 'me-too' venture no longer exist. In addition, certain sectors are facing decline, for instance, old-style traditional provision shops (i.e. grocers) and hardware stores located in the neighbourhoods. While relying on their convenience in being closer to the residents for their attraction, they are faced with a decline in consumer preference for large well-stocked supermarkets and 'Do-It-Yourself' type stores located in shopping malls. Such a competitive environment promotes as well as inhibits entrepreneurship. Those who are able to identify niches will be able to succeed. However, there are those who do not wish to venture in the light of this situation.

Resources for venture creation

Access to and availability of finance is critical to new ventures. While there is an entrepreneurial infrastructure in Singapore, an established banking industry and a growing venture capital industry, a new start-up will, more likely than not, face difficulties in obtaining finance. Hence, when a young professional has identified a worthwhile entrepreneurial opportunity there may be no financial resources which they can readily access. The loan officers in banks function as bankers and place great emphasis on the entrepreneur's track record and ability to provide security for the loans (Tan, 1996). The venture capitalists in Singapore do not employ investment criteria far different from those in the USA. Few of them, however, focus solely on new start-ups preferring to have a mix of investments (Tan et al., 1997).

Apart from venture capitalists who could provide the start-up equity capital, the capital market provides another source. However, the current criteria for flotation on the Singapore Stock Exchange are rigorous. Hence, a new start-up, from the very outset, would not be able to obtain equity financing from the public. Furthermore, the government guaranteed finance scheme, administered by the approved financial institutions, does provide funds to local enterprises. New start-ups may apply and would obtain financing when, as is the case with banks and venture capitalists, the business proposition has adequate merits and is perceived as potentially profitable. Hence, it is no surprise to find that most studies into the sources of finance for start-ups in Singapore find that it comes from private funds (Wong *et al.*, 1994; Law *et al.*, 1995). The entrepreneur in the following case study clearly illustrates this difficulty in obtaining finance for new ventures. It remained a key issue that is borne out in his story and continues to be an area in which he has a keen interest. In fact, he subsequently examined the issue of finance for SMEs in his dissertation for his MBA degree.

Socio-cultural factors

Opportunism

The opportunistic trait that was identified among the early entrepreneurs is still present in Singapore. However, it can give rise to those who seek short-term gains rather than for the longer term, which has serious implications. In particular, most new start-ups do not utilize technology as a competitive advantage, and commerce and services are the two most popular sectors for new start-ups. Meanwhile, there is a need for technopreneurship, for entrepreneurs to start high-technology ventures, and for those entrepreneurs who are able to establish a mark on the global marketplace through products or services with intellectual property rights.

Education

It has been noted that the education system seems to be the cause of many problems inhibiting entrepreneurship, such as the fear of failure, and a lack of creativity and innovation (Wong *et al.*, 1994) It is felt that the education system in Singapore, with its emphasis on channelling children into various 'streams' and specializations based on their examination and test performances, stifles creativity, innovation and/or entrepreneurship. It has been reported in the media that there is a lack of an entrepreneurial spirit among young Singaporeans today, and that Singapore tertiary students are generally not interested or are not willing to be self-employed or to start their own businesses, preferring job security and relatively high paying jobs (*The Straits Times*, 16 July and 3 January, 1993). The examination orientation of the education system has also been accused of being responsible for this situation, which has resulted in curriculum changes. For example, the most recent announcement by the Minister of Education was on the introduction of creative thinking in schools. The results of these changes will be known only some time in the future.

While it has been noted that there is a lack of the entrepreneurial spirit among tertiary students, it is not totally absent. In a study with tertiary students, 47 per cent of a stratified sample drawn from two universities and three polytechnics in Singapore were identified as possessing an entrepreneurial spirit (Tan *et al.*, 1995). This was defined using the six key characteristics of entrepreneurs that have featured in the literature: risk taking; locus of control; innovative; leadership qualities; strong determination; and achievement-orientation. Employing a questionnaire, which was administered in group interviews, it was found that tertiary students lacked entrepreneurial spirit when they were assessed on a stringent rating scheme (answering the questionnaire positively for any four of the six key characteristics). It was also found that of the students who possessed entrepreneurial spirit, 51.3 per cent had work experience and 42.4 per cent did not, and that this work experience is associated with entrepreneurial spirit.

However, one wonders if the results might be different if a national programme of entrepreneurship development was to be formally introduced into the education system. Further, the existing entrepreneurship and small business management courses are not compulsory for tertiary students. The association of work experience and entrepreneurial spirit would imply that the policy of some tertiary institutions in placing the students in attachments in business and industry is sound and may contribute to the development of entrepreneurs.

While graduates from the tertiary institutions may prefer to be employees, there is an indication from anecdotal evidence that a number of them seriously consider entrepreneurship later in their working lives. Sources of entry into an entrepreneurial career would be from work experience and into a related sphere of business, as our example of the stationery entrepreneur in the case study illustrates. He chose to learn from a stationery house before commencing his own business, and another entrepreneur began his biotechnology and agri-tech firm after working for a multinational biotechnology firm.

Low tolerance for failure/shame

In general, Singaporean society has a low tolerance for failure. Failure at one's job or business carries with it perceptions of castigation and ruin, which is hardly conducive to risk taking. This begins in the schools with the education system where the parents emphasize the need for their children to attain good grades in their schools, which has as its corollary a fear of failure. A local term has been coined to refer to this ultra-cautious behaviour, it is called *kiasuism*, based on a Chinese dialect term meaning 'afraid to lose', which roughly equates to fear of failure. Wong *et al.* (1994) in their survey of 44 entrepreneurs found that this factor weighed heavily in the minds of the respondents as a factor inhibiting entrepreneurship.

Empirical findings on the role of social, cultural and economic factors

This section reports the findings of a recent study that examined the effects of the social, cultural, economic and government factors as discussed in the earlier sections on entrepreneurship. There has been considerable interest in the effects of culture on entrepreneurship in recent years. However, the relationship between the environment in a country, embodying the cultural, economic and regulatory factors, has not been the subject of extensive scrutiny. The studies referred to earlier examined selected variables, were descriptive in nature, or postulated a model as in Wong *et al.* (1994). This motivated Tom Begley and myself to embark on an international research project on these issues. As part of the project, a study on Singapore was conducted. It sought to identify the socio-cultural factors that operated in Singapore and their impact on perceived feasibility, perceived desirability and entrepreneurship intentions.

It also examined the relationship postulated in Shapero and Sokol (1982) between these factors. They presented a model of the larger-scale precursors to starting a business that remains the point of reference for subsequent studies in the area. They argue that providing a reasonable supply of entrepreneurs first requires an environment congenial to creating potential entrepreneurs. Thus, policies may need to be identified and established to address both the perceived feasibility, and the perceived desirability of entrepreneurship, in order for there to be more potential entrepreneurs. These factors are seen to be products of cultural, social and environmental factors, which help determine which actions will be seriously considered and subsequently taken.

The social and cultural factors that enter into the formation of entrepreneurial events are most felt through the formation of individual value systems. Perceived feasibility is critical to understanding planned, intentional behaviour by influencing intentions through situational perceptions of feasibility (Krueger and Brazeal, 1994). Although the environment may be conducive to entrepreneurship, and the individuals may possess the required perceived desirability and perceived feasibility, they remain inert until something disrupts or displaces that inertia. The displacement is often negative, such as job loss, but can easily be positive, such as an inheritance.

The empirical research sample comprised 110 MBA participants at the Nanyang Technological University in Singapore. Students in MBA programmes were chosen as the sample because they should be knowledgeable about the environment for business in the country, and are typically in the early to middle stages of their careers, a time at which entrepreneurial thoughts and desires are viewed as high. As our intention was to assess the views of local residents regarding their country's business environment, non-Singapore citizens were excluded. The research instrument was designed to obtain information from the participants on the socio-cultural, economic and governmental factors, and the impact of these factors on the environment in Singapore for the promotion of entrepreneurship. The questionnaire that was administered also sought information of potential entrepreneurs in setting up a new business (which we shall call entrepreneurship), and details relative to personal characteristics.

Observations

First, the empirical study showed that one of the four socio-cultural variables, the social status of entrepreneurs, predicted the desire and intention to start a business. The higher an individual perceives the status of entrepreneurs to be, the greater is that individual's desire and intent to become one. Second, a modest relationship was also found between the value of innovation and desire to start a business. In this case, the relationship was negative indicating that people who believed innovation was highly regarded were less likely to want to start a business. Third, although it had been hoped that economic and governmental factors would predict feasibility, these relationships failed to be significant. This is astonishing as economic and governmental factors are more likely to influence one's perceived self-efficacy in starting any business, especially the general or specific availability of financial support, which should directly influence one's perceived feasibility to form companies. The only explanation that can be offered is that economic and governmental influences could be too remote to sway a potential entrepreneur's perceptions of feasibility directly. For instance, the impact of certain legislation may have been lessened by the time it reaches the potential entrepreneur.

The study serves to highlight the influence of socio-cultural, economic and governmental factors on entrepreneurship. It is but an exploratory study that provides some interesting findings, which confirm the notional expected links between the social status of entrepreneurs and the desirability and intention to become one, and the value of innovation and entrepreneurship, although not in the expected direction. It is surprising that shame of failure, while predicting desirability, did not have any significant relationships with feasibility and intention. The presence of government support, availability of labour supply, competition and finance, contrary to expectations did not predict feasibility, desirability or intentions. One should therefore temper the observations made earlier with these preliminary findings. While the preference for employment, the Central Provident Fund, the effect of education were directly examined, the study did not investigate all the factors that have been discussed in this chapter.

Chapter summary

Entrepreneurship will continue to be a mainstay for Singapore's economy. The challenge is to groom local enterprises into growing ventures that will graduate as Asian MNCs. The driving motivation for entrepreneurship development in Singapore remains continued, sustained, economic development and not job creation. The Singapore environment has factors that auger well for entrepreneurship development including: government supports systems in the form of an entrepreneurship infrastructure; established capital markets; excellent location as far as transportation is concerned; and a good education system. However, whether entrepreneurship will flourish is dependent on external and internal factors. While we have examined some of the internal factors through the perceptions of individuals, there is more to be fathomed. One observation that can be made is that the element of the opportunity cost of entrepreneurship as opposed to another alternative, say employment, may be a factor that will play a significant role.

Finally, returning to entrepreneurship in the larger context of a wider definition, unlike other countries, where it is confined to the private sector and only to business, Singapore is believed to be unique. In this context, it can be considered an enterprise in itself where many individuals are entrepreneurs as defined widely. Hence, the label 'Singapore Inc.' has been applied to Singapore. There are government-linked companies managed by civil servants which account for 'state entrepreneurship' (Lee and Low, 1990). Pioneering ministers have also been called 'entrepreneurs' and recently a public servant, Philip Yeo, chairman of the Economic Development Board, was awarded an entrepreneurship excellence award. Singapore has also benefited from entrepreneurs in social and charitable work in the areas of education, health and the poor. These entrepreneurs were not necessarily rich merchants turned philanthropists, but included volunteers – ordinary members of society.

This concept of a wider definition is introduced to indicate to the reader that Singapore's past success and continued success in the future could be explained by this expanded understanding of entrepreneurship. As a consequence, the factors influencing it will differ in kind from those affecting what has been traditionally understood as entrepreneurship. However, the larger categories will still apply: environment factors, motivational factors, cultural factors at the national and organizational levels, and perhaps even the ideological factors for it may be a system of values that are held by the citizens of the nation-state.

Case Study: The Stationery Entrepreneur

Background

When you consider his credentials and employment history, you would probably be puzzled why a successful young sales manager would leave his second job to become an entrepreneur. Mr Tan is a qualified professional accountant. He had secured a prime position as financial controller in his prior company and was rewarded with a S$20 000 Mercedes Benz in the early 1970s (a similar car would fetch S$200 000 today). In this regard, the sentiment is not dissimilar to the social norms when he left his job to enter the stationery business. Society did not expect that of him and could be said to 'frown' on such behaviour. Today in Singapore, while there has been progress, the same sentiments still exist although entrepreneurship, in starting a business, has gradually become accepted as a career alternative for a professional.

Today, he is a successful entrepreneur, whose businesses included one in Malaysia, another in Indonesia, and another in Australia. These businesses have been successfully developed and sold to other multinational companies. In the years leading to the sale of the businesses in Malaysia and Indonesia, he had two joint ventures in stationery manufacturing with a major German stationery manufacturer. His present business is a company in Singapore and another business in Indonesia. He has been in business a total of 19 years.

From high flying executive to walking stationery salesman entrepreneur

The young Mr Tan, who graduated with an accountancy degree, was not just an ordinary graduate. He was also extremely intelligent and an accomplished national chess champion, who is internationally ranked as a chess master. In fact, as he sat across from the lunch table where this interview took place, he recalled the number of national chess champions he had trained. He talked about his choice of industry sector:

> Switching from an executive position to the stationery business was a big jump but I made my preparations. I joined the leading stationery distributor for nine months to learn the ropes. Before I left, I was responsible for some of the main product lines of the old firm. A number of these products were in stationery and office equipment. So I went into the stationery business with an understanding of the trade.

A number of manufacturers of stationery decided to use him as their distributor and agent. He had seen the opportunity in the marketplace. Most of the stationers were Chinese speaking while the manufacturers (i.e. the principals) were Westerners, who could speak English. As the profit margins on stationery were small, apart from his previous employer, none of the big companies were interested in selling stationery. After all, as he put it, 'Would you rather sell a national television set where you made more per set or would you rather sell rulers and erasers where you probably had to sell a hundred to obtain the same margins?' He saw his niche in being able to 'tango' with the principals and at the same time 'parley' with the local stationers in their local tongue – the Hokkien dialect. It was a strategy that worked. Furthermore, a few of the principals chose to follow him from his previous employer. One of them became his long-term business partner, which until a recent friendly parting of ways, led to manufacturing concerns in Malaysia and Indonesia.

Factors inhibiting the business start-up

When he left employment to become his own boss, not only did friends and family try to dissuade him, even the customers he was attempting to sell to had difficulty swallowing the fact.

> My first customers were the ones who used to order from the old firm. They knew me and used to see me drive down the row of shops where almost all the stationery shops were located. They recognized me and my Mercedes Benz.

> That was before I sold it and appeared before them carrying a brief-case with my first product: a German brand of correction fluid. I walked those streets. A sharp contrast to driving grandly in the status symbol. I can still recall their disbelief and wonderment. I literally had to beg them to buy my products.

> Those first six months, I did little business. But, my efforts brought attention to the name of my company.

> A few of them purchased the smallest pack of correction fluid possible. These were the sympathy orders. The small pack was six bottles. One of them dutifully bought six from me each fortnight.

Apart from the socio-cultural inhibitor mentioned earlier, Mr Tan remembered the difficulty in obtaining finance.

> When I was the manager in a big company with a salary, bankers came to see me. They wanted to lend money to the company. When I quit, I went to see the same gentlemen who graced my office and they turned me down. They did not want to know me anymore.

> One of them was kind enough to see me. He was the only one who actually bought me a meal and listened to me. No, I did not receive a loan. Only some advice and an explanation why bankers were not interested in new ventures like mine.

> All I had were some savings of S$6000, the Mercedes Benz which I sold, and my determination to get going. I am grateful to one financial institution. Till this day, even though I can get cheaper capital from other sources, I still borrow part of my needs to support this institution. The general manager then dared to risk it with me when others would not.

As to government assistance at that point in time, it was non-existent as the focus was on foreign investment and manufacturing.

What does he think about the situation today for would-be entrepreneurs?

On government support and assistance

I studied the tax incentives and schemes as part of my Master of Business Administration programme. It was part of my final module under Advanced Taxation. All of them are targeted at manufacturing concerns. It does not help those who want to become entrepreneurs and be involved in trading. An agency house like mine would not get any support. To start a business in manufacturing would require a great deal of finance and no banker will lend you money if you are just starting out.

I have not applied for government support but would like to tell of an experience I had with one government statutory board, who was my landlord. I knew the Chief Executive as a school mate so I approached him to voice my hope that the landlord would reconsider the rental for my new lease. I drew his attention to the fact that they were raising my rent by 300 per cent! His reply simply was, 'You should know the government's position: If you cannot afford to pay the rent, go and work for someone.' That speaks volumes. It is quite clear that the government policies are highly selective in the types of businesses and particularly, those with high value-added and growth potential.

On finance

The situation is still the same. No bankers will extend money to you if you are just starting out. Two questions are foremost in their minds: 'What security do you have?' and 'What is your track record?

Now that I look back, it only occurred to me on reading Wayne Long's book *Entrepreneurship and Venture Development*, that bankers are not in the business of sharing your risk. I always thought that bankers should, since they are making money from me through my business, share some of my risk.

On acceptance of entrepreneurship as a career

I do not think the situation has changed. The amount of salary I had to forgo may have been larger but the sentiments are the same. I left a position as sales manager responsible for all the lines of an agency house to start my business. It was no mean sum: S$8000 a month. Any university graduate leaving his/her job for entrepreneurship would have to exchange their salary for uncertainty. In this present day and age when there are jobs, that is still an insensible decision to most people.

The future

The interview ended with an expression by Mr Tan on the prospects of any would-be entrepreneurs.

For one's business to be a success, a few ingredients are required. One is intelligence and analytical skills. You need these to make wise decisions about the business: be it products or services. Second, is strategic fit, which some call 'luck'. Third, negotiation skills; these are vital. Just consider my recent success in selling two of my businesses to a major multinational corporation and a likely joint venture with another, all of which require no equity injection on my part.

Case study review

Mr Tan exhibits the full range of Timmons's themes. Factors contributing to his entrepreneurial behaviour are presented in Table 6.1.

Table 6.1 Factors contributing to Mr Tan's entrepreneurial behaviour

Category	*Factors*
Antecedent influences	• He is committed to life-long learning through the formal education system and observation. • He brings intelligence and sound analytical skills to bear on risk management. • He exhibits a 'trader' instinct and impressive selling and negotiation skills.
Incubator organization	• His business has developed directly out of an incubator organization, the experience from which acted as a trigger for entrepreneurial action in its rejection, and as a strength to bring to bear on his business's development.
Environmental factors	• He is a deviant from social norm of his country. • There is limited access to finance for new and young businesses which hinders growth potential. • Due to the constrained nature of the domestic market, he has developed an international approach to business development.

7

Australia

Dianne Wingham

Key feature summary

Australia has a strong tradition of entrepreneurship, in part due to the high number of immigrants within its population. It continues to support and stimulate entrepreneurial activity, particularly in relation to the small business sector. Key features affecting entrepreneurship are:

- Over time, through its immigration policy, Australia has grown a population that has the potential to exhibit strong entrepreneurial tendencies. It has a history of individualism and an ambition to achieve which continues through the changing ethnicity of the current immigrant groups.
- Within a stable political, economic and social structure there is a high propensity for migrants to start-up their own businesses. Within a stable political, economic and social structure these enterprises are making, and will continue to make, vital contributions to the national economic and social welfare.
- Extensive political intervention policy has been introduced in support of the small business sector. This has taken the form of incentive arrangements, deregulation and legislative simplification, and government subsidized training and consultancy services. However, the highly legalistic, prescriptive formal environment continues to represent a challenge for small businesses in general.
- Migrants coming to Australia are able, in significant numbers, to maintain their business networks in Asia, the Indian Ocean region and Europe. In addition, small businesses are forming networks and alliances to develop new products and services targeted at emerging markets.
- Within Australian society individualism and entrepreneurship are accepted as norms. Furthermore, there is a high level of risk tolerance found in the prevailing management philosophy. This reflects a culture that is receptive to supporting risk, uncertainty and ambiguity which are generally accepted as central features of entrepreneurship.

Introduction

This chapter specifically focuses on the small business sector in Australia, and the factors that contribute to the high degree of participation of entrepreneurs in the business environment. In particular, it highlights the increasing maturity of this sector, which is exhibited in the form of the acquisition of essential skills to sustain the enterprises, the recognition of the importance of quality assurance in the international marketing place, and the evolution of more informed political interventionist strategies. The subject of the case study, Strong and Casey Freight, clearly illustrates the very basic trials, tribulations and joys of business development and management which are confronted by numerous small business owners. Specifically, it emphasizes the skill content and balance that are required in order for founding entrepreneurs to sustain their initial business idea and enthusiasm.

Australia: an overview

With a history of more than two centuries of dependence on primary industry, Australia no longer lives entirely off the 'sheep's back'. Although still the world's largest exporter of meat and wool, agriculture now accounts for only 5 per cent of Gross Domestic Product (Australian Bureau of Statistics, 1996). The country is undergoing a period of economic and social change, positioning itself as a major player in the fastest growing region in the world – the Asia-Pacific Rim. In addition, Australian export markets have moved away from their traditional Eurocentric focus towards Asia, which now accounts for 60 per cent of merchandise export.

For the first part of the twentieth century Australia adopted a protectionist policy. This enabled trade unions in highly protected industries to successfully push for increased wages in excess of productivity improvements, especially during the 1960s and 1970s. Industry and labour markets, not exposed to the forces of competition, were largely unresponsive to changing economic circumstances resulting in productive inefficiency due to resource misallocation. Throughout the 1980s Australia experienced slow growth in productivity, declining international competitiveness and reducing real living standards. By the late 1980s productivity in Australia grew at only 61 per cent of the OECD average compared with 75 per cent in the 1960s and 89 per cent in the 1970s (Australian Bureau of Statistics, 1996).

When the Hawke labour government came into power in 1983 there began a significant swing towards economic liberalization. This has tended to follow global trends and the emergence of market-oriented economic rationalism as the predominant ideology in the economic debate governing trade policy. Today, bipartisan political support exists for trade liberalization, with both major political parties proposing substantial tariff reductions over several years. This move would result in Australia becoming one of the least protectionist of OECD countries, having been one of the most protectionist for so many years. In addition, Australia is progressively working towards reducing trade and investment barriers in the region under its agreements with the Asia Pacific Economic Co-operation (APEC), and is urging other countries to progress the rate of tariff reduction. In 1996, Australia's general applied tariff on imports was reduced to a maximum of 5 per cent, with further cuts expected by the year 2000.

The Australian government actively encourages direct foreign investment in most areas of Australian industry. In 1992 the government relaxed its foreign investment policy guidelines. Consequently, small foreign investors, acquiring or starting businesses valued at less than AU$50 million do not normally need government approval. Limitations do exist on foreign investment in certain 'sensitive' industry sectors, particularly residential real estate, the media, telecommunication and civil aviation. Currently, the USA has the highest level of investment holdings in Australia valued at

AU$89 billion, followed by the UK with a portfolio worth AU$72 billion and Japan with AU$51 billion (Australian Bureau of Statistics, 1996).

In order for business to be able to meet the challenge of competing in a more open economic environment, rapid microeconomic reform to complement the liberalized trade policy is vital. Greater labour market flexibility and a supportive infrastructure are seen as an essential foundation for the development of more efficient industry. Increasingly, government economic policy has centred on sustainable growth and microeconomic reform. Market deregulation in particular has been a high priority in a bid to increase the competitiveness of Australian firms and reduce barriers to trade. Consequently, economic growth has averaged 4 per cent over the last four years supported by high capital expenditure and a low inflation environment (Small Business Development Corporation, 1996).

Population profile

Australian society is a heterogeneous representation of origins and cultures. Until recently a dominant British culture, the society has undergone a significant transformation in the post-Second World War era. The population has been built by a constant influx of immigrants over the years. It is still significantly European in origin, but is aligned substantially with the USA and Asia. The extent that immigration has been allowed over the years has resulted in a concentration of the major population centres of Australia around its extensive coastline. The need for increased population, and for the development of specific areas and regions has been reflected in the mode of structuring the immigration policies. Historically, two general categories of migrants have been sought:

- The migrants entering Australia on an assisted travel scheme commonly referred to as the '£10 Scheme', to provide skills and to generally boost the pool of employees in the new land. This was accompanied by those entering to facilitate family reunions, or to start a new life with prospects of adventure and changing fortune. In addition, it included a series of special groups of political or humanitarian migration schemes.
- Alternative migration programmes brought immigrants to Australia to undertake specific developments. Generally, conditions were harsh, and gradually the population of these isolated settlements filtered back toward the urban regions.

As a consequence of a high proportion of migrants in the population, there has been a history of individualism among the Australian settlers over time. This continues through the changing ethnicity of the current immigrant groups. What has been observed by business 'watchers' has been the extent of assimilation. Deakin, when speaking on the Immigration Restriction Act in the Federal Parliament in 1901, said of the diversity of immigrants at the turn of the twentieth century:

> It is their inexhaustible energy, their power of applying themselves to new tasks, their endurance, and low standard of living that make them such competitors ... It is the business qualities, the business aptitude, and general capacity of these people that make them dangerous ... (quoted in Hale, 1992, p. 2)

These qualities as identified nearly a century ago continue to be represented in the small business entrepreneurs currently starting business in their new country. Their capacity for work, their need to achieve, and their dedication to their business are now being recognized by many employees and business people today as the types of attributes that established businesses must try to instil in their own employees. For only in this way will business have any hope of surviving in an increasingly competitive environment. Indeed, it can be concluded that, through its immigration policy, Australia has grown a population that has the potential to exhibit strong entrepreneurial tendencies, and many of the migrants are key instigators of small business activity.

Furthermore, Williams (1992) maintains that enterprises owned and operated by immigrants to Australia (classified as a person or persons born in another country, and migrated to Australia after the age of five years) are making, and will undoubtedly continue to make, vital contributions to the nation's economic and social welfare. Through significant longitudinal research, he identifies the extent of small business involvement by migrants to Australia. This is relative to the percentage of migrants involved as both employees and entrepreneurs within the small business sector (Table 7.1).

Table 7.1 Immigrant participation rate in small business ownership/employment

Place of birth	Owner/Manager		Employees		Total	
Outside Australia		%		%		%
Immigrant	13 096	22.84	83 203	24.54	96 299	24.29
Non-immigrant	1947	3.40	12 886	3.80	14 833	3.74
Total born overseas	15 043	26.24	96 089	28.34	111 132	28.03

Source: Williams (1992).

The migrants coming to Australia are able, in significant numbers, to maintain their business connections in Asia, the Indian Ocean region and Europe. Markets as well as social structure reflect these evolving alliances. An increasing number of international corporations are locating their regional headquarters in Australia to service the booming Asia-Pacific region. They are attracted by the skilled labour force, advanced communications infrastructure, a stable political environment and the high standard of living. Australia has an effective 'non-partisan' reputation that enhances trade within the region.

Significance of small business

The small business sector is seen as having been the driver in Australia's economic turnaround over the past decade. It is regarded as the 'engine room' of the economy, and responsible for much of the innovation and employment growth. Encompassed under broad definitions of small and medium-sized enterprises (SMEs), the Australian government recognizes the major role small businesses play in its economy, where over 80 per cent of manufacturing exporters and 65 per cent of service exporters are defined in this way (Hine and Kelly, 1996). In fact the Carmichael Report (1994) confirmed that the small business sector is a vital contributor to the overall performance of the Australian economy, with a contribution of 96.9 per cent of all business operations in the private non-agricultural sector and a significant and growing 56 per cent of private sector employment. Since 1985, employment in the sector has grown at an average annual rate of 3.6 per cent, more than twice as fast as total employment, and as a share of the total employment it has risen from 39 per cent in the period 1985–86 to 45 per cent in 1993–94 (Australian Bureau of Statistics, 1996). Consequently, successive federal and state governments have taken care to become involved in the formalization of small business policy.

Specific examples of political intervention are as follows:

- **Incentive arrangements**: are being offered by the federal and state governments, including discounted tax rates and the provision of land and facilities. This does not only relate to corporate entities. Small business migrants are also taking advantage of current policy to invest and set up residence through a number of the incentive arrangements.
- **Deregulation and legislation simplification**: of the labour market, the finance sector, transport, communications and public utilities. Another key push has been to facilitate the provision of a 'level playing field' between the eight Australian states and territories. This is resulting in a larger and more consistent domestic market for many goods and services.

It is proposed that changes in policy are needed which will assist the growth of the small business sector, and which recognizes the peculiar culture of small business owner/managers. Furthermore, policy requires to more closely reflect the growing awareness by governments that small business is a discrete, powerful sector. This is beginning to happen. For example, recent increases in the capital gains rollover time for reinvestment of profits from the sale of a small business effective from 1 July 1997 has resulted from meaningful dialogue between government, the Australian Chambers of Commerce and Industry and the Australian Small Business Associations. This is another step in the simplification of regulation to facilitate small enterprise business compliance.

Definitional debate

Despite this proven significance of the small business sector in Australia, the government's application of broad definitions results in a failure to recognize the disparities which exist within this heterogeneous group. Furthermore, for a number of years, governments have merged the big and small business sectors together, and have responded in policy decisions to the most influential of these parties – big business. This lack of formalized clarification for the parameters of small business definition is seen as a reflection of this culture. It is a situation that is mirrored in a number of other countries, and therefore government policy often fails to adequately target support strategies.

The disparity over the years between the definition of small business adopted globally has resulted in nations seeking to define their own perception of the phenomenon. Thus, definitions that are advanced by participating nations will vary. However, the description in each case in many ways defines the prevailing culture and attitudes of business monitors and governments toward these entities at one particular point in time. The outcome has been that researchers and policy-makers who have sought an objective definition have resorted to a number of different ones. These either specifically include or exclude other segments of the business community. This practice has contributed to the level of difficulty found in assessment and analysis of cross-cultural small business practices and environments. For example, few cross-country comparative studies have been undertaken to specifically identify the planning practices of small businesses that employ fewer than 21 employees (one quantitative parameter of a definition favoured in Australia), or to reflect the cohort of constraints in small businesses in general.

Within Australia, a number of definitions are applied, which are given credibility in the arena of small business research (Table 7.2). The Wiltshire Committee (1971) description attempted to cover a number of eventualities and scenarios, spelling out the areas of personal control. By general definition, a small business is seen to exist in the majority of enterprises having fewer than 100 employees. Further, the definition chosen by the Australian Bureau of Statistics (1988) relied upon the number of employees being 20 or fewer, regardless of industry or industry activity. A small business may be defined under the Beddall Report (1990) on the basis of two major criteria: the number of employees; and whether it is or is not a manufacturing firm. Ang (1991), based on an agency perspective, reverted to an expanded description, and suggested an appropriate form of a small business defined through a series of established operational and philosophical criteria. There is, therefore, a great deal of agreement in the principle of the definitions, but a clarity and cohesion in the adoption of a national definition to facilitate global comparison is lacking.

Table 7.2 Australian small business definition criteria

Wiltshire Report (1971)	A business in which one or two persons are required to make all of the critical management decisions (finance, accounting, personnel, purchasing, processing or servicing, marketing and selling) without the aid of internal specialists, and with specific knowledge in only one or two functional areas.
Australian Bureau of Statistics (1988)	A business having fewer than 20 persons is referred to as 'small' irrespective of the industry in which it operates.
Beddall Report (1990)	A small business may be defined as one which employs up to 20 persons in the non-manufacturing sectors; and up to 100 if a manufacturer. It should also be independently owned and managed, be closely controlled by its owner/managers, who also contribute most, if not all, of the operating capital, and have the principal decision-making functions resting with the entrepreneurs.
Ang (1991)	A small business possesses most of the following characteristics: it has no publicly traded securities; the owners have undiversified personal portfolios; limited liability is absent or ineffective; first generation owners are entrepreneurial and prone to risk taking; the management team is not complete; business experiences the high cost of market and institutional imperfections; relationships with stakeholders are less formal; and it has a high degree of flexibility in designing compensation schemes.

Small business environment

Management practices and workplace cultures

The increasing environmental volatility and turbulence is escalating the pressure on small business owners/managers in Australia to plan for the future directions of their organizations. Many small businesses often rely on the continued steady rate of business development, based on the current level of sales as the best future estimates of growth. In the current environment, unfortunately, there have been a number of small businesses that have been askew in their estimates. However, as a further sign of a maturing small business sector, there is a growing reliance on more scientific market indicators (DEET, 1991; Monash University, 1994) as a means of determining future growth.

The benefit to small business of more scientific indicators is that they inform them of the forecasted trends and fluctuations, determined from consolidated knowledge and experience of the industry. Such data serves to limit risk, assisting in the development of an enhanced understanding of a new culture and industrial environment. The availability of these consolidated theoretical and practical data, coupled with the government investment in training to facilitate the growth, is a significant promoter for small business growth in the subregions.

This is leading to a reduction in the levels of reliance on the judgement of individual entrepreneurs, which is frequently based on instinct, industry experience and/or historical data. General observations suggest that small business owner/managers are slowly developing management practices and workplace cultures that narrow the skills gap between them and their larger counterparts. Implementation of plans and strategies has implied significance, representing a change within the internal business culture of many small enterprises.

Skills training

Promoters of growth in the form of skills training required by owner/managers to facilitate the implementation of more sophisticated planning practices are increasingly available in the form of short courses and seminars. However on the negative side, current work practices, the cultural imperative of the 'self-made-man' at work and compliance pressures often preclude attendance. Therefore, there are generally widely differing levels of skills available within small businesses. Along with other planning inhibitors, this has resulted in a wide disparity between the level to which small business owners/managers have relied on planning as a strategic tool. A flow-on effect of this disparity has resulted in significant differences in levels of access among the sector to financial support, through highly structured government funding programmes and tenders.

Legalistic, formal and prescriptive environment

A further factor that both contributes to and constrains small business owner/managers is the legalistic, prescriptive and formal environment in which they are forced to operate. This applies whether they are simply conforming to compliance requirements or are advancing their own growth through accessing funding, training, export or development programmes. Businesses aspiring to trade with government departments, and those wanting to export, require to become confident with the relevant planning skills. These skills are vital in an environment of competitive tendering that has resulted from increased international interaction. The attraction of foreign investment in Australian companies has emphasized the importance of compliance with standards set at industry level, and often by potential customers. This accountability and reliance on documentation to ensure compliance is a particularly significant cultural change for small businesses.

Small business opportunities

Australia is a fertile country that abounds with small business opportunities. Currently, key sources are derived from the following areas:

- **Workplace reform:** the Australian workplace is undergoing major reform. Corporations and government agencies are streamlining their operations and out-sourcing 'non-core' activities. Government and bureaucracy have used this process to affect savings and to achieve strategic goals. As services are still required in many cases, these are now sourced through a network of systems such as contracting out, outsourcing, hiving-off and subcontracting. These are all seen as major contributors to 'new business' growth within the small business sector in both domestic and commercial markets. This has resulted in strong growth in the number of small firms servicing the business and public sector. In particular, accounting, legal, human resource, marketing and information technology firms are developing specialized niches and looking across traditional boundaries for new markets. More than one in five new jobs generated in the last decade have been in the business services sector (Australian Bureau of Statistics, 1996). While the corporate sector has redefined itself through cost-cutting and revised development strategies, the small business sector with its inherent flexibility has grown strongly, forming networks and alliances to develop new products and services for these emerging markets.
- **Lifestyle**: the face of Australia is changing. Australians are now living longer, having children at a later age, working longer hours and are more discretionary in their purchasing behaviour. For example, the proportion of people in the population aged 65 will double within the next 25 years (Australian Bureau of Statistics, 1996), and the longer working hours and higher per capita incomes are seeing many of the household tasks previously done within the home outsourced. This is an area in which franchises have already made strong inroads with outsourced home cleaning, maintenance and security becoming common practice over the last few years.
- **Consumer behaviour**: One distinctive characteristic of Australian consumers is their rapid take-up of new products and services, especially those related to information and communication technologies. According to the Australian Bureau of Statistics (Australian Bureau of Statistics, 1996), 99 per cent of Australian households possess a television set, 80 per cent a VCR, and 30 per cent a personal computer. Business usage of information technologies and communications equipment is also particularly high.

- **Recreation and tourism**: the Tourism Forecasting Council expects just over 6 million people to visit Australia in the year 2000, more than double that visiting in 1993. The tourism sector is already gearing up for the Sydney 2000 Olympics which is expected to create considerable demand for new services and facilities. Tourism has overtaken a number of other industries in its importance to the national economy and is currently Australia's single largest export industry. The profile of the overseas tourist is changing. Tourists are not only coming in at the top end of the market but there are also increasing numbers of budget tourists seeking out Australia's unique lifestyle and countryside (Small Business Development Corporation, 1997).

Financial assistance and support

The commonwealth and state governments operate a number of financial assistance schemes including subsidies, grants and loan guarantees. Without the benefit of an effective venture capital market over the years there had, until 1984, been restricted access to venture capital for small business and entrepreneurial venture activity. With the advent of the government licensing of management and investment companies (MICs) in that year, limited direct benefits have resulted due to restrictive investment criteria, and a small capital base. However, the flow-on effect has been to stimulate interest in the small business sector, and there is now a growing perception in the financial sector in general, of the value of its contribution to the viability of the low capital-base business. Consequently, many banks are actively pursuing the small business market.

In addition, financial assistance extended by the National Industry Extension Service (NIES) has been the route for a number of small enterprises to the development of a more professional approach to business management. The NIES scheme has enabled owner/managers to employ a multiplier agent duly accredited for consultancy assistance. The hiring of consultants suggests that NIES grants have been an important source of assistance in overcoming the resource-poverty related constraints peculiar to small enterprises (Glen and Weerawardena, 1996).

Although most of business related literature currently available continues to reflect the big business structure, the NIES scheme has enabled owner/managers to bridge the gap and to apply many appropriate fundamentals to their own business. Access to, and acceptance of, the programme are very much a function of the entrepreneurial intensity of the owner/manger, the degree of external advisory assistance, and the size of the enterprise. These variables, individually, and through interaction with others, influence the degree of planning sophistication achieved by small enterprises (Glen and Weerawardena, 1996).

Chapter summary

Currently, entrepreneurial opportunities certainly do exist through product and service innovation in Australia. New entrants to these markets will be found among both the immigrant and the established business groups. However, changes are taking place at an exponential rate, and entrants need to evaluate their opportunities very carefully, but will be able to take advantage of the increased technological development in Australian society. This is coupled with the risk tolerance found in the management philosophy, reflecting social culture. Within the context of the following case study, these factors present new promoters and inhibitors of entrepreneurial behaviour. Chief among the promoters is the continuing market deregulation. In particular, this will assist the growth of Casey's new firm that stands to benefit from the reduced barriers to trade.

The outlook for Australia is yet to begin reflecting the optimism of the boom days. There are, however, a number of indicators that point to a more sustainable growth pattern, which will be supportive of the development and growth of a business environment favourable for the small business. Small and big business operators are beginning to feel the benefits of economic reform, increased competition in the marketplace, and co-operative practices. The door to new markets and opportunities through regional trade with the APEC bloc is just being opened. The federal and state governments are formulating legislation designed to advance internationally perceived issues. Furthermore, standardized delivery and quality has increasingly become a priority.

However, the author is of the opinion that room exists for some interventionist economic policy, even within the realms of rising liberalization. This intervention needs to take a form that will bring about high levels of investment into human capital, with provisions being made for the continual access of workers to retraining throughout their working lives (Hale, 1992). Only in this way will Australia have businesses capable of meeting 'world best standards', resulting in the production of high quality goods and services, produced by a highly skilled and flexible work force.

It is predicted that the development of the Australian small business sector in the coming decade will be stimulated by the range of factors identified in this chapter. Undoubtedly, the most dominant of which is the asset of a population that is characterized by individualism and a burning ambition to achieve. When combined with the stable political, economic and social structure and the advantageous strategic trading position of Australia, all things being equal, it would appear that the entrepreneurial potential of the country should be unlimited.

Case Study: Strong and Casey Freight

Casey and Strong Freight operates within a niche market in Western Australia, and a general service market across Australia. The general market is by way of an extra service to existing clients. The business is located within the transport and storage sector, which has undergone considerable change in the past 20 years, and there are a number of different practices that are unique to this sector. It has minimal barriers to entry, provided the owner/managers is a homeowner, and it holds a certain mystique. There are upward of 6000 (Table 7.3) participating businesses in this industry sector in the subregional area of the state of Western Australia, and it employs in excess of 15 000 people.

Figure 7.3 Small business numbers and employment by industry (1994/96) – Western Australia

Industry	Number of small businesses	Employment
Construction	16 400	37 800
Property and business services	13 800	39 400
Retail trade	13 600	48 800
Manufacturing	7600	40 400
Personal and other services	6100	13 400
Transport and storage	6000	15 200
Health and community services	5300	19 100
Wholesale trade	4900	20 000
Cultural and recreational services	2900	6400
Accommodation, cafes and restaurants	2100	13 000
Finance and insurance	2100	5500
Education	1500	4500
Mining	500	2500
Total	**82 800**	**266 000**

Source: Small Business in Western Australia – Fact Sheet (December 1996).

Background

The first venture into business by William Casey was with his friend Gordon Strong with whom he had completed his apprenticeship in the mechanical engineering field. The arrangement was initially in the form of a partnership, a popular form of business arrangement at the initial stages of a small business. After taking some external professional advice, given while playing golf with their accountant, the partners decided that it was in their best interests to form a company. There were only family representatives on the Board, and the two men saw their wives as providing some clerical support in the home-based office in the early stages, but always viewed the business as belonging to the two male 'partners'. This perception remained throughout the 23-year life of the business.

The only times when the female partners were called upon to participate (other than to be telephone receptionists or to act in a clerical capacity for brief but regular times – staff holiday or sickness relief, and other contingent emergencies) was to agree to allow the family homes to be used as equity for successive business loans. This was necessary as the business grew in size and the capital outlay for vehicles increased with their load capacity. These elements of uncertainty, and personal risk contributed substantially, but by no means fully, to the eventual sale of the business at a considerable profit.

One aspect of small business that is of considerable importance, and yet is rarely covered by writings in the area, is that it is invasive, especially generally during the early entrepreneurial phase. A major factor in the establishment of a number of family businesses in Australia is the flow-over into family life, and the impact of such activities. This can take the form of the accounts being prepared each evening on the kitchen table, and the home telephone used for incoming business calls. Most participants in a current study report that they were totally unprepared for this aspect of their business, and admitted to varying degrees of discomfiture with it (Wingham, 1997). This factor also contributed, but in an unquantifiable way, to the eventual sale of Strong and Casey Freight. At this time, the principal entrepreneur, William Casey, was 48 years old, about to become divorced, and had two children. One a girl aged 26 years old and a boy aged 22. Gordon Strong was also 48 years of age.

The early days

Casey and Strong had begun their business with, what they termed, a 'healthy dissatisfaction' with where they currently worked, and a total lack of management and administrative skills. This was coupled with blind faith in their ability to 'do things better', and a huge overdraft supported by their family homes, which meant that they had to work 14-hour days and seven days a week, driving the two trucks which stood in the front garden at Gordon's home.

The form of the business was designed to take advantage of the mechanical skills of the pair, and they soon discovered that although doing their own repairs saved money, it did not generate any income. This led them to consider two approaches:

- taking on drivers and conducting their own repairs and maintenance; or
- taking on one driver and sharing the driving of the other vehicle, and the maintenance of both.

They chose the latter and now they were employers, they realized that they had never seriously considered this as a reality.

Trading environment

In the era when Strong and Casey Freight was established, a substantial amount of the goods moved around Australia were carried by internal transport departments of big businesses. A significant reduction in in-house fleets was experienced during the 1970s and 1980s. This was often not noticed by the general public because transport contractors were required to comply with often prohibitive requirements of the contract. This included transporting exclusively the goods of a single contractor, and carrying the livery of that business, always in good condition, and at the expense of the contractor.

Contract prices were cut throat, and contractors were tempted to cut corners. This resulted in the stringent enforcement of regulations governing the time a driver could spend on the road, and the load capacity of vehicles. While Strong and Casey Freight were not able to avoid these government regulations, they remained outside the single contract market, and developed a niche market in short haul heavy and bulky goods. This was augmented by general freight when it was available. A great deal of this freight was primary industry goods, and was subject to market fluctuations. The inconvenience of this factor was offset by the proximity to the drivers' homes resulting in a more stable work force of men living at home with their families. In addition, the restrictions on driving times, which worked against the single independent owner/operator not tied to a company, were able to be used to the advantage of Strong and Casey Freight as they had a number of drivers located across the state.

The financial market for transport was tight throughout the life of Strong and Casey Freight. There was no time during negotiations over the years that the business was able to obtain money without the collateral of the directors' homes. This was a contributory factor in the final decision to sell the business, as it was on the verge of a take-over, and the non-participating directors refused to forfeit the mortgages. The financial constraints were lessened as the business grew in size, and began to employ subcontractors, thus reducing the need for more vehicles. The financial strength of Strong and Casey Freight also meant that they could maintain a newer fleet of vehicles, being able to purchase for their own tax advantage. This strategy served to attract the work that was regular, paid well, and was less likely to be subject to the business failure of the client.

Challenges of business development and planning

As the business became established and expanded, the paperwork grew. It was soon beyond the kitchen table stage. Local authority intervention, spurred on by neighbours and residents in the suburb, insisted that the business relocate to a more commercial location. This was done – but not before relationships in the street had become quite strained. This was another factor which had been overlooked by the pair – the need to maintain co-operative relationships in the residential environment. Due to the combination of these factors and the lack of skills of the entrepreneurs, Strong and Casey Freight looked like closing down within 18 months of start-up.

A chance comment caused the pair to rethink their *laissez-faire* approach to business development and planning. They called a meeting. Table 7.4 lists the key issues that they identified and addressed. The pair soon realized that some of these issues were symptoms of their own lack of skills, and others were the result of under-capitalization. The remainder were simply problems which any entrepreneur would have to deal with in the normal run of business. The pair said that if they had been aware of all of them, they would have found trading into profit altogether too daunting. So Casey and Strong then sat at the kitchen table of Casey's home and mapped out the future of the business. They had realized that a plan was needed, and this in itself was a huge step forward.

The new era

Consequently, over time there were changes. Casey found that the administration appealed to him far more than the hands-on driving or mechanical work. Hence, he took over the management of the business. This was insofar as obtaining work for the growing fleet of trucks and their drivers, hiring and firing, and the management of the accountant and office staff, and the accommodation for a growing business. Strong maintained control of the workshops and the vehicle maintenance. He also ordered supplies of parts and accessories for the vehicles, enforced

Table 7.4 Key issues for the partners of Strong and Casey Freight

Entrepreneurs' motives	• To be their own boss. • To maximize their earning potential to provide a business for their children to inherit. • To give them freedom to spend time with their families (they had previously lived and worked away from home, earning good money, but without family life).
Partners' skills (on commencement)	• Mechanical engineering: 'we could do anything with a truck'.
Partners' skills (acquired since commencement)	• Negotiation (bank, suppliers, customers). • Contract formulation. • Seeking legal help, and protecting their own interests, through increased knowledge of legal costs and liabilities of the business. • Time management. • Administration. • Taxation, employment legislation and industry specific (some awareness but not the skill needed to facilitate smooth running of the business). • Communication with each other and employees.
Recognized skill deficiencies	• Planning and forecasting. • Quotation writing – to include sufficient cover for contingencies without pricing the business out of the market. • Debt collection. • Control of accounting and stock. • Purchasing parts, spares and fuel (on the road). • The need for insurance, still perceived as a cost to the business, and therefore left until the final notice each year.
Skill deficiencies recognized at a later date	• Lack of market definition, which meant wasted time and resources going after unobtainable jobs. • Failure to recognize a niche market. • Business procedures and record keeping.

relevant government regulations, and was responsible for the hiring and firing of the drivers and mechanics. The distribution of responsibilities worked well for the remainder of their working relationship. They became more skilled and confident in their roles. Casey even found time to join the local Chamber of Commerce and Industry, began addressing apprentice classes, and became interested in the theoretical side of the business.

End of the road

The partners were not unduly disturbed when an attempt to take over a small competitor resulted in a take-over offer for Strong and Casey Freight. After resisting the initial approach and resuming business as usual, a further offer was made, which both men agreed to accept. The business relationship ended with some of the motives for entry identified in Table 7.4 satisfied. They had achieved their aims of being successfully self-employed, and had gone some way in maximizing their earning potential. They lived at home for the duration of the business, and Strong subsequently continued to do so. However, the effect of the strain of repeated mortgaging of the family home, coupled with the long days and continued seven-day working, took their toll on the Casey family which split up. One significant issue that was not achieved was to provide a business for their children to inherit. The age disparity and the gender imbalance made this a difficult issue. Although it was addressed several times over the life of the business, it was seen as contentious and neither man felt comfortable with this level of contention. The inheritance issue was therefore avoided, and resolved through its disappearance on the sale of the business. On reflection, Casey admits that the partners needed for one partner to have significant management and administrative skills. It was often luck and inherent good timing which had protected them from their own skill deficiencies.

Epilogue

With the business successfully traded into a well-negotiated sale, the directors chose to retire. William Casey has since returned to the same industry sector, establishing a new company – Casey Transport. He reports that the level of skills training take-up is still low in the sector, and there are still the old 'shoestring' operations represented. He has, however, observed an increase in visibility of young companies with entrepreneurs under 30 years of age, and with a more professional approach to long-term involvement in the business. Casey optimistically anticipates that business ventures will one day be negotiated on face value, and not require the mortgaging of family homes to support purely business relationships. He feels that this will be a significant sign that 'bureaucracy' is taking small business seriously.

Strong and Casey maintain that the greatest single promoter of their entrepreneurial behaviour was the increased access to government subsidized training in the form of management courses. The greatest single inhibitor was perceived by both to be the cumbersome and prescriptive taxation system. Specifically, were the Provisional Tax imperatives that they perceived as making small businesses pay tax twice in one year. A close second was the ease of entry to their particular industry sector. This resulted in some ill-equipped businesses setting up and, occasionally, led to price wars and were generally disruptive to business relationships.

Case study review

William Casey and Gordon Strong exhibit the full range of Timmons's themes in an implicit, rather than aggressively explicit manner that presents a 'low key' entrepreneurial approach. Factors contributing to their entrepreneurial behaviour are presented in Table 7.5.

Table 7.5 Factors contributing to William Casey's and Gordon Strong's entrepreneurial behaviour

Category	Factors
Antecedent influences	• The motivation for their entrepreneurial action was life-style driven in a desire to spend more time with, and provide for, their families. • They display a strong work ethic. • They are committed to life-long learning through experience and participation in training programmes.
Incubator organization	• Their business has been directly developed from an incubator organization the experience from which acted as a trigger for entrepreneurial action in its rejection, and as a strength to bring to bear on their business development.
Environment factors	• Their behaviour is not deviant from the social norm in their country. • Constrained access to funding led to the use of personal assets as security which placed considerable stress on the business and families. • The existence of opportunities for business consultancy and advice benefited the entrepreneurs. • Business is developed on intuition rather than market research and formal management information.

8
Eastern Europe: Slovenia

Miroslav Glas

Key feature summary

Slovenia represents a country in transition from a centralized to a market economy. As such the promotion of a culture which sustains and encourages entrepreneurship is seen as an issue of significant import. Key features affecting entrepreneurship are:

- The systematic deprivation of private enterprise and the limited function of the market as a consequence of state regulation and control from the 1950s to the 1980s served to significantly suffocate the spirit of enterprise in Slovenia. It was only evidenced in the form of craft shops that were permitted by law, and by socialist entrepreneurs acting intrapreneurially within nationalized enterprises.
- Traditionally, Slovenians have not been classed as exhibiting entrepreneurial traits. The collectivist culture, dependency upon the state, historical subordination by external powers, and strong egalitarian values relative to the even distribution of social and material gains have combined with a conservative formal education system that rewarded obedience and diligence, and suppressed innovation and creativity.
- In the late 1980s a period of transition from a collective to a market economy began, pushed by severe economic recession, rising unemployment, a process of deregulation directed at enabling private initiative, and a strong underground economy, and provided the populace with an illustration of how living standards could be improved through entrepreneurship. Thus, began a new era of entrepreneurship that took place within a reformed institutional environment combining market economy, private ownership and political democracy with inconsistent degrees of success.
- Until 1988 entrepreneurship was viewed as a phenomenon intertwined with capitalist greed, for material gains through the exploitation of others. Slowly the attitude towards entrepreneurship is becoming more widespread and positive. However, the new society needs time to take root within people's conscience before the Slovene national can be described as 'collectively programmed' to recognize the value of, and need for, a truly entrepreneurial culture.

Introduction

This chapter coherently presents the historical and present day account of an extremely complex subject area. It successfully meshes the social, political and economic issues of import in Slovenia – a country very much at the embryonic stage of transition from a collectivist to an entrepreneurial culture. The content moves through time, introducing the different values, attitudes and behaviours that are emerging within Slovenian society bringing with it the 'new age of entrepreneurship'. These transitions have been enabled by a new institutional environment; a market economy; private ownership of business; and political democracy. A comprehensive summary of factors promoting and/or inhibiting entrepreneurship in Slovenia is presented. The case study is of a company called Jasksa d.o.o., which produces magnetic valves for the domestic and international marketplace. It was first established as a craft shop in 1965 and has traded through the transitional period. The entrepreneurial attributes of the founding entrepreneur, Stane Jaksa, are thoroughly analysed.

Entrepreneurship in Slovenia

The development of entrepreneurship in Slovenia must be considered in the context of its historical framework. It is only since 1991 that Slovenia has evolved as an independent state, and been able to create its autonomous political and economic system. Earlier, the opportunities for entrepreneurship development depended substantially upon Slovenia's strategic role within its former political formations; the Austro–Hungarian monarchy ruled until 1918 followed by Yugoslavia, often without consideration for the specific social and economic conditions within Slovenia. Moreover, after 1945, the central planning system essentially destroyed the private sector through confiscation, nationalization and agrarian reform, leaving only small agricultural holdings and craft shops to private owners. The specific collectivist culture resulted in a limited role for entrepreneurship. It was only during the 1980s, after a long period of recession that the Slovene economy moved towards a market economy, with its traditional structural characteristics (Kovaè, 1991). This new society still needs time to take root within people's conscience, and to develop a coherent value system. Currently, existing social groups share fairly controversial values, and the government is pragmatically looking for a minimum level of consensus, erratically changing its views on entrepreneurship.

It is difficult to say if at any time in history Slovenia could be considered a true entrepreneurial society. Historic subordination by external powers is a contributing reason as to why Slovenes failed to develop strong political and business elite. There was a lack of leadership capable of imposing a national vision. A large part of enterprise was performed by businessmen of German, Austrian and Jewish origin. The fundamental culture of Slovenes focused on production and work, quite in line with the catholic fashion of *ora et labora*.

Historical roots

Geographically, Slovenia is at the crossroads of commercial routes from the Southwest to the Southeast of Europe, and from Western Europe to the Near East. This results in a rich inflow from the various cultures. As a small nation it developed a tough culture of survival. For centuries, Slovenia existed on agriculture and some alternative sources of gains such as driving cargo from Trieste to Vienna. In addition, various industries and trades developed regionally, for example linen in Gorenjska; straw hats in Domzale; Idrijan lace; wood products of Ribnica; and metal works throughout Gorenjska.

The evolution of relatively strong indigenous crafts was supported by domestic resources during the nineteenth century, and imported capital from Vienna and Berlin co-financed the industrial growth. The process of industrialization began in the mid-nineteenth century, with the railroad construction from Vienna to the Adriatic Sea. In 1852, there were 116 factories with approximately 6600 workers, which grew to 441 factories with 36 200 workers in 1912. The inter-war period has seen further industrialization, with foreign capital as the majority owner of larger companies. In 1938, there were 1601 industrial plants in Slovenia employing five or more workers, representing a total of 65 825. That is to say an average of 41.1 workers per plant. From this group, 50.2 per cent of the firms employed up to 10 workers, 84.2 per cent represented small firms according to existing criteria (up to 50 workers), and only 2.7 per cent of firms were large firms, employing 39.5 per cent of all workers.

The tradition of entrepreneurship in Slovenia is truly represented by crafts and artisans. At the beginning of the nineteenth century, crafts were well developed, supplying the domestic and broader Austrian market. The process of industrialization concentrated the crafts mainly into services, with a modest representation in the manufacturing of goods. There were 15 000 craft shops around the year 1850, craftsmen were well organized in professional associations and some integrated into larger co-operatives. After 1945, the government intervened radically into the ownership and organization. In 1948, most of larger craft shops were nationalized, with state, co-operative and private shops existing since then. The state has limited the enterprising spirit of craftsmen through:

- controlling the size of the craft business: previously only a maximum of three employees, five since 1964 (with a multiple of them in 'joint' craft shops established by two or more craftsmen), and 10 since 1983;
- restrictions on the area of business premises;
- restricting crafts to selected list of activities.

Towards the end of the 1980s, the government allowed for different trades to register as crafts, such as small shops, therefore circumventing the otherwise strict regulations on private businesses. This resulted in a growth in the number of businesses categorized as 'craft shops' and employees therein as can be seen from Table 8.1.

Table 8.1 Development of craftshops in Slovenia (1939–1990)

	1939	1945–46	1951	1959	1970	1980	1990
Craftshops	21 632	15 154	16 872	14 273	12 790	14 349	34 747
Employees*	34 971	24 290	36 617	36 376	40 825	46 473	55 309

*Owners and apprentices not included.
Source: *Encyclopaedia of Slovenia* (Anon, 1994).

In the 1980s, the crafts industry assumed an important source of employment, with good work attitudes and strong commitment. It offered a possibility for personal gains through private initiative. Due to a lack of supply, it was possible to earn high incomes which were not significantly taxed by the weak tax authorities. The craftsmen became synonymous for wealth, conspicuous consumption, large houses and expensive cars. In addition, part-time crafts provided many employees in the state sector with better living standards.

Socialist entrepreneurship

Entrepreneurship that followed 1952, during the period of effective liberalism and greater market role in the internationally open economy, is an often-neglected area. Entrepreneurship did, in truth, develop and establish itself within the socialist economic sector. During the period 1952–60, a large number of workshops and small firms grew into medium- and large-sized companies, throughout Slovenia. The managers of these companies shared many features generally associated with entrepreneurs. These include:

- searching for business opportunities, although primarily in the domestic market, with a focus on import-substitution items;
- negotiating financial investment and political support by local politicians and bankers;
- creating entrepreneurial teams; and
- developing solid loyalty among employees, sometimes related to a strong local adherence.

Nevertheless, this environment differed in many important aspects from a true market environment, in particular in the terms of risk. As a 'suppliers market', the domestic market was heavily protected from the foreign competition. Exports were subsidized and the interest rate for loans was relatively low. Some entrepreneurs created true 'gazelles', competing successfully in demanding foreign markets, although the majority of Slovene firms were focused on the Yugoslav market. However, these 'socialist entrepreneurs' were not allowed to share the ownership of companies as a reward for their excellent performance. Even their earnings were severely restricted. Thus, their motivation was primarily through rewards such as: self-satisfaction; personal reputation; high social status; and the opportunity to acquire unique benefits and perks including housing loans, travel abroad, business gifts, and the use of the company car.

Periodically, the political elite feared the power of these successful businessmen and reacted with new restrictions. The economic reforms in 1965 strengthened remarkably the role of the corporate management, however, by the end of the 1960s, politics again removed many leading managers under the disguise of 'a struggle against technocratism'. The transformation of enterprises into 'organizations of associated labour' undermined further entrepreneurial efforts. Management was put under the tight control of politics and the self-management hierarchy. This significantly hindered the initiative and flexibility of many entrepreneurs.

The period of transition

More than at any time in the history of Slovenia, the real awakening of entrepreneurship occurred in the 1980s, when the political and economic changes in the countries of Eastern Europe reached Yugoslavia. The adverse national sentiments in Yugoslavia, as a result of the substantial differences in the development among republics, complicated the whole transition process acutely. Many phenomena towards the end of 1980s pointed to the inevitability of change. These included the:

- administration allowed different businesses to register under the cover of 'crafts' which enabled private initiative to gain momentum;
- strong underground economy demonstrated how employed people searched for alternative ways to improve their living standards;
- economic recession caused many problems for larger companies and artificial mergers quickly dissolved, raising the unemployment levels dramatically;
- Yugoslav market disintegrated due to national tensions, for example, Serbia started a political boycott of products from Slovenia.

In 1988, the Slovenian parliament passed the Enterprise Law, which allowed the formation of enterprises with mixed public and private ownership. This process of deregulation, in particular with respect to foreign trade and company registration, quickly encouraged a wave of new start-ups. In addition, the Law on Crafts (1988) allowed up to 10 workers per shop and extended the crafts status to a number of new activities. Furthermore, the government sponsored initiatives to develop a support network for small and medium-sized enterprises (Glas *et al.*, 1997). In 1991, the parliament in Slovenia passed the Law on Small Business Development, which provided the following:

- assistance to newly defined small businesses;
- the allocation of budget resources to implement government measures to foster further development of small businesses;
- the establishment of the Small Business Development Fund.

With 1989, a new era in the development of entrepreneurship began in Slovenia. This took place within a reformed institutional environment combining a market economy, private ownership and political democracy. The wave of start-ups, mainly in the form of limited liability companies, took off. There were 3755 companies in Slovenia in 1989, mainly established with social capital. The key features of the macro- and microenvironments that provided for the radical changes are presented in Table 8.2.

At the beginning of the 1990s, Slovenia declared itself an independent state. The short engagement with the Yugoslav Army in 1991, followed by the war in Croatia and Bosnia, and the United Nations ban on exports to Serbia led to a sharp decrease in business transactions with other Yugoslav republics. The larger companies were affected by a dramatic fall in sales, the break in their financial flows, and the process of dramatic organization downsizing. Many of them lost large amounts of capital in the territories of other Yugoslav republics. They slowly captured new markets in developed countries elsewhere in Europe. However, this was generally achieved through selling at substantially lower prices. As a consequence of these problems in established companies, many enterprising individuals started their own businesses. In addition, the Employment Office began to promote the self-employment programme, into which many skilled workers entered during the period 1991–96. Despite all these unfavourable events there was a romantic period for entrepreneurship during 1990–93.

This resulted in a sharp decrease in the rate of growth in the number of new companies in 1994, at least partly offset by sole proprietors as can be observed from Table 8.2.

Table 8.2 Business environment in Slovenia: basic economic information

	1990	1991	1992	1993	1994	1995
Economic parameters						
Growth rate of GDP	−3.4	−9.3	−5.4	2.8	5.3	3.9
Inflation (%)	549.7	117.7	201.3	32.3	19.8	12.6
Employment (1000)	818	746	692	666	647	642
Unemployment (1000)	44	75	103	129	127	122
Business ventures						
Incorporated business	14.957	23.348	36.448	47.734	51.038	51.875
Individual craftshops	33.484	34.380	35.650	35.911	34.607	–
Sole proprietors	–	–	–	2.157	10.643	57.802
Part-time crafts	N/A	12.699	12.021	11.255	10.563	–

Source: Statistical Office of Slovenia, various publications.

Privatization in Slovenia was slowed considerably in comparison to other Central European (CE) countries as a heated debate on efficient methods and social equity raged. However, due to the model chosen, privatization did not contribute to the entrepreneurial culture in Slovenia as expected. This was due to:

- the majority of socially owned companies implemented a scheme of internal ownership, which distributed ownership among employees with management not able to gain the controlling share;
- there were only some spin-offs from companies taken over by entrepreneurial teams;
- the process of restructuring has not been implemented to its fullest extent and only a modest amount of foreign capital has been invested.

Therefore, privatization did not serve as a real opportunity for entrepreneurs to take over existing companies. Instead, entrepreneurs focused more on growing new small ventures, which demanded a lot more time commitment in order to capture strong market positions.

Furthermore, the Company Law (1993) and Law on Crafts (1994) substantially altered the behaviour of Slovene entrepreneurs in their choice of the legal status for their ventures. Higher amounts of start-up capital and new extensive accounting and record-keeping requirements diminished the interest in companies. However, from the number of incorporated businesses (Table 8.2), only about 60–65 per cent actually operated, which is still a higher percentage than in other East European countries (Ljuhto, 1995). At this time, crafts ceased to be segregated as a particular type of venture and they became mainly a form of sole proprietorships. Part-time crafts were abolished as a type of initiative for additional earnings.

Cultural issues

Clearly, the tradition of entrepreneurship in Slovenia is truly and deeply rooted in crafts, which tended to exhibit only modest growth. Later, the socialist period of 1945–88 interrupted the continuity in private venturing, and developed a radically different political and business environment. Until 1988, entrepreneurship was often viewed as a phenomenon intertwined with capitalist greed for material gains, through the exploitation of others. The positive features of entrepreneurship, such as innovation, creativity and risk-taking, were forgotten (Plut and Plut, 1995).

The systemic deprivation of private ownership and limited functions of the market severely suffocated the development of a real entrepreneurial culture. Moreover, in a business environment dominated by politics, the stimulation of an entrepreneurial spirit in larger companies was limited. In addition, the Slovene people in general have never nurtured a strong business-oriented ethos, which in itself mitigates against the promotion of a strong entrepreneurial culture. Furthermore, few attractive role models for younger people exist within the country, or among emigrants.

Experts in psychology and sociology do not claim strong entrepreneurial potential in Slovenes. In his research into the Slovene national character, Musek (1994) assessed the following as fundamental personal attributes:

- introverted, inward-looking personality – correlated with egoistic, restraint behaviour, rather weak incentive to responsible group action and co-operation;
- unstable emotions – depression, oppressiveness, feeling of misfortune and guilt, pessimism;
- psychotic behaviour – tendency to dominance and dogmatism;
- discipline, diligence, ambition, and envy.

Essentially, only discipline and diligence coincide with entrepreneurial traits. These are opposed by very strong anti-entrepreneurial features of envy and emotional instability. Later honesty was added as the fundamental strength of Slovenians. As much as we could challenge these assessments, the reality is that conservative education has in the past rewarded obedience and diligence. Business skills, flexibility, innovative and creative attitudes did not bring recognition or career advancement. Consequently, the socialist period suppressed innovation and creativity, reducing the concept of innovation from the broad Schumpeterian concept to plain technical improvements.

This situation is further compounded when combined with the historic strong egalitarian value, which has been considered the substance of an anti-business or anti-entrepreneurial culture. Supanov (1970) emphasized the value of egalitarian distribution of social, not only material, rewards. This was irrespective of other conditions, such as differences in skills and abilities, and functional divisions in the economic, social and political structure. Interpretations of 'equality' vary among Slovenians. Antonèiè (1993) found different criteria of distributive justice in his research. The majority were in favour of functional equality, according to economic performance, or merit pay. However, it represents a problem for an entrepreneurial culture that is concerned with wealth creation and often results in 'inequality' in the distribution of resultant wealth.

Thus, it can be observed that the operation of the entire Slovene economic-political system generated many economic, social, psychological and general barriers to an entrepreneurial venture. These are summarized as:

- the collective decision-making process hindered the development of entrepreneurial networks and the assertion of individual initiatives;
- the lack of private savings and limited accessibility to credit money at commercial banks made it difficult to start new businesses;
- a strong social egalitarianism did not properly reward creative efforts;
- the prevailing embedded welfare mentality did not encourage private savings or the attention to business opportunities for individual action;
- resistance to changes in society interfered with individual dynamics;
- a lack of encouragement and feedback as inadequate incentives limited the pursuit of promising opportunities, and created a shortage of innovation and creativity;
- risk avoidance through obedience to the system discouraged 'trial and error' attitudes, and learning from mistakes in business behaviour;
- complacency among managers and professionals believing in the uniqueness of the self-management system discouraged the pursuit of alternative actions;
- mistrust towards people not belonging to the ruling party made it difficult to create entrepreneurial teams;
- the dependency attitudes towards the state limited individual dynamics;
- a romantic nationalist feeling resulted in many barriers to foreign investment and control;
- envy, a strong national characteristic, together with an intolerance for diversity discouraged the search for profitable ventures;
- a culture of positive thinking and trust was not highly developed;
- corruption and profiteering emerged as a substitute for true entrepreneurship;
- the educational system did not promote creativity, critical observations and problem solving among the youth.

The entrepreneurial community in the 1990s

The transition period introduced new horizons to business opportunities and entrepreneurship claimed high political esteem, as the search for new products and markets with job creation potential were high national priorities. It was seen as the panacea that would solve the mass of problems accumulated throughout the decades. Unfortunately, the needs for dramatic restructuring of the Slovenian economy surpassed the ability of entrepreneurs and the resources Slovenia marshalled to meet the challenges of being an independent state. It was a disappointment to people when the new 'age of entrepreneurship' did not live up to expectations. Negative features of entrepreneurship began to emerge. For instance, not all entrepreneurs were ideal employers. In addition, a number of rapid bankruptcies of speculative ventures occurred. These outcomes of entrepreneurship not only destroyed the illusions of an easy success story, but also raised serious complaints relative to crude profiteering, impassive lay-offs of personnel and general exploitation.

The political and economic changes of the 1990s set free some of the best entrepreneurial traditions in Slovenia. In the beginning, Slovenia fairly successfully managed to create an enthusiastic climate for entrepreneurship, particularly within the small business sector. With no thorough analysis available, we could speculate that the wave of entrepreneurship mostly involved certain groups of potential entrepreneurs. These groups were:

- employees from middle and larger social firms working closer to customers and the marketplace, who viewed their own enterprises as a means to bring forward business ideas that would have been difficult to develop within a conservative business environment;
- middle management, experts and individuals who built upon their expertise, now free from the excessive burden of the restructuring troubled companies;
- successful craftsmen from the younger generations who were growth oriented;
- freelance professionals in different trades drawing upon the boom in business services;
- the unemployed relying on assistance from the self-employment programme.

The majority of these people built upon their true inherent entrepreneurial culture. However, the rest of the society was still slow in developing the same kind of behaviour. This was generally due to the lack of business skills, different attitudes and demotivation arising from the difficult times they had lived through. Furthermore, in the 1990s, the government began establishing a belief in the value of entrepreneurship, but later let the promotion of an entrepreneurial culture falter. The initial momentum was lost when confronted with the growing demands of larger companies for government assistance in order to delay social tensions.

Considering the wide range of limitations and barriers to the promotion of an entrepreneurial culture, it is a surprising to identify a strong performance in the number of start-ups in the early 1990s. Slovenians stubbornly made their way into entrepreneurship, with less foreign official assistance, and less foreign capital than other CE countries. Following the Anglo-Saxon experiences, during the 1990s Slovenia developed a number of providers of business services. It experimented with different forms of the entrepreneurial infrastructure, such as business incubators and technology parks, support institutions of National Government Offices (NGOs), government-sponsored units, and new financial institutions. There is, however, quite a distinction between generations in different ages, with the younger developing the true potential for dynamic entrepreneurship.

Chapter summary

Analysis of the following case study and entrepreneurship research (Glas *et al.*, 1997) in Slovenia reveals different patterns of promoters and inhibitors over time, as the government support dwindled and small business failed to become the core focus of government support. The most striking changes in the business environment concerning entrepreneurship are presented in Table 8.3.

Table 8.3 Promoters (+), inhibitors (–) and neutral (∅) effects on entrepreneurship in Slovenia

---

Political intervention
- relative stability of key macroeconomics measures (+)
- substantial deregulation and simplification in early 1990s (+), reversal later (–)
- strong support for entrepreneurship/small business in some regions (+), but hardly backed up by appropriate resources (–)
- privatization process reached the stage of company restructuring (+)
- financial assistance: national/local small business development funds (+), still restraints in the attitudes of commercial banks (–), short supply of venture capital (∅)
- small business support network under development on the local/regional level (+)
- plans for new industrial/crafts zones (+), incubators (∅), technology parks (+)
- export promotion abroad (+)
- small business information system (∅)
- tax policy withdrew substantial tax stimuli for innovation, investment, job creation (–)

Entrepreneur(s) social development
- new concepts of distributive justice enhance innovation and creativity (+)
- strong beliefs in the (over)protective role of government still persist (–)
- entrepreneurs do not fear to get higher rewards (+)
- quality of life and work satisfaction became more important (+)
- social tensions due to the excessive social differentiation along income and wealth dimension (–)
- networking among entrepreneurs still weak (–)

Promoters/inhibitors in social structure
- high unemployment encouraged active employment policy (+)
- service economy is gradually evolving, providing new opportunities (+)
- process of de-industrialization scared a lot of employees (–)
- women are still underrepresented among entrepreneurs (–)
- large companies continue to control vast resources (–)

Entrepreneurial behaviour mobilization
- barriers to foreign capital prevent new managerial approaches (–)
- entrepreneurs are increasingly ignorant of politics and government (+)
- environmental consciousness awakening on cost of consumerism (+)
- still strong product-driven approach (–)
- low private savings (–), strong risk-averting attitudes (–)
- preference for total ownership of ventures (–), lack of the culture of team work (–)
- new attitudes toward financial management (+)

There is no doubt that entrepreneurship has taken root in Slovenia. Furthermore, there is a need for further start-ups, with new groups of entrepreneurs entering the process of venturing. However, a strong social and economic impact is also expected from the growth of existing ventures. This expectation may result in changes in the behaviour of entrepreneurs as a result of the following events:

- specific measures of the government and National Government Offices to support growing businesses;
- a positive attitude of large companies to develop subcontracting;
- clusters of companies around their core businesses;
- a culture of co-operation and networking strengthening among entrepreneurs.

Currently, there is a growing consensus among people in local and regional communities that they have to take social and economic development into their own hands, confronting the clear tendencies to the over-centralization of political and economic power. Slowly, the public attitude towards entrepreneurship is becoming more widespread and positive. However, entrepreneurship in Slovenia still has a long way to go to catch up with the developed market economies of Western Europe. The government has an important role to play in enabling this process to run smoothly by providing an appropriate mix of 'hard' and 'soft' support for entrepreneurs. The whole Slovene society has to recognize the need for a new breed of dynamic entrepreneurs, in order to participate in the technological process, and to grow a new, healthy, economic structure. Slovenian entrepreneurs have to seize all the advantages of the new entrepreneurial culture to fulfil their visions and ambitions, and those of their nation.

Case Study: Jakša d.o.o.

Jakša d.o.o. is a company with a long tradition, which has experienced entrepreneurship under the socialist system and during the transition. It is known as a famous Slovene family business. Stane Jakša, the founder, is a recognized entrepreneur in Slovenia, holding the Prize of Small Business Owners, presented by the Chamber of Economy of Slovenia, and the Award for Innovation from Eureca, Brussels.

The company was established in 1965 as a craft shop, which focused on the production of magnetic valves. Today, it is a limited liability company with a product mix of over 600 types of magnetic valves for the control of water, air, gases, steam and hot water. In addition, special applications are designed specifically for customers. The company is managed by the founder's son. Sales turnover amounts to over 1 million DEM per year, and it employs 11 workers, seven of whom are family members. In addition, the company manages a subcontracting network for metal parts, which produces the electronic and plastic components used in the assembly of valves. In 1997, the company moved to new premises in an industrial zone that should cover its requirements for the following 10–15 years.

Personal history of Stane Jakša

In 1965, the founder and his wife wanted to earn more than their jobs provided, so they resigned. The entrepreneur had had a job in a company producing fire-alarm equipment. The craft shop started to produce fashionable electrical rings, but was searching for new products. A company called Gorenje, a large producer of domestic appliances, decided to produce washing-machines. They were looking for subcontractors, to make valves and pumps. Jakša chose to make the valves. In February 1966, after a number of setbacks they developed a prototype and the production was scheduled for November 1966. Production expanded from 7000 pieces to 450 000 within 10 years, with Jakša being the exclusive supplier to Gorenje.

During 25 years of co-operation with Gorenje, Jakša maintained the continuous development of new types of valves, although he was unhappy about the attitude of the large company towards subcontractors. He extended his product range to Siemens in Germany during the period 1975 to 1997, competing with Italian and American producers. This trade had to cease due to the price being 'squeezed' by Siemens. Jakša was not very happy, as competitors constantly undercut his company's profit margins. Then the business with Gorenje became uncertain due to delayed payments during a period of high inflation that exercised continuous pressure on the company's liquidity. Jakša decided to focus on customer-designed application of valves. In 1990, he had a 25 per cent market share of the Yugoslav state and 25 per cent of sales in other export markets. The independence of the Slovenian state caused substantial loss within these markets and the company started to search for new customers in other European countries. By 1995, it was again on a stable development path.

Entrepreneur's personality

Stane Jakša is an entrepreneur toughened through hard work, competitive struggles and disputes with the prevailing politics of the time. His personality involves the characteristics of an entrepreneur, such as:

- (technical) creativity and innovation;
- resource gathering;
- the founding of an economic organization;
- the chance for gain under risk and uncertainty.

He often remarked that the timing of his start-up was wrong, as 1965 was the year of the economic reform which restricted growth and investments. This made it very difficult for new firms to find a niche in the market. However, he managed to find and identify a venture where his technical skills played an important role, and his tenacity secured the first contract with the large customer.

He strongly asserts the view that his key advantage is continuous innovation and the association with the reputation of a trustworthy partner. Looking at some of the attributes generally associated with entrepreneurs (Timmons, 1985; Brockhaus and Horwitz, 1986) his personality is interpreted as summarized in Table 8.4.

All these attributes point to a strong personal will and determination. Stane Jakša represents those entrepreneurs that have taken the chance in the former political system to perform a kind of small industrial activity under the status of crafts. His technical skills dominated the operations and the culture of the firm is very much focused on production and customers, not on financial gains.

Key cultural promoters and inhibitors

Jakša plays a kind of individualistic game, and the existing entrepreneurial culture does not have a strong impact on his behaviour. In other words, it is neither a promoter nor an inhibitor. Nevertheless, his company record still expresses some ingredients of the environment. For example:

Table 8.4 Jakša's entrepreneurial attributes

Attribute	Description
Business ethics	• Takes pride in personal honesty and integrity, and in the assertion that there were no complaints relative to quality, delivery schedules, or financial performance. In some instances, his strong personal ethics were maintained at the financial cost of the company.
Decision making and planning	• The decision-making process tends to be slow, is final and irrevocable, even if it results in financial losses. The planning process is a family affair, and although the entrepreneur is not a strong proponent of a formal planning process, he values clear and accurate management information.
Environmental intuition and self-confidence	• Environment intuition and sensitivity is the basis for his strategic decision making. This results in him not seeking a complete set of information, which could represent a weakness in the current dynamic environment.
Initiative and responsibility	• His inclination to take the initiative and to bear the whole responsibility is almost excessive. Although he had the support of his wife and, later, children he strongly dominates the company even after formal retirement.
Need for achievement and opportunity focus	• His motivation grew from the desire for money, into the need to develop new products, to bring in new customers. Focused on the business of magnetic valves, he was presented with an opportunity in the form of customer-designed valves, covering the new more sophisticated applications, and adding value for customers.
Power and trust	• Although he does not need strong formal power, he remains the personification of the company, and is proud to be trusted to decide on the distribution of rewards. Formally retired, he continues to live for the company, maintains the relationships with customers, and handles public relations.
Risk management	• He has operated in this industry sector for 30 years, feels comfortable with his technical competence and does not consider entering a new sector. He manages risk and uncertainties through hard work and honesty, and expects his workers to share the same attitude. He presents conservative optimism, cautiously avoiding potential threats, rather than exploiting new opportunities. He avoided uncertainty by building on long-term personal relationships, quality and timely deliveries, continuous innovation and improvements in the value to customers.
Self-belief and values	• He strongly believes in what he is doing, and that his performance is not accounted for by luck or chance.
Tenacity, ambition and rewards	• Tenacity is a strong attribute of his personality and his motives are inspired more by the ambition to develop a strong reputation than by the rewards in monetary terms. He never planned to grow to a factory capable of mass production.

- Gorenje decided to create the network of subcontractors, free from discrimination against small private businesses, that provided the opportunity and initial growth of the company;
- the legislation allowed for a form of joint craft shops, with partners employing up to five workers each, with Jakša, his wife and his sister employing 15 workers;
- he worked with efficient subcontractors:

He ignored the cultural inhibitors, developing a strong personal culture, heedless of the behaviour and attitudes of both administration and society. In particular:

- He considered state intervention as an inhibitor, because the state always wanted to control businesses. In 1977 he was subject to an inquest that caused disturbances in commercial operations due to the temporary requisition of documents. The mistrust of the government relative to successful businessmen continues to bother him.
- His operations were hindered by high taxes. In some years, he was the most important taxpayer in the municipality. However, he still considered tax as a given fact. It was important to him that they were determined, and his attitude was to comply with the law in order to concentrate on business and to avoid any conflict with tax authorities.
- He did not like the attitude of banks towards small businesses, however, it did not bother him since he preferred to use his own financial resources.

The business philosophy of the entrepreneur is projected in the following SWOT analysis of Jakša d.o.o. as presented in Table 8.5.

Table 8.5 SWOT Analysis: Jakša d.o.o.

Strengths	Weaknesses
• focus on quality*	• not fully occupied capacities
• continuous research and development (R&D) activity	• no systematic marketing
• financial self-sufficiency	• poor after-sale services (abroad)
• good organization of production	• demands for advance payments from customers
• flexibility (proper equipment)	• large stocks
• up-to-date equipment	• strong charisma of the entrepreneur – pressure on the successors
• vast business experience	• strong family-oriented culture
Opportunities	Threats
• wide application of products	• strong competition at home and (in particular) abroad
• opportunities to enter new markets and develop new product lines	• possibilities for new entrants
• co-operation with consultants	• recession in the customer industries
• network of committed partners	

*Jakša d.o.o was the first small enterprise in Slovenia with the ISO 9000 standard.

The strong family culture in the company is a weakness in the sense that the company does not promote non-family staff, thus, not attracting non-family managerial personnel. This is not an problem in production and R&D, where the son continues the father's tradition. However, it is an issue in the area of marketing, especially as a strong engineering culture leads to the understatement of the important commercial issues. There is no suitably skilled family member to address this weakness, which accounts for some of the negative attributes of the company.

The entrepreneur is aware of some of his strengths and weaknesses, but is blind to those that do not correspond to his personal set of beliefs. Furthermore, the commercial weakness seems to be less important to him than the technological advances. This is due to Jakša not being overly interested in expansion and short-term profit maximization. His answers to the challenges from the changes in the environment are focused around quality, personal relationships with customers, technical expertise, and honesty and good faith in the business. He is dedicated to solving customers' problems with sound design, continuous co-operation, and incremental improvements. These attributes give him a competitive advantage in the domestic market where he can provide direct personal contacts and advisory services to customers. However, in the export market these strengths are more difficult to deliver. Consequently, he is working on the creation of a network of skilled partners indigenous to the individual foreign markets in which he wishes to participate.

Through this analysis, four key characteristics of the company can be identified. These are:

- family management employment practices;
- entrepreneur's personal set of beliefs which bound thinking;
- low company growth and profit motivation;
- competitive advantage is seen to be achieved through product/service quality, relationship management and business ethics.

Views on the current cultural environment

Jakša considers the current business environment critically from two aspects:

- the product/quality attitude which is lacking in many 'new-born' entrepreneurs;
- poor government attitude towards the small business sector.

He mostly deals with small business partners abroad, and believes in the future of a strong SME sector in Slovenia. However, he does not recognize that government assistance is a key promoter of entrepreneurship. He shares the opinion of other established entrepreneurs that the government has to ensure a stable macroeconomic environment, encouraging tax policy, and together with financial institutions the access to the capital on the same terms as foreign competitors.

Jakša does not believe that the current cultural environment as truly conducive to successful entrepreneurs for the following reasons:

- entrepreneurs are not adequately recognized by the public in terms of social status and economic contribution to the country's wealth;
- the system of formal education provides neither proper knowledge and skills nor promotes the business attitude among youth;
- the work ethic of employees is generally far lower than what Jakša demands from his workers;
- no recognition of the need for, and the value of, innovation.

However, reflecting on the past, Jakša does not consider the current cultural environment as a strong impediment on his business. The company does not really depend on the broad public as suppliers or customers. According to his views, his direct relationship with the most important customers is the best assurance for further development of the company.

Visions of the future

Jakša considers the company as his lifetime project. He does not believe it to be necessary that either him or his son should in any respect change their business attitudes. His vision focuses on the existing core business and the R&D expertise as the cornerstone for the company's strategy. In the future, he intends to:

- continue with the existing core business persisting in the concept of customer-driven operations in the market niche;
- improve the organization and economics of operation through CAD-CAM procedures, tighter cost control and well-managed information systems;
- ensure the high quality of products and personal contacts with important customers in Slovenia, providing the same kind of advice and after-sale services abroad through a network of committed partners;
- further develop the network of subcontractors who will share the same quality-centred approach;
- consider fresh fields of applications of valves to bring new customers and to provide a more complete range of products.

The key concept remains not the growth in the quantity of production, but covering the profitable market niches and developing committed customers. Business is not considered simply as a wealth-producing activity, but rather as the way of a meaningful life, combined with satisfied customers and pride in the status of being a trustworthy businessman. The company has to grow into a strong source of welfare for the family, balancing the financial rewards with the satisfaction drawn from innovation, quality, solving the problems of customers, occupying the lead market position in Slovenia and being a respected producer in the industry, in Europe at least.

Case study review

Stane Jakša exhibits the full range of Timmons's themes. Factors contributing to his entrepreneurial behaviour are presented in Table 8.6.

Table 8.6 Factors contributing to Stane Jakša's entrepreneurial behaviour

Category	Factors
Antecedent influences	• He possesses strong social, business and work ethics. • His business development has been influenced by the support of his family, and the degree to which it has become dependent upon it. • He has a strong personal will and determination for the business to survive despite having to trade within a politically difficult regime.
Incubator organization	• His business has developed directly out of an incubator organization the experience from which acted as a trigger for entrepreneurial action in its rejection, and as a strength to bring to bear on his business development.
Environmental factors	• He is a deviant from the social norm within his country. • His business has survived within an extremely exacting environment, which has contributed little in terms of support. • Due to the constrained nature of the domestic market, he has developed an international approach to business development.

9

Europe: Scotland

Frank Martin and Susan Laing

Key feature summary

In recent years, Scotland has experienced extensive political intervention relative to the stimulation of an entrepreneurial culture, which has been relatively successful. Key features affecting entrepreneurship are:

- In recent years within Europe interest in entrepreneurship has increased. It is believed that future prosperity is dependent upon growing a significant pool of entrepreneurial talent that can be motivated to create vibrant, indigenous businesses to contribute to local economies and societies.
- In research carried out by Scottish Enterprise (1991–93), the regional economic development organization, it was found that Scotland had a low business birth rate in comparison to other regions in the UK. Reasons which were presented were relative to: industry structure dominated by large firms; inefficient technology commercialization ability; under-developed informal support networks; and limited access to funds and fear of financial failure due to under-capitalization.
- It was found that Scotland has a substantial latent pool of people interested in entrepreneurship but that it had a low conversion rate. Consequently, political intervention measures were designed to redress this situation. One such measure is through involvement in the formal education system in the form of inclusion of enterprise and entrepreneurship studies in the curriculum from primary school to university level. This represents an investment in a long-term strategy, the effects of which may not be evidenced for several decades.
- The intervention driven by Scottish Enterprise is a significant example of a comprehensive, co-ordinated policy specifically designed to alter the dynamics, attitudes, values and beliefs of the culture of Scotland's society over time.

Introduction

This chapter focuses on a specific government initiative that has been designed to promote and sustain entrepreneurial behaviour in the long term. It outlines the nature of a national policy initiative in the higher education sector, aimed at increasing the rate of new firm formation in Scotland. The basis of this initiative is a major enterprise development strategy, identified as the 'Business Birth Rate Strategy'. This strategy developed by the main Scottish public sector enterprise development agency, Scottish

Enterprise, is the promotion of an enterprise culture to the population of Scotland as a whole. Within this overall promotion are actions aimed at specific segments of this population. This chapter details those actions specific to university students. The case study is based on David Wares, a university graduate, and his company Display Products Technology. This provides an example of the desired achievement as a consequence of the described political intervention.

The importance of entrepreneurship in Europe

A wide range of factors have contributed to the interest in entrepreneurship in Europe. The principal reason has been the most recent economic recessionary period with its associated impact on employment, particularly in manufacturing. Other influences include:

- the switch in employment emphasis from manufacturing to services;
- the move by large firms to prune their overheads by subcontracting or outsourcing;
- the encouragement of management buy-outs;
- the growing interest among a substantial minority of the middle class in exercising independence and finding alternative lifestyles which include small business as an option;
- changing technological and communication advancements which facilitate home working and smaller scale enterprise viability.

Garavan and O'Cinneide (1994) conclude that there is now a wide acceptance within the European Union (EU) that:

> future prosperity hinges on the creation of vibrant indigenous businesses that are deeply rooted in the local economy.

For this to occur there is a need to expand the pool of entrepreneurial talent to develop and manage new business ventures. In the UK this was recognized by all of the major political parties, and in Scotland it manifested itself in the development of the Business Birth Rate Strategy.

Definitional debate

The process of defining entrepreneurship is something of an industry itself. Among the useful definitions that apply in the context of this chapter are the following.

Kao (1994) defines an entrepreneur as:

> a person who undertakes a wealth-creating and value-adding process, through incubating ideas, assembling resources and making things happen ... entrepreneurship is the process of doing something new (creative) and something different (innovative) for the purpose of creating wealth for the individual and adding value for society.

The trait approach to entrepreneurship offers an understanding that focuses on the personality or psychological profile of the individual. Researchers have sought to identify and extract personality traits that might be considered uniquely entrepreneurial.

Carson *et al.* (1995) defines entrepreneurial traits as:

> personal characteristics that have been distinguished entrepreneurs from other groups in the population.

Carson *et al.* (1995) has provided a list of the most common traits.

- need for achievement;
- risk-taking propensity;
- self-confidence and locus of control;
- creativity and innovative behaviour.

Carson *et al.* (1995) has four main criticisms of the trait approach as presented in Table 9.1.

Table 9.1 Criticisms of trait approach

- The inability to differentiate clearly between entrepreneurial small business owners and equally successful professional executives in more established organizations.

- The emphasis placed on identifying the supposed key trait that is most characteristic of the entrepreneur. The single trait approach seeks to identify and prioritize the specific aspects of a person's personality that are deemed to be particularly entrepreneurial.

- Lack of recognition of entrepreneurship as a dynamic process. The entrepreneur will be required to adapt continuously and change their psychological frame of mind and outlook as the venture grows and changes.

- The deficiency in attempting to link traits to behaviour. This usually omits the importance of the individual entrepreneur's situation, and the influences emanating from the entrepreneur's overall situation. This neglect is an obvious explanation for the low correlations recorded between traits and behaviour.

The extent to which this approach contributes to our understanding of entrepreneurship as a concept and the process of business start-up has, over the past 20 years, created a great deal of debate. The literature on this debate is certainly extensive. It is summarized by the authors as:

> we lack a generic definition of the psychology of the entrepreneur and the relationship of psychological traits to both the initiation of a new venture and the growth of new enterprises ... it might be beneficial to concentrate research efforts, not on the psychological characteristics of entrepreneurs, but on determining why they succeed or fail.

Basically the conclusion we can arrive at is that the trait approach, in isolation, cannot be used to explain entrepreneurial behaviour. We need to look at what entrepreneurs do and why they do it.

Are entrepreneurs born or made?

Gibb (1996) discusses the degree to which entrepreneurial attributes are innate, can be acquired, or formally learned. Equally importantly, is the degree to which entrepreneurial attributes are contingent upon the job or task in hand. It can, for example, be argued that creativity is only measurable and meaningful within a particular context of task and roles.

The viewpoint is supported by Garavan and O'Cinneide (1994, p. 4) who comment:

> ... the debate on whether entrepreneurs can be taught still rears its head from time to time. Successful new ventures are as much the result of a driving entrepreneur with an abundance of luck and timing. The literature suggests that, on balance, it is desirable to come from two learned, successful entrepreneurial parents; it is also beneficial to gain work experience and get adequate education. This scenario will substantially enhance the probability of success ... Equally there are so many factors that are unrelated to genetics and support the counter paradigm 'entrepreneurs are often made, not born'.

From the foregoing, it seems logical to assume that, entrepreneurial attributes are likely to be stimulated by the nature of the opportunity and other work circumstances in the entrepreneurial business, and developed by experience. The strength of the stimulus, brought by the opportunity, on entrepreneurial attributes will be a function of the nature of the business, and of the environment in which it is operating.

Furthermore, in adopting Gibb's (1996) argument, it is reasonable to also state that the entrepreneurial attribute thresholds required, to enter into, and survive in business, will vary with respect to the nature and type of business. In particular, they will be unpredictable in relation to a number of factors depending on the simplicity or complexity of the production and marketing environment in which a business operates; in addition to the degree of certainty or uncertainty the business faces in that environment.

The process of entrepreneurship

Recognition that individuals require different entrepreneurial skills in different situations is critical. The role of an educator is to support individuals in developing themselves to take advantage of business opportunities that arise in the marketplace. To allow this to occur, research must provide answers to:

- How do entrepreneurs think?
- What actions do entrepreneurs take?
- How do entrepreneurs generate new ideas for business ventures?
- How do entrepreneurs develop their businesses?

Timmons *et al.* (1990) suggests that successful entrepreneurs share a number of common behaviours and attitudes. He lists:

- working very hard;
- copious quantities of energy;

- working with commitment and dedication;
- working with a competitive zeal;
- striving for excellence and the desire to win;
- enjoyment of changing conditions, economic or otherwise;
- treating failures as experiences to be learned from for the future;
- the satisfaction of control, and knowing that they influence the lives of many others.

Timmons *et al.* (1990, p. 11) sums up by stating:

> Successful entrepreneurs are those who have a flair for creativity and innovation and are primarily driven by opportunity and its attendant change.

The ability to exploit opportunities and cope with change will depend on the entrepreneur's ability to take decisions.

Carson *et al.* (1995, p. 8) concludes that:

> ... the entrepreneurial process is an action oriented way of thinking and behaving, which determines the way in which individuals approach their jobs and responsibilities, how they acquire resources, manage people, market their enterprise or produce products.

Entrepreneurship and culture in Scotland

In 1993 Scottish Enterprise published the results of an extensive research study into: new firm performance; the business environment; entrepreneurial potential and cultural issues. Specifically, the research was concerned with why Scotland creates so few new companies in relation to other parts of the UK.

Key research findings

The research indicated that Scotland had fewer companies per head of the population than both southern England and the rest of the UK. The new firm formation figures given in the study are shown as Table 9.2.

Table 9.2 New firm formation by region

	New companies per million population	% of stock
Scotland	1807	52
West Midlands	2818	53
South East	4801	57

Note: Growth companies defined as companies created since 1978 with over 50 employees in 1990.
Source: Dun and Bradstreet.

The analysis of these figures promoted the view that with fewer companies per capita than in other parts of the UK, a given company birth rate, measured as a percentage of the stock, generated fewer new companies. An additional problem identified was the number of new companies that subsequently grew to more than 50 employees in the same period. Table 9.3 profiles this position.

Table 9.3 New independent growth companies by region

	Growth companies per 1 million population	*Growth companies as % of all new companies*
Scotland	76.9	4.25
West Midlands	85.6	3.04
South East	117.1	2.44

Note: Growth companies defined as companies created since 1978 with over 50 employees in 1990.
Source: Dun and Bradstreet.

Analysis of the detailed figures indicated that growth companies are most likely to come from manufacturing. While constituting 17.2 per cent of all Scottish new ventures, manufacturing accounts for 38.5 per cent of those with over 50 employees. Unfortunately while Scotland performs relatively well in the certain industries, e.g. construction, textiles and electronics, it under-performed relative to the target area of the West Midlands, the hub of the manufacturing industry in the UK.

The reason for low levels of new business start-up was found to be a consequence of Scotland's historical legacy, specifically relative to:

- the dominance of large companies and the loss, through take-over and business failure, of headquarters' functions;
- high-tech ventures suffer from difficulties in converting technology ideas into growing businesses;
- traditional industries such as textiles do generate start-ups, but have failed to achieve significant growth;
- the lack of Scottish-based multinationals means a lack of demanding customers for small firms;
- informal networks are of vital importance to the development of new businesses, however, in Scotland networks are relatively restricted, closed, unco-operative and underdeveloped;
- worry about lack of funding is by far the largest single cause of prospective entrepreneurs deciding not to proceed with establishing a business, and widespread concern also exists that many new ventures fail because of under-capitalization.

Unexploited potential

One reason offered within the study for Scotland's perceived low rate of new firm formation was that few Scots living in Scotland were interested in setting up their own business. A MORI survey of 1600 people in Scotland, 1600 elsewhere in England and Wales and 500 each in the USA and Germany revealed a wide range of propositions. A summary of these is given below.

- The British, including the Scots, believe entrepreneurs are willing to take risks, and place considerable importance on making money. Few believe that entrepreneurs are concerned about job security and only 10 per cent believe they care about people.
- Scotland has a large latent pool of people interested in entrepreneurship but a lower conversion rate for both men and women than in southern England with 0.39 as against 0.63 for southern England. This is calculated as a percentage of the population who run their own business divided by the percentage who are latent/potential entrepreneurs.
- Compared to other countries, fewer Scots believe entrepreneurs contribute positively to the economy. In the case of Scotland 43 per cent of those interviewed agreed that entrepreneurs are of vital importance to the economy as opposed to 34 per cent in England and Wales. The main difference is with Germany 65 per cent and the USA 93 per cent.

Additional findings include:

- It was found that successful entrepreneurs are restricted to a narrow grouping within Scottish society. Over-represented groups include men aged 35 to 54 years old, while under-represented groups include women, the young (under 35) and 'blue collar' groups (the working class).
- The most significant explanatory variable over time inhibiting business creation has been found to be the low rate of home ownership.

Resulting political intervention measures

Thus, in an attempt to close the gap between Scotland and the rest of the UK, in terms of the number of new businesses created, Scottish Enterprise's Business Birth Rate Strategy (1993) set out the main policy priorities as follows:

- Unlocking the potential: persuading a larger number of people set up a business.
- Improving the business environment: encouragement given to new starts by informal and formal business support networks.
- Improving access to finance: helping potential entrepreneurs gain access to appropriate funding to develop their business.
- Widening the entrepreneurial base: unlocking the untapped potential among women, the under-35s and non-home owners.
- Developing start-ups in key sectors: obtaining more new starts in the important sectors of manufacturing, high technology and business services.
- Supporting growing companies: increasing the number of starts that subsequently achieve substantial growth, across the spectrum of business activities.

These priorities have been addressed through the provision of appropriate formal institutions and programmes, accompanied by a more informal approach in acting as a catalyst to establish for example:

- **The Business Forum**: modelled on the MIT Enterprise Forums in the USA, the forum provides a regular meeting place for entrepreneurs. It provides support, practical case histories, promotes networking and fosters links.
- **LINC Scotland**: acts as the main body for promoting informal investment, and operates a database linking investors with investment opportunities.
- **National Seed Capital Fund**: the encouragement of new pre-start and start-up funds for growth-oriented businesses. The fund makes relatively small, early stage investments in new and growing businesses, with conventional venture capital coming in at a later stage.
- **From Primary to Plc**: to improve the contribution made by the formal education system in order to increase the knowledge and understanding about business, finance and the role of the entrepreneur among young people, and to stimulate a stronger sense of identification with the business culture.

It is to this final provision, within the Scottish formal education system that our discussion now turns.

Teaching entrepreneurship

The concern to increase the pool of actual entrepreneurs and enhance the image of entrepreneurship has seen the development of a number of initiatives by Scottish Enterprise. Among these has been the strategy that has the title 'From Primary to Plc'. This strategy seeks to promote the possibility of entrepreneurship as a career through the creation of a positive image towards being enterprising to the education sector within Scotland. Children from primary to secondary school levels are now exposed to exercises and activities within schools that promote enterprising activities including entrepreneurial activities. This is carried on into the further and higher education sectors. In terms of the universities, Scottish Enterprise has provided funds in one form or another to six of the 13 universities located in Scotland. These universities have established Centres for Entrepreneurship whose main long-term objective is to offer, as far as is practical, every student the opportunity to take an entrepreneurship course during their time at university.

Garavan and O'Cinneide (1994) highlight the need to increase the *pool* of entrepreneurial talent, and then *improve the ability* of these entrepreneurs to manage new and growing businesses. The foregoing are the minimum prerequisites to subsequently allow the future prosperity of the economy to be realized.

The reasons why entrepreneurship has faced so many impediments to achieving academic acceptance predominantly relates to the 'lack of a body of knowledge' within established boundaries which academics felt safe and secure. The efforts made by academics, most notably Hills (1988), Davis *et al.* (1985) and Vesper (1993), to understand the role that entrepreneurship takes within the educational curriculum have faced much cynicism from opposing academic colleagues. Specific possible explanations, according to Davis *et al.* (1985), as to why scholars largely ignore new enterprises are presented in Table 9.4.

Table 9.4 Reasons for omission of new enterprise from academic curricula

- Small is by connotation less worthwhile than large.
- 'Small business' has been a low-status endeavour.
- A record of mediocre quality research.
- Greater potential for funding from mature 'large' businesses.
- Sophisticated management practices reside in larger firms.
- The functional organization of business schools contributes to making entrepreneurship 'an elective' or a management discipline, thereby narrowing the focus.
- Lesser quality data from new versus mature company – consulting projects.
- Entrepreneurship is a fad.

Objectives of entrepreneurship education

An important principle to be remembered proposed by Vesper and McMullan (1988, p. 5) is that:

> … education *cannot make* entrepreneurs, but it can offer students the opportunity to learn about entrepreneurship, and develop a mind set in graduates.

Thus, the development of students in such a way allows students to achieve learning outcomes as presented in Table 9.5.

Table 9.5 Desired learning outcomes of entrepreneurship education

- Greater knowledge about entrepreneurship and how it works, including the wide arrays of different ways in which entrepreneurship is implemented.
- Knowledge of business basics, but without the elegant academic refinements entrepreneurs don't find helpful.
- Greater ability and tendency to spot new business opportunities before others do.
- Greater ability and tendency to respond to business opportunities with virtuosity.
- Vision that reaches more extensively in both detail and future time in designing potential ventures.
- Enhanced capability to stimulate other people to share those future visions.
- More entrepreneurial in their thoughts and actions.
- More knowledgeable about the career opportunities open to them.
- Informed about common characteristics in successful businesses.

Source: Vesper and McMullan (1988).

It is proposed that the aim of teaching should be to progress entrepreneurship as an academic discipline, and to extend the body of knowledge in terms of what is known about entrepreneurs and the entrepreneurial process. The ability to engender an *entrepreneurial spirit* in students will be the outcome of this rapidly expanding process.

What to teach?

According to Gartner and Vesper (1994), entrepreneurship educators view the practice of business in a different way from educators in other business courses. The skills and knowledge necessary to understand issues regarding business entry are different from the skills and knowledge necessary to understand the operation of an ongoing business entity. Initially entrepreneurship courses focus on the 'hands-on' practical aspects of business that are often overlooked or de-emphasized in other management or business classes. Furthermore, the basics of entrepreneurship are fundamentally different from the basics of management. For example, Gartner *et al.* (1992) comments that an important part of entrepreneurship education involves dealing with the uncertainty inherent in business entry. This aspect of uncertainty in new business creation is in essence the foundation of entrepreneurship curriculum development. Educators must expose the degree of uncertainty and focus attention on:

- new product development;
- new services;
- new markets;
- new organizations.

Gartner *et al.* (1992) concludes that it is not the ability to tolerate ambiguity or uncertainty that is an important feature of entrepreneurship, but the ability to take uncertain situations and transform them into non ambiguous events that appears to be the essence, and indeed, spirit of entrepreneurship.

Pretorious (1996) undertook research in South Africa, Ireland and Russia to investigate the expectations of students relative to entrepreneurship education. The key findings of this research are presented in Table 9.6.

Table 9.6 Expectations of students about entrepreneurship education

The subject preference in an entrepreneurship course
1 Starting a new business
2 Identification of business opportunities
3 To think creatively and implement
4 Leadership skill development
5 Financial management for small business

Unsuitable topics in an entrepreneurship course
1 Commercial aspects
2 Analysis and interpretation of financial statements
3 Income tax issues
4 Workforce management
5 Finalizing of contracts/social responsibility of entrepreneurs

The balance which must be achieved from the findings in Table 9.6 relates to what students primarily wish to study and what is important that entrepreneurship students *should* study.

Gibb (1994) argues that entrepreneurs derive their knowledge needs from their business problems and opportunities. This important link between knowledge needs and business development can be seen from Table 9.6 and underpins three outstanding characteristics of the entrepreneur's approach to learning. Gibb (1994) cites these characteristics as:

- the desire for knowledge on a *need to know* basis;

- a concern for knowing *how to* do things;
- an equal concern for *with whom* the knowledge will be applied.

Entrepreneurs learn from doing, therefore to engender an entrepreneurial culture in the educational curriculum requires the establishment of learning situations which allow students to *apply* the knowledge that they have acquired. This first step takes into account Gibb's (1994) 'need to know' and 'know how' characteristics of entrepreneurial learning. Secondly, and equally important, is the requirement for educators to realize that successful entrepreneurs recognize patterns which lend themselves to the building of successful businesses. In other words, those who make mistakes, learn from the situation and avoid repeating them. Entrepreneurs build networks of people who allow them to develop their business ideas into business opportunities. The more frequently they go through this process, the more adept they become at it. Timmons *et al.* (1990, p. 11) refers to this as:

> the process of fitting pieces into a three-dimensional jigsaw puzzle.

The final dimension which Gibb (1994) calls 'know who' should also be incorporated into the learning situation, in terms of the nature of participation and involvement required of the learning students. This, in educational learning terminology, is referred to as reflective learning through to active learning. Entrepreneurship education to be effective should be *active,* allowing students to demonstrate their learning through *skills attained and attitudes developed.*

Scottish Enterprise with their 'Centres for Entrepreneurship' initiative target students across disciplines such as engineering and computing schools with entrepreneurship education. As part of a consortium programme between Napier University, the University of Stirling and the Robert Gordon University such a strategy was adopted. One of the universities (Napier University, Edinburgh) specifically targeted engineering and computing students for 'elective' (free choice) studies by:

- specifically targeting communication campaigns;
- giving priority over business students for places in classes concerned with entrepreneurship studies.

However, even with such positive discrimination towards the engineering and computing students, the business, and especially marketing management, students accounted for over 90 per cent of the class composition. If one is to adopt a marketing approach to curriculum development and target markets, it is essential to understand the market that one is operating in and then focus on the key market segments. From the experience of the USA, and the Scottish universities' experience to date, it must be concluded that academia should concentrate their efforts on offering courses to the *key* markets.

In the Scottish university sector the most accessible market appears to be *under- and postgraduate* students in the *business schools*. At undergraduate level, classes are offered by approximately 10 universities throughout Scotland. Only three specialized masters programmes are offered with many MBA programmes offering a range of entrepreneurship or small business-type topics. However, at this point in time, no Scottish university has yet developed the opportunity for a student to concentrate on entrepreneurship, and exit with a major in entrepreneurship at the undergraduate level. Interestingly, since 1997 the University of Stirling offers students across disciplines the opportunity to major in their chosen subject and take entrepreneurship as their minor honours subject.

The entrepreneurial learning situation is one which each of the Entrepreneurship Centres in the six universities in Scotland will need to address in their own way. Some are likely to approach it on the basis of reaching out to the wider student body, that is not only to business students but also to students in other disciplines. Others may concentrate on business-only students. The universities' initiative is very new with few direct business start-up examples to date.

Chapter summary

The following case study provides an example of what would be an ideal outcome for any one of the university Entrepreneurship Centres and for Scottish Enterprise, namely the creation of a successful manufacturing-related business by a young technically trained graduate. Although not a product of any university entrepreneurship programme, David Wares represents the ideal student candidate. He is a technical graduate who gained industrial experience and then moved to create a successful enterprise. David was 'inclined' towards an entrepreneurial career from his time at university, but required the initial 'push' of possible unemployment to start the process going.

Scottish Enterprise's Business Birth Rate Strategy is an example of political intervention designed to alter the dynamics, attitudes, values and beliefs of Scotland's culture. The vision adopted has been enlightened and is now one that poses a question. Just how much more can we achieve in Scotland, in terms of business creation, if only more students of David Ware's profile can be successfully endowed with the 'enterprise culture'? The aim of this process is to deliver to students an entrepreneurship programme which, at some point in their career, will help them to positively consider entrepreneurship as an attractive and real alternative to paid employment or unemployment. This represents a long-term strategy, an investment in the nation's future, aimed at effecting a significant cultural change. Furthermore, the outcomes may not be fully exhibited for a number of decades to come.

Case Study: Display Products Technology Limited

David Wares had a problem. Having initially decided to leave IBM when his current contract expired to start his own business, Display Products Technology, he had been offered a permanent position with a very attractive package. His dilemma was compounded by conflicting views from his potential partners and his family. Should he stay or should he go?

Background

The idea for Display Products Technology (DPT) was developed by David Wares, a 26-year-old test engineer with IBM, after a series of events had left him wondering where his career within IBM was going. As a contract employee rather than permanent staff, David was concerned about the uncertainty of his position. This was most evident when in early 1993, with his four-year contract running out in October of that year, he had still not had a satisfactory meeting with his manager to discuss his future.

David had developed a significant specialism in liquid crystal display (LCD) technology and regarded himself as something of a guru in this field. He enjoyed the challenge of this new technology and was concerned that, with the market failure of IBM's new LCD monitor and the loss of local control over the development of the IBM notebook computer, he would be unable to continue to work in this area at IBM. All the indicators pointed to the use of LCDs as the display products of the future and David wanted to capitalize on his expertise. In February 1993, David decided to seek some advice on setting up his own business. He approached Glasgow Opportunities, an advisory service for start-up and small businesses, to discuss his ideas for a consultancy business.

He was advised to carry out some market testing of his idea and approached a number of companies using LCD panels in their products, including Compaq and Apple. It quickly became apparent that there was a need for a service but not simply for consultancy. All LCD panels were manufactured in the Far East and when there was a problem in manufacturing or with a warranty claim by a user it was necessary to ship the panel overseas for testing and repair, an expensive process. During his conversations with the computer manufacturers and LCD panel manufacturers he realized that in many cases the LCDs need not have been despatched, at considerable cost, to the Far East. Either the units were beyond repair and should simply have been scrapped locally, or the fault lay not in the LCD panel but in the computer itself. No one in Europe had the skills to test the panels so all faulty LCDs had to be shipped.

There it was – the opportunity David was looking for. He decided to set up a screening service for testing faulty LCDs and to this end David produced a business plan and set up DPT. From his discussions with Glasgow Opportunities, his local business support agency, David knew that he would not be able to develop the business to its full potential on his own and he tentatively discussed his plans with two friends Bill and Ted. Bill, a qualified accountant, was a financial controller with a Glasgow-based motor dealership and Ted was a sales executive with as computer reseller, also based in Glasgow. Both Bill and Ted were excited by David's vision and agreed to support him. David would leave IBM when his contract expired and would be joined in the future by his two friends from their respective employers as and when the business could afford them.

The horns of a dilemma

David was now very excited by their plans and was counting the days until the end of October. However, one morning in July his boss threw a spanner in the works. He called David into his office saying that he had some very good news for him:

Boss:	David – great news. I have managed to persuade the guys upstairs that we should give you a permanent position with the company. That work that you did on the LCD monitor project was noticed up the line. Like me they believe you have a great future with us. Here is an offer letter, just a formality really. I have managed to get you a big increase too. Isn't that great?
David:	Eh...yes. Great.

That evening:

David:	What on earth do we do now? This offer is really good. I'm confused.
Bill:	I don't think this changes anything. You have already decided to leave and you shouldn't let this change your mind.
Ted:	Yes. The opportunities for DPT are too good and we must go for it.
David:	What do you mean we! I'm the one that is leaving not you. You two still have the security of a job and a salary. This offer would give me that too.
Ted:	David, we both have families and a mortgage – you don't.
Bill:	Look David. Before today there was only one way forward. You were going into the business full time and we were working with you in the evenings and at weekends. We are not suggesting that this changes at all. We are just as committed to DPT as you. Have you spoken to your mother about this?
David:	Yes. She is hasn't said much but I think that she would be happier if I accepted and 'had a proper job'!
Bill:	So what are you going to do?
David:	I don't know. I'll sleep on it and talk to you tomorrow.

Background information on David Wares

David Wares' fascination with science and how things worked began at school and when it came to choosing a university course he settled on a practical science course specifically in a new area. He chose laser physics and optoelectronics at Strathclyde University in Glasgow and graduated in 1989 with a BSc Honours degree. His frequent comments to his friends that one day he would be a millionaire seemed increasingly unrealistic as, along with the rest of the new graduates, he started the arduous task of applying for a job through the graduate recruitment 'milkround'. He quickly found out that the only potential employers in his discipline were the major defence contractors. As David puts it:

> I was naive. I had not thought about where my course would lead me and I found myself staring at offers of employment from companies that made things that were designed to kill people. Even though I needed a job I felt that there was no way I could work in such an industry.

A career in IBM Development

David's brother was by this time working for IBM and clearly enjoying it. He suggested to David that he approach IBM, which he did, and he secured a four-year contract at the IBM development laboratory in Portsmouth.

Although the work was predominantly in electronics David quickly picked up the relevant knowledge and was put on a development project looking at the analogue design of colour monitors. With the backing and encouragement of his manager he was awarded a patent in 1990 relating to the automated adjustment of user controls (brightness and contrast).

He was selected for an IBM Graduate Experience Module and returned to Scotland on a secondment to the manufacturing development team working at Greenock. Here he was involved in designing test processes for both monochrome and colour liquid crystal display (LCD) monitors. In view of the specialist nature of the LCD which represented a major new step for IBM the test engineer's role was combined with that of procurement engineer which involved frequent visits and liaison with the Japanese manufacturers of LCD panels. In particular he gained access to DTI in Japan which was a manufacturing joint venture between IBM and Toshiba where he was able to more fully understand the manufacture of LCD panels.

A move into manufacturing

Structural changes at Greenock meant that responsibility for LCDs was moved away from David's area into mainstream laptop PC manufacturing. David decided formally to move from development into manufacturing as a test engineer, which was regarded by some of his development colleagues as a backward move. However, it gave David the opportunity to pursue his dream of becoming an 'LCD guru' by remaining with the product.

At one point, faced with a tight deadline, David and some of his new colleagues formed a project team to resolve a problem that they were faced with (not LCD related). This was a radical step within IBM where functional boundaries were strictly observed and the team took responsibility for planning, budgeting, capital expenditure requisition, business process development and reporting on the project. As David explained:

> It was like having your own business. We now had to consider what the financial effect of working overtime would be on the outcome of the project instead of simply authorizing it. It was not easy but we all learned a great deal.

The project was an outstanding success and the team attracted attention from the senior management who were anxious to learn why it was that the original problem was solved in such a beneficial way.

Frustration sets in

In early 1993, David's enjoyment of his job started to wane when his former colleagues from the development team in Portsmouth were relocated to Greenock with substantial relocation packages. His sense of inequity was compounded with the discovery that these individuals were all on permanent contracts whereas he was still on a four-year contract which was due to expire in October of that year. No one at IBM had even talked to him about the options that were open to him in spite of the profile that he now enjoyed. He felt extremely let down and made up his mind to leave IBM when his contract expired and set up his own business. He did not want to be at the behest of an employer again.

Evaluating the options for self-employment

His first thoughts were to act as a consultant to Original Equipment Manufacturers (OEM) who used LCD panels. While still at IBM he approached his local Enterprise Trust and was persuaded to undertake some market research. During this process he established that there was potential for a screening and repair facility. Because of the high cost of the LCD panel, when a defective panel was discovered during the manufacturing and testing process, the OEMs had to ship them back to Japan for rework which was an expensive exercise. The companies that David spoke to seemed enthusiastic about a service that would allow them to establish which panels were not capable of being repaired and which therefore need not be sent back to Japan, thus saving time and costs.

Decision time

David prepared a business plan with the help of the Enterprise Trust. An off-the-shelf company was purchased in July 1993 and renamed Display Products Technology Limited and David started to plan for the day he could leave IBM in October. He began to approach a variety of sources of finance. Things were going according to plan until David's manager called him in one day to make him an offer of a permanent contract. Little did he know that David had other plans. The package on offer was very attractive and David now had a tough decision to make.

He boldly made the decision to take up the entrepreneurial challenge. DPT began trading in the early part of January 1995. At start-up the firm employed five people offering a 10-day turnaround for repairing colour LCDs as opposed to a 90-day turn-around for repairs coming back from Japan. Funding for the start-up was secured from the public sector Local Enterprise Company and British Steel Industry. As part of the start-up process David Wares enlisted the services of David Brain, former vice-president of Unisys in Scotland. As a member of the firm's Board, Mr Brain was given responsibility for overseas marketing and the financial aspects of the business.

At the start-up phase DPT was handling 1500 units per month with the aim of moving to 5000 LCDs per month within two years. By April 1996, the company had expanded to a work force of 30 employees and a turnover of £2 million. Wares himself believes that DPT is on an upward growth curve:

With the global computer industry set to turn out about 600000 defective – but repairable – LCD panels this year, there is ample potential to ramp up DPT's present modest production,

Case study review

David Wares exhibits the full range of Timmons's themes. The factors contributing to his entrepreneurial behaviour are presented in Table 9.7.

Table 9.7 Factors contributing to David Ware's entrepreneurial behaviour

Category	Factors
Antecedent influences	• He brings intelligence and sound analytical skills to bear on risk management. • He exhibits a 'trader's' instinct and impressive selling and negotiation skills.
Incubator organization	• The business has been directly developed from an incubator organization the experience from which acted as a trigger for entrepreneurial action in its rejection, and as a strength to bring to bear on his business development.
Environmental factors	• He is a deviant from the social norm within his country. • The funding environment was receptive to such a high technology business opportunity. • He made extensive use of the formal environment which exists to support entrepreneurial action. • He developed the capability to expand international market potential.

Note

The case study forms part of a series of case studies developed on behalf of Scottish Enterprise to highlight the role of the entrepreneur in the creation and development of a business. It was prepared by John Anderson of Price Waterhouse, and Frank Martin, University of Stirling. Copyright © Scottish Enterprise 1997.

10

Scandinavia: Finland

Antero Koskinen and Markku Virtanen

Key feature summary

Traditionally, Finland has not had a culture that strongly supported entrepreneurship. That is not to say it was actively against it, it was more that the society was neutral on the matter. Key features affecting entrepreneurship are:

- Finland hosts a diverse culture which, historically, has not been supportive of entrepreneurship. Appreciation of the actual and potential benefits arising from entrepreneurship has more recently grown as a consequence of high unemployment levels and economic recessionary pressures. The social impact of higher levels of entrepreneurial behaviour will not be fully reflected until some point in the future. However, a significant cultural insight is provided in the use of terminology relative to the 'negative selection of entrepreneurship' as an alternative to unemployment, and the 'shock' effect such a selection has on family and colleagues.
- A model is presented by Koskinen that enables comprehensive understanding of how entrepreneurship, culture, society, the economy and business development and management are interwoven within Finland. This serves to cut across wide-ranging academic debate that often adds an unnecessary level of complexity to the 'discipline' of entrepreneurship.
- Through the promotion of self-employment and small business start-up political intervention policy has been designed to foster full employment. In the period 1980 to 1990 this has consisted of widening entrepreneurial training and education, stimulating new venture creation and self-employment particularly in technology-based enterprises, and addressing general economic pressures experienced by small businesses. However, this has been to the neglect of the service sector. In the 1990s the central objective is to improve the real competitiveness of small businesses by intensifying the activities of the SME sector, and to specifically support those which are innovative and growth oriented.

Introduction

Since its independence in 1917, Finland has developed from an ancient class society to a market economy with a diverse entrepreneurial culture. The factors that have affected this development could be assumed to be quite similar to other market economies. However, they are also dependent on other factors including the historical development of Finland before independence, the Second World War and the geo-political location. Historical development could be divided into five different stages:

- the era before independence;
- the beginning of independence to the Second World War;
- the Second World War to the middle of the 1970s;
- the middle of the 1970s to the end of the 1980s;
- the development in the 1990's.

Within this chapter, analysis concentrates primarily on the current development even although, from the perspective of cultural context, more profound analysis of historical development might be reasonable. The justification for this approach is that there does not exist a thorough analysis of the historical development of entrepreneurship in Finland and official statistical data is not comparable. The first small and medium-sized enterprise (SME) policy programme was published in 1993, although the Consultative Committee for Small and Medium Sized Businesses (Industry) was established in 1978.

The Finnish political climate and atmosphere have not previously supported entrepreneurship and small businesses (Katila, 1991). Trade unions and interest groups have had a significant influence on the values connected with work such as salaries, working times and vacation, but the primary focus is generally on large companies (private or state-owned). In this sense the deep recession and high levels of unemployment at the beginning of the 1990s may have been the 'wake-up call' that has raised the appreciation of the benefits of entrepreneurship and small businesses within Finland.

This chapter commences with a definitional debate relative to the complex theoretical framework of entrepreneurship that has evolved. Debate progresses through the application of a model developed by Antero Koskinen which facilitates understanding of cultural, social and environment relative to small business development. A comprehensive account of the Finnish industry structure, SME policy and its outcomes is provided. Finally, the case study of Saimatec Engineering clearly illustrates the key issues highlighted throughout the chapter as influencing the process of entrepreneurship in Finland.

Theory and definitional debate

It has to be asked why is it so difficult to explain and predict entrepreneurship by approaching the subject through established theories. As Morrison *et al.* (1998) state, the process of entrepreneurship is essentially a fundamental, basic, human creative act where the entrepreneur plays a central role, and entrepreneurs are products of their environment. Is understanding of this 'act' really dependent upon a complex army of theories?

Busenitz and Lau (1996) emphasize the linkage between the personal variables of the entrepreneur and the environment, stressing that the propensity to engage in entrepreneurial activity is a function of cognition that is affected by the individual entrepreneur's cultural values. After studying development factors and phenomena of several countries, Wilken (1979) emphasizes the wider ramifications of entrepreneurship. He believes that when it has some influence on the growth and development of industry this impact should relate to, and be incorporated in, economic as well as in social, cultural and political connections and characteristics.

Furthermore, Järvinen (1948) states that if we think only about material development in culture we are in danger of labelling its central premise through the concept of entrepreneurship. This perspective is considered to be restrictive, ignoring the immaterial cultural and non-economic factors involved in the development process. Moreover, according to Szczepanski (1980), culture is formed by material and immaterial products of mankind, as well as values and identified norms of behaviour. These are objective and adopted in all communities and will be transmitted to other societies and subsequent generations. Thus, entrepreneurship should be seen as a reflection of ethical economic culture (Weber, 1976), a continuation of economic culture (Heikkilä 1979, Vesikansa 1979), and as a creator of new, regional entrepreneurial culture (Harisalo, 1988).

Over the years, entrepreneurship has become linked to the development of economies, cultures, social structures, and sectors of industry and technology in specific eras differently (Hoselitz, 1951; Haahti, 1987). In these wide contexts entrepreneurship has been interpreted synonymously with small businesses. It has generally been regarded as a phenomenon that creates new business but little attention has been paid to what kind of businesses are created. Some definitions of entrepreneurship, especially in the new venture creation literature, have differentiated between small businesses and entrepreneurial ventures. Drucker (1986), Kirchhoff (1991) and Hornaday (1992) state that not every new small business is entrepreneurial or represents entrepreneurship. They argue that entrepreneurship refers to the ability of new firms to create innovation. Gartner (1989) criticizes this kind of differentiation because he believes that it answers the wrong question and does not consider behavioural aspects.

In the 1930s, Schumpeter (Kilby, 1971) introduced the meaning of entrepreneurship to be a generator of economic change. He defined entrepreneurship as assembling production factors into a new combination and called this a process of 'creative destruction'. The process creates something new: new products or services; markets, organizations; and new ways to produce and deliver products or services. Thus, he saw the role of an entrepreneur as an innovator. Schumpeter's definition gave a new connotation to entrepreneurship and offered an alternative to the traditional equilibrium theories of economics. His main reasoning was that the fundamental task of explanation about economic behaviour was to find non-economic factors which were connected to the activity of individuals in the market (Greenfield et al., 1979). According to Schumpeter, entrepreneurship and entrepreneurs are instruments that change and improve the economy and society. He saw entrepreneurs as decision-makers but he also considered social reality to be a holistic entity in which decisions and choices are made under fluctuating social circumstances and contexts.

Allardt and Littunen (1972) consider the issue of the basis of social changes as the most essential problem of social activity. This issue deals with individuals, citizen groups and their consciousness about the possibilities for change; the influences of change and legitimacy as well as their own opportunities to generate changes. The conflict about the origin of change in idealism and materialism is interwoven with production technology but could also be linked to basic issues of entrepreneurship. For example, is entrepreneurship dependent on idealistic or materialistic starting points and how does large-scale entrepreneurship increase at different turning points of societal change?

In spite of different definitions, entrepreneurship can be seen as *a sign of structural change* in *social and market characteristics*. Entrepreneurship creates changes but, on the other hand, it is a process that also originates from change (Boime, 1976; Bagby, 1988). It represents a human creative act, which is intrinsically linked to the environmental and cultural context. The concept is much more holistic than simply an economic function. It is composite of material and immaterial, idealism and pragmatism. The extent to which it is supported is influenced by the degree of tolerance of change within the host society.

The Koskinen model

In an attempt to cut through the complexity of the theoretical frameworks and to present a clear account of the process of entrepreneurship as related to small business, Koskinen (1996) introduces a model of development tracks and arenas. It highlights the differences relative to the development of start-up firms in Finland. The model is based on a longitudinal study of 82 start-up small businesses during their first five years in operation. He divides the holistic concept of business into four arenas: financial; market; organizational/operational; and entrepreneur. He believes that the management of business transactions, and the balance and acceptance of challenges are the most important factors in starting a new business, not knowledge in any specific area of activity.

Evidently, the entrepreneurial process generates the power to mobilize the venture, while financial margin and credibility determine the direction of the development track in a small business. Financial margin and credibility result from the balanced development and mutual dependency of the different functions of a small business, while the four development tracks are called growth, stable, unstable, and declining firms (Koskinen, 1996). In the following analysis we describe the development of an average, hypothetical, firm in the various tracks. We believe that this approach may be more informative than seeking some specific firm that could be described more particularly.

Entrepreneurship: culture, society and economy

One way to approach the understanding of entrepreneurial cultures is to classify them according to national development, the nature of activity and motives. For example, Hietala (1987) suggests that three kinds of cultures will be needed in post-industrial service-oriented society: large business; small business; and self-aid and neighbour-aid. He characterizes large business culture as a capital-intensive industry that uses high levels of technology and economies of scale in production. Basic values are hard, masculine, egoistic and emphasize success. Small business culture is labour intensive with small-scale tailored production, and semi-hard values. Belief in entrepreneurship and freedom of action constitute the basic values. Hietala combines scenarios of self-employment, experimental production, house and community work with self-aid and neighbour-aid culture. The development of this culture is characterized by smooth, green, non-egoistic, solidarity and feminine values.

Hietala's classification can, to some extent, be accepted but the suggested characteristics could also be criticized. This is especially relative to the generalization of the value contents of large businesses, which is not convincing in times when 'green', smooth values are highlighted in businesses in general. It could be argued that business strategies are formulated according to prevailing attitudes and values. Thus, the businesses take advantage of the driving forces and values of the society. In this way, the changing social environment also transforms the values of businesses.

In addition, Hietala considers the significant influence of 'push' factors in entrepreneurship as:

- the *negative* selection of entrepreneurs in that their only alternative is unemployment, including a large proportion who are poorly educated, and those who have interrupted their education to become entrepreneurs;
- the *shock* influence in the environment affecting those who start their businesses, such as the negative reactions of family and close colleagues to the choice of an entrepreneurial career.

Growth track entrepreneur

The following characterization of a growth track entrepreneur in some sense confirms the conclusions of Hietala but also opposes his views:

> *The entrepreneur in a growth track*
>
> Typically a middle-aged, not very well educated, married man who has a technical vocational degree. This education supports his productive know-how but not the other business functions. Often his parents are also entrepreneurs. He has a long previous employment and experience in responsible tasks. His career has been stable or continuously advancing, but he has considered an entrepreneurial career for five years. He has organizing skills, seeks goal-directed co-operation with other people and knows how to stand up to competition. High achievement, diligence, and expert knowledge encourage him to carry out the work he knows and wants to do.
>
> He values self-employment, flexible working conditions, livelihood, and maintaining his family and also receiving recognition from the environment. He proceeds systematically to create an active enterprise and considers alternatives that will secure sufficient growth. He is an enterprising, skilful, goal-directed person evolving into an owner-manager (Koskinen, 1996).

Declining track entrepreneur

In the self-aid/neighbour-aid culture, Hietala considers the meaning of acting entrepreneurially to be evidenced in two factors and the manner in which these factors are valued. First, is the valuation of community activity of unemployed people and the redefinition of unemployment. Second, is the valuation of small business based on the hobbyist activities. If we analyse the characteristics of the firms in Koskinen's (1996) study we find that majority of these characteristics are common to the firms in the declining track.

The entrepreneur in a declining track

This includes young and old men and women. They are divorced more often than other entrepreneurs. They had a middle-class childhood home and no previous contacts with entrepreneurship but usually they are better educated than other entrepreneurs. More than 50 per cent of them have been certificated to an upper intermediate educational level. They have considered a business of their own for a long time. Getting start-up money was more important to them than to other entrepreneurs.

Usually they have no previous experience in entrepreneurship, in responsible jobs or in business life. Their career has been stable or mainly declining and they have been working in firms employing fewer than 20 persons. The last period of unemployment lasted longer than other periods. Female entrepreneurs emphasize planning and creativity whereas male entrepreneurs mainly value making their own decisions, working hard and making money. They really believe that they will always succeed by working hard.

They value self-realization and self-development. They try to operate creatively and independently while enjoying the results of their work. These entrepreneurs dreamt about employing and supporting themselves and they want to unite work and hobby. They have, however, more problems than others arising from neglect of important issues and questions, unsuccessful choice of partners, and health problems. They lack financial resources and collateral and thus have failed to secure income financing and external capital. Their expert knowledge is insufficient and family problems drain their energies. Their business is growing and personal resources and support of their partners are not sufficient to sustain it (Koskinen, 1996).

Unstable track entrepreneur

An individual who is caught up in the turbulence of social and economic changes has to fight with the difficult personal problem. For example, should one trust the common development processes of society, solve the problems independently or seek an intermediate form, such as to become an entrepreneur by using the society's support? The entrepreneur in an unstable track could be considered a product of a turbulent environment. Analysing the background of unstable track entrepreneurs reveals that they may represent the entrepreneurs with the greatest growth potential in the future.

The entrepreneur in an unstable track

Typically a middle-aged or younger married man who has known entrepreneurship from his childhood home. His intention period to become an entrepreneur is short. He is not very well educated but may have an upper technical college education with some entrepreneurship training. His work experience varies but usually he has no experience in business life. A stable career with short employment periods is a typical characteristic of this entrepreneur, who possesses the ability to organize and to interpret other people's behaviour.

He values creativity, is diligent and persistent, energetic and achievement-directed. This entrepreneur makes his own decisions, creates something that is his own and develops himself by studying. He is enterprising in developing his venture. Due to being involved in different phases of the work, he gets more experience and satisfaction observing evidence of resultant business improvements.

His goal is to support himself and earn a decent living through reasonable efforts. Finding his own place and having the opportunity to operate independently on his own terms heighten his self-esteem. Most of his problems are linked to finance and lack of collateral. Changes in family relations, additions to the family or accidents are also exhausting problems. However, he is an entrepreneur who seeks a place and venture of his own and tries to attain his goals through different experiments (Koskinen, 1996).

Stable track entrepreneur

Cole (1971) connects entrepreneurship, the role of choice of the entrepreneur and the decision characteristics to the social sciences, history and environment. He believes that ideology and environment, which are typical of the society, have an influence on the entrepreneur. The forces that are important in society and in a private enterprise are strongly connected with the history. The entrepreneur in a stable track has a relatively long working history in very small businesses. This may be one reason why these entrepreneurs prefer to keep their businesses small and stable rather than attempting to grow their firms.

The entrepreneur in a stable track

Usually is a middle-aged or older married man. Often he knows entrepreneurship from growing up as the only or eldest child. He has long considered becoming an entrepreneur. Unemployment and getting start-up money made the decision topical and possible. He is not well educated. His vocational education is of either lower or middle degree, either commercial or something other than technical.

He has a lengthy but fragmented employment history. He has no experience in responsible tasks or entrepreneurship. He has worked in very small enterprises. He very much prefers practical work and operations and always tries his best. He can also easily stand up to crises.

He values diligence, energy and exactness. He is active, persistent and realistic. He develops himself. He appreciates planning and variety in work. He keeps himself abreast of the times and considers his customers' interests. To him, it is very important to be able to employ himself. Independence, the opportunity to act as an entrepreneur, putting his ideas into practice and using his expertise heighten his self-esteem.

If he attains his goals, then the well being of his family and good friends is very important to him. Problems arise if the living standard is not what he desired or if family conflicts or sudden illnesses divert his energies. He is a prudent self-employed person who utilizes his own abilities, and is a craftsman with high self-esteem (Koskinen, 1996).

New growing track enterprise

Many expectations are connected with the individual who decides to become an entrepreneur when society is changing. These include the innovativeness of entrepreneurs and the new wave of development in the society where the different political guidelines and programmes are based. However, we should always remember the wide diversity of enterprises and entrepreneurs. Koskinen's (1996) characterization of a growth track entterprise reveals that these firms have many generally identified characteristics but innovativeness is not explicitly emphasized.

A new growing track enterprise

Turnover increases quickly, resources are efficiently allocated, equity is raised and effectively used, however, risks involved with debts are taken to support the development of the enterprise. In the beginning, fast growth burdens the solvency of the enterprise and high profitability expectations require a strategy of continuous growth, flexible financing and operational solutions. Achieving the growth objectives and creating financial margin strengthen the continuous development. Financiers find that the activities of the enterprise are credible in the financial arena.

A growing enterprise has natural access to the local market at the start-up phase and appropriate market operations support the selective widening of operations. Successful networking strengthens the image and competitiveness. Customers rely on the enterprise and support the company's endeavours to improve its market position.

Quality management, the propensity to apply new working methods and flexible adaptation of production create an effective basis of activities in growing ventures. The drive and continuity of growth follow from a willingness to reinforce ownership, to change the structure by acquisitions, and balanced adaptation of supply to demand. Internal development of effective communications, and open external relationships are also significant features in the development process of a growing enterprise.

> The entrepreneur's skills and know-how, work experience and practice, and taking responsibility are important starting points for a new entrepreneur. The ability to work with others, set goals and objectives, and make conscious efforts to achieve the goal support the enterprise's managed growth. When family communication is in good condition, the entrepreneur receives valuable confirmation from this arena to make a full commitment to entrepreneurial activity (Koskinen, 1996).

It is clear that wide-ranging cultural and environmental factors have a significant influence on generating the intention and orientation of entrepreneurship, as well as the establishment and development of new ventures (Koskinen, 1995). The Koskinen model answers the question as to how these factors direct and regulate the development tracks of businesses in different situations and cases. These factors could be categorized as processes of change in the environment generally referring to the structure of institutions and industry, and the policies which reflect the objectives of environment, specifically, SME policy which directs the development of entrepreneurship. These aspects are now addressed.

Development of Finnish enterprises in the 1990s

Finnish statistics from 1989 to 1995 suggest that it is difficult to deduce the connection of entrepreneurship and culture to the number of enterprises initiated. The hypothesis could be that if new firm creation decreases, then it is an indication that the level of entrepreneurship has decreased. In fact, Finland's economic recession that started in 1990 reduced the number of enterprises, whereas economic growth in 1995 led to their increase for first time in the decade (Statistics Finland, 1997). These figures suggest that entrepreneurship should have decreased up to 1995 but our argument is that it in fact has increased during recession.

Can it be explained as *'forced entrepreneurship'*, created through unemployment? The huge unemployment and resulting change in environment and social context, that we have, and continue to experience, has probably changed entrepreneurial attitudes and values in the long term. Thus, its social impact on the behaviour of the population will not be reflected until some point in the future. However, unemployment has resulted in altering the attitudes of decision-makers, who in turn have created solutions, for example through changes to tax laws, designed foster entrepreneurship.

According to Statistics Finland (1997, p. 28) an enterprise is defined as follows:

> ... an economic activity carried out by one or more persons for profit-making purposes. Enterprises are natural persons (self-employed), legal persons (e.g. limited companies, co-operative societies, savings banks or economic associations), public financial institutions or unincorporated central government enterprises.

In 1990, the number of enterprises was at an all-time high with over 218 000 firms which employed 1.4 million people. In 1991–94, the number of enterprises decreased by 15 per cent, and the number of employees in them by 27 per cent. In 1995, there were approximately 190 000 enterprises employing 1.1 million people. Compared to the previous year, the number of enterprises rose by 2.4 per cent and the number of employed in them by 4.4 per cent. Medium-sized and large firms represent only 1.5 per cent of the total number of firms.

These changes are indicated in the number of enterprises, employees and the amount of turnover. It is significant that the number of medium-sized firms decreased in 1990, whereas the number of enterprises in the small and large firm classes increased by 5 per cent at the same time. Relative negative change in the number of firms was the highest in the class of medium-sized businesses, approximately 15 per cent in 1992. They also decreased their employees relatively more than small and large firms, but their turnover did not decline at the same rate. On the other hand, large firms decreased their number of employees in 1990, while employee numbers stayed at the same level in medium-sized companies, and increased in small firms. It should be noted that medium-sized companies increased their turnover in 1993 by 10 per cent, whereas turnover of small businesses declined.

We may deduce that the small firm is slower to adapt, and lagging behind the development of medium-sized and large companies. We can suggest several reasons for this phenomenon. It could be because small firms:

- have a poorer level of planning and information systems and thus do not recognize or understand 'the weak signs' which could warn them in time;
- are extremely diverse and many of them seem to lack awareness of changes in the environment;
- are more likely to imitate other small firms, rather than larger firms which have been in the market for years.

The latter reason is supported by Brittain and Freeman (1980), who investigate how individuals act in establishing new firms, and how clusters of industries develop. They believe that an individual establishing a new firm looks for imitation models to create new businesses. Often they are based on their own, or others' experiences. Thus, it has been argued (Stinchcombe, 1965; Brittain and Freeman, 1980) that new firms are not created in the brains of an entrepreneur as a completely creative process without external influences. It is more probable that the entrepreneur will imitate an existing firm, which has been discovered to be successful. In this way entrepreneurs perceive this strategy as a means to alleviate the weaknesses of a new venture.

Political intervention

Frequently, entrepreneurship has been considered to be the most efficient way to create new working opportunities and prevent unemployment. Scase and Goffee (1980) emphasize the importance of the small business sector as employers and subcontractors for special products and services; the producers of small-scale technical innovations; and one of the driving forces of market variability. SME policies and programmes deviate from each other in different countries but enjoy parallel starting points and objectives. This is generally accepted as the: promotion of entrepreneurship and the development of SME activities in ways that strengthen their survival potential but do not distort the competitive mechanisms of a market economy.

The current main objective of Finnish political intervention is to introduce policy measures that foster full employment, the stable development of prices and balance of payment and growth. In Western economies today, unemployment is a significant problem. Thus, the main goal of policy-makers could be divided into two categories:

- to create new working opportunities;
- to alleviate the problems of unemployment.

The origins of Finnish SME policy

In Finland during the 1970s and 1980s, SME policy has been partly regional and partly employment policy. Regional policy has been constructed from several actions of social policy. Employment policy has usually concentrated on the solving of unemployment problems caused by structural changes in society. The Ministry of Labour is mainly responsible for employment policy measures. Previously, new job opportunities were generated through public works programmes, but in the 1980s an increasing amount of activities and measures were introduced to promote self-employment and small businesses (Vartiainen, 1982; Ilola and Aho, 1988).

SME policy has been a compact but weakly identifiable part of regional policy. Different emphases have been highlighted in the subthemes of SME policy according to the prevailing circumstances (Ministry of Interior Affairs, 1991a). Regional policy has used financing, including subsidies and tax relief, as an instrument to generate a lucrative environment for new and existing firms in different areas. Thus, public financing organizations under the supervision of the Ministry of Trade and Industry (MTI) have played a major role in implementing regional policy. Such activities as training, counselling and consulting, and research and development (R&D), have been used as instruments in all these organizations.

Illustration: Kera Ltd

In addition to the regional offices of the MTI, the Regional Development Fund (Kera Ltd) was set up in 1971 to promote and finance SMEs in the development areas of Finland. Kera is a state-owned credit institution operating throughout Finland. Its activities are governed by a special Act which outlines the framework but gives Kera freedom and flexibility in its operations. The promotion of start-up enterprises and corporate development play an important role in Kera's operations. Development loans are targeted at the holistic development of corporate activities. Kera also has special loans for start-ups and for female entrepreneurs.

One regional policy task has been to promote stabilized regional development by renewing the structure of production. Measures have been directed not only at SMEs but also at large firms, and they have been found to have a great influence on geographic location decisions of firms. However, the location decisions of firms are also dependent on several simultaneous factors (Lehmusto, 1987, Tiihonen and Virtanen, 1991). Lehmusto states that the investment funding of industry, availability of professional labour, status of the credit market, and factors connected with economic growth have an influence on location decisions. Thus, both 'push' factors in the current site, as well as 'pull' factors in the developing area affect location decision making.

Focus of SME public policy

The first real efforts to introduce a specific SME policy were in 1978 and 1980. The Consultative Committee for SMIEs (Small and Medium-sized Industrial Enterprises) was formed in 1978 and was composed of political decision-makers, leading official of central ministries and organizations from industry and commerce. As an advisory board to the Ministry of Trade and Industry the Committee was charged with the following tasks:

- to evaluate and follow systematically the development of profitability, competitiveness and financing possibilities in SMIEs;
- to deal with development activities in the administration, products and production, marketing, financing, consulting and training and research in SMIEs;
- to propose development measures in the above areas;
- to propose central infrastructure policies and SMIE environment prerequisites.

The emphasis and focus of industry, manufacturing and technology can be observed in the name of the Consultative Committee for Small and Medium Sized *Industrial* Enterprises. Currently, the emphasis has changed and the Committee is focusing on the entire sector of SMEs. As central areas of emphasis, in its first report the Committee suggested (CommR, 1983):

- improving the competitiveness of firms by decreasing their labour cost burden;
- improving the financial structure of firms to support a rise in equity financing as well as to increase their ability for risk taking;
- developing education and training to offer better fundamental information about establishing a firm and to provide the special know-how needed to establish firms in different regions of the country;
- intensifying consulting, training and other development measures to increase the reformation ability of SMIEs and to accelerate the transfer and adoption of new technology;
- developing the fundamentals and activities of financing organizations owned by the state, especially from the perspective of start-up businesses and firms which renew their products.

The Report of Technology Committee (1980) dealt with specific activities directed to SMEs (CommR, 1980) and introduced measures to develop the SME sector such as:

- allocating funds for product development;
- making product development services more effective;
- developing existing information and consulting services and establishing new ones;

- analysing the feasibility to establish new development companies for technology transfer purposes.

The technology focus is also highlighted in regional policy. One sign of this orientation is the planning of regional technology policy programmes (Virtanen, 1991). In the 1990s, the focus has changed towards more service-oriented activities.

Illustration: TEKES

The Technology Development Centre (TEKES), established in 1983, is a national organization that promotes technological research and development and co-operation between companies, universities and research institutes within Finland as well as internationally

---

SME policy and new entrepreneurs

The Ministry of Labour initiated a start-up funding experiment at the end of 1984 (Legal Act Nr. 702/84), which is one example of implemented SME policy. It began to grant start-up subsidies to entrepreneurs and unemployed people who intended to establish a new firm, and who had some previous entrepreneurial experience and sufficient education to run the business. The experiment was launched nationally (Koskinen, 1986). By the end of 1985, over 6000 applications were received, with approximately 41 per cent (2550) of the applicants being accepted.

This experiment raised conflicting feelings and also opposition in the world of commerce. Some members of the population hoped that the era when the entrepreneurs were enticed by offering money rewards, and start-up funds, would soon be over. However, subsequent developments revealed that start-up subsidies have become one of the most important instruments in the reduction of unemployment and creation of new enterprises. In addition, the attitudes of entrepreneurs have changed. It is generally believed that (Virtanen, 1996, p. 232):

> A start-up subsidy of FIM 50000 is a proper way to support new ventures. Mainly this is a psychological element which allows you to operate for some months.

New jobs, taxes and benefits for society were used as measures of the social importance of the start-up finance experiment (Koskinen, 1986; Ukkonen, 1987; Ilola and Aho, 1988). It was concluded that the payback period of the funds invested in start-up subsidies was estimated to be relatively fast.

New guidelines of SME policy

The Consultative Committee has published two SME policy programmes (Committee Report 1/1993; 1/1996). These were a result of the efforts of a working group whose

objectives of SME policy in the 1990s were to increase production by over 5 per cent and exports by approximately 10 per cent annually. Four measures to reach these objectives were recommended:

- the increase of equity and securing the availability of credit;
- the increase of productivity and elasticity of cost flexibility of labour;
- deregulation and increase of competition;
- the use of know-how to increase production and export.

Thus, the central objective of SME policy in the 1990s has been to improve real competitiveness by intensifying the activities of the SME sector. Moreover, the goal to strengthen the economic base has sought to improve the preconditions for growth of SMEs. The Committee has stated that resources should be allocated especially to entrepreneurial ventures and family enterprises. The updated SME policy programme (Committee Report, 1996) seeks to strengthen the SMEs' position in three key areas of activity:

1 *Development of environment and infrastructure through the*:
   - simplification of administrative practices;
   - objectivity of taxation;
   - reduction of labour costs of SMEs;
   - improvement of the position of SMEs in the money markets.
2 *Development of working life in SMEs through the*:
   - development of human resources;
   - development of co-operation and flexibility in working life.
3 *Promotion of projects which intensify the growth and competitiveness of SMEs through the*:
   - support of the growth of SMEs;
   - improvement of networking and R&D services of SMEs.

Contribution of political intervention and evaluation of SME policy

In 1995, the MTI published an evaluation of the 1993 SME policy programme (Committee Report 1/1995). It concluded that the majority of the measures proposed in the programme had been fulfilled. However, the degree or rate of implementation of renewal measures was not evaluated. Paasio and Heinonen (1993, p. 82) introduce research findings relative to the implementation of Finnish SME policy. They asked:

> How well have the Ministry of Trade and Industry, Regional Development Fund (Kera Ltd), Technology Development Centre (TEKES), Federation of Finnish Enterprises (previously SYKL, at the moment SY), local entrepreneurship organizations, commercial secretaries, Finnish Foreign Trade Association (UL), municipalities and chambers of commerce managed the implementation of SME policy?

Entrepreneurs gave only moderate grades to any of the named organizations. The entrepreneurs' own organizations (SYKL and local entrepreneurship organizations) obtained the best evaluations, while the municipalities were assessed as the weakest in implementation. The most successful entrepreneurs generally gave above-average scores. Understandably, the entrepreneurs who had scaled back or terminated their activities were the most negative. Both entrepreneurs and external evaluators appreciate the activities and measures which have supported the establishment of new businesses (Niittykangas, 1985; Koskinen, 1986). However, Finnish entrepreneurs appear not to value SME policy particularly highly, even if its main goal is to support the creation of new job opportunities (Niittykangas *et al.*, 1992). They also explored the factors affecting SMEs, how they adapt to changes in their environment, and also the effectiveness of SME policy. They conclude that SME policy should be thoroughly reconsidered. From their findings emerged references for the direction of development. They recommend the following:

- patience, predictability, attention to the quality of R&D services, expertise and special know-how should be increased in development organizations;
- clarification of the roles in different organizations;
- more orientation on the future and success of the firms;
- transfer of know-how to the SME sector;
- SME input in all of the legislation formalization.

More specific needs for development were identified in the fields of taxation, R&D activities, bankruptcy law reform and indirect labour costs. The respondents highlight the need for equality in the implemented policy. It should be equally directed to export firms as well as to the domestic market, to high technology companies as well as to traditional firms, and to different size classes, regions of the country, and sectors of industry.

Other issues arising from public policy intervention, or the lack of it, which have been identified by the authors are as follows:

- **Venture capital**: a significant aspect in developing SME policy measures in Finland is that of venture capital. Public sector funds have been dominating the market and some crowding-out effects may exist as a result (Virtanen, 1996). This is especially the case relative to regional markets, where public authorities should carefully differentiate between subsidies and venture capital. It is possible that the mixture of different financing instruments may lead to the collapse and failure of the whole market.
- **Unemployment**: SME policies and programmes should foster entrepreneurship and thereby create new job opportunities. However, these aspects are not explicitly mentioned as objectives of Finnish SME policy. The authors suggest that economic growth has been considered a prerequisite for development and thus an indirect measure to increase employment. However, focusing on growth ignores the role of different production factors – labour and capital – as growth contributors. In general, official policies in Finland have favoured capital intensive manufacturing and technology and ignored the labour intensive service sector.
- **Education**: entrepreneurship should be encouraged at universities and research institutions to create the basis for knowledge-intensive ventures. Such efforts are increasing. Academic entrepreneurship courses and programmes, as well as business start-up incubators have been established in universities and the '*1995–2005 Decade*

of Entrepreneurship' project has established an advisory professor group to promote its activities. These activities are not widely encouraged in current Finnish SME policy programmes, which target education and training mainly at the vocational level. However, life-long learning and knowledge intensity are emphasized in information technology strategies. Thus, it is recommended that the entrepreneur's learning process and mental development should be more explicitly highlighted in official programmes.

Chapter summary

In this analysis we have introduced the framework of Finnish entrepreneurship which in some respects resembles the Scandinavian practice but certainly also deviates from many characteristics of entrepreneurship in Sweden, Norway or Denmark. In Finland the meaning of entrepreneurship in the establishment of new businesses has been highlighted in public presentations, but not in practice. Conflicting attitudes exist because the politicians emphasize the importance of entrepreneurship but do not identify dynamism and the importance of appropriate incentives. However, recognition of some of these weaknesses suggests that attitudes are changing and entrepreneurship is being viewed more positively, especially as a creator of new employment opportunities.

From statistical analysis it was generalized that small firms tend to adjust to economic changes slower than medium-sized or large businesses. Possible explanations for this kind of behaviour were presented as imitating behaviour and the level of planning in small businesses. Through the application of Koskinen's model we progressed discussion from the general to the particular in considering the different tracks and arenas in which small firm entrepreneurship may follow and operate following start-up. This enabled the development of a comprehensive understanding of how entrepreneurship, culture, society, economy and business development and management are interwoven.

The focus of Finnish SME policy has been on industry and technology. It has been 'decentralized' under the supervision of several ministries and no holistic efforts took place until the 1990s. Reorganization of different administrative institutions and sectors may have a positive effect in the future. However, more attention should be paid to the service sector to relieve unemployment. Finnish SME policy has concentrated on industry whereas almost all services have been excluded until Kera and the Ministry of Trade and Industry introduced service-related measures in the mid-1990s.

The SME programmes have emphasized different areas and activities at different times. For example, entrepreneurs' knowledge and strong efforts to widen entrepreneurial training and education were emphasized in Finland in the beginning of the 1980s. When unemployment increased in the middle of the 1980s, new venture creation and self-employment were weighted more. At the same time the introduction of high technology was promoted. Economic growth altered the unemployment problem as the lack of professional labour and internationalization displaced neo-entrepreneurship at the end of the decade. At the same time, attention was mainly paid to European integration and managing of growth. At the beginning of the 1990s, the growth expectations persevered but because of the severe recession the focus changed to address basic economic pressures such as high unemployment, financial problems and crises in enterprises.

From the policy perspective, the challenge is how to develop durable measures that are not dependent on cyclical fluctuations. One possibility would be to create an entrepreneurial culture that encourages entrepreneurship in all the levels of society, and throughout the hierarchy of business operations. Decision-makers who understand the problems and motivations of an entrepreneur can set norms and regulations that support a more enterprising environment. Academic entrepreneurship is an appealing long-term solution that could be considered as an opportunity since it is timely, durable and attractive. In the future, we need more advanced level entrepreneurship education and training to create a more advanced entrepreneurial culture. The goal at the beginning of the twenty-first century should be the University of Entrepreneurship where knowledge-intensive entrepreneurs and researchers of entrepreneurship adopt enterprising attitudes and acquire a cross-scientific, holistic perspective on entrepreneurship.

Case Study: Saimatec Engineering Ltd

Background

Saimatec Engineering Ltd, which produces machinery and equipment, in particular roll packing systems for the wood and paper industry, started in the town of Imatra in 1981. In 1986, it moved to Savonlinna, the home city of the entrepreneur and managing director, Seppo Rasimus. According to the Koskinen model Mr Rasimus represents a 'growth track entrepreneur' and exhibits the range of associated characteristics.

The entrepreneur, who was born into a farming family, trained as an engineer and prior to creating the venture he worked for 13 years with the Enso Corporation as a product manager. The job description included product development, planning, marketing and sales tasks, giving him a strong experience in logistics. On the basis of this experience he decided to experiment in a career as an entrepreneur, independent of large organizations.

Saimatec Engineering began as a limited partnership and transformed to a limited company at the time venture capitalists became involved in 1991. In 1981, the entrepreneur had difficulties in acquiring start-up funding and that is why the firm started from its Imatra location as Mr Rasimus found it easier to raise funds in this region. Thus, the venture was financed by a bank loan and a start-up subsidy from the Ministry of Trade and Industry.

Motivation, commitment and risk characteristics

Mr Rasimus's main motivation to become an entrepreneur was the aspiration to experiment to find out if it was possible for him to succeed, and to have the opportunity to manage in a different way to what he had experienced in a large company. He wanted to establish himself as an independent operator in his industry sector. The commitment to his firm is illustrated relative to the equity holding. Mr Rasimus personally owns 80 per cent and his wife 5 per cent, and currently, he has also committed personal financial guarantees to the company.

He states that the management of risk taking is a natural and a crucial part of entrepreneurship. Mr Rasimus reckons that if he had been in anyway risk adverse he would not be in business for himself. When asked what kind of risk attitude entrepreneurs generally have, he points to a postcard sent to him by a friend. On it is the phrase 'fear of credit institutions'. He says, 'when I saw this I identified myself with it'. This insight emphasizes that entrepreneurs are not without fear of the risks they take, particularly those of a financial nature. However, they learn to manage such fear and risks.

Opportunity and main products

When it started Saimatec Engineering was purely an engineering office offering only consultancy services. Currently, the company produces machinery and equipment for the wood and paper industries, and a sister company, in which Mr Rasimus has a major stake, takes care of production. Although the company received its first order relatively quickly, the entrepreneur believes that he faced problems during the early days in persuading large prospective customers that his company was reliable. He is of the opinion that, 'in Finland large enterprises have generally had a very critical attitude towards privately owned small businesses. The attitude has changed partly because of providing proof of product reliability and through references from previous/current clients'. The transformation from a purely consulting to a holistic operation that incorporates production as a component of the business can be clearly seen in the development of the venture. Furthermore, it resulted in doubling the firm's turnover!

The entrepreneur started his venture independently. A management team was not established until 1994, when the growth of the firm and the market demand were such that it was desperately needed. Mr Rasimus perceives customer-based technical and tailor-made solutions, and operationally and functionally competitive technology as the most important factors providing the competitive advantage of the venture. 'Price is not a decisive factor. In fact we know that we frequently secure sales because we offer the most advantageous solution – not the lowest price', he states proudly.

The maximum percentage of total sales which have gone to export amount to 80 per cent, on average it is approximately 50 per cent. This market is important to Saimatec as, 'when we had the deepest recession in Finland we did not get any invitations to submit tenders within the country for two years. If we had not had our export market we would have literally starved', remembers Mr Rasimus.

Venture capitalists recognized in Saimatec an opportunity for sustained growth and trusted the ability of the lead entrepreneur to motivate and drive forward this product development oriented company. From the entrepreneur's viewpoint the main motives to seek venture capital investment were the need to increase credibility within the world of business; the requirement to internationalize the firm to strengthen the export market; and the desire to honour the existing obligations that the company had to customers and employees.

Challenges and rewards

Mr Rasimus believes that the most serious financing problem is, and continues to be, that of insufficient collateral to support loan finance. 'Money will always be available. Nobody has refused to finance my firm, but the question is where can I get sufficient collateral to fuel a growth business', he agonises. Long-term business development, keeping the company on a growth track, has been Mr Rasimus's most challenging entrepreneurial task. On the other hand, the feeling of success when a project has been completed or some tender has been accepted, he considers to be the most rewarding part of his career as an entrepreneur.

External support and the future

As previously mentioned, the entrepreneur received a start-up subsidy provided by the Ministry of Trade and Industry. Saimatec Engineering has also been involved in impressive product development activities which have been financed by the Technology Development Centre. In addition, the company used finance from the Regional Development Fund (Kera Ltd) at the time when it granted financial subsidies. Furthermore, financing for export promotion from the Foreign Trade Association and employment subsidies from the Ministry of Labour were also accessed. 'We have taken full advantage of all the subsidy instruments we were aware of. This has worked well for Saimatec', said Mr Rasimus.

However, the entrepreneur feels strongly that the creation of a venture should not be based on support systems. 'The authorities are currently eager to push people into entrepreneurship. Generally, they lead you to believe that it is easy to start a business, and it certainly isn't', Mr Rasimus asserts. As a consequence, in Finland the profile of people setting up in business is changing to one that is dependent on government subsidies and who are not fully aware of the challenges that they will face, or are equipped to deal with.

Mr Rasimus concludes that he foresees a stable and promising future for Saimatec Engineering. He is extremely proud that the company has become significantly involved in international business, attracting strong interest from abroad which he believes will contribute to sustaining the company's 'growth track' and success.

Case study review

Mr Rasimus exhibits the full range of Timmons's themes in an implicit, rather than aggressively explicit manner that presents a 'low key' entrepreneurial approach. The factors contributing to his entrepreneurial behaviour are presented in Table 10.1.

Table 10.1 Factors contributing to Mr Rasimus's entrepreneurial behaviour

Category	Factors
Antecedent influences	• He brings intelligence and sound analytical skills to bear on risk management. • Family support and influence has had an important positive effort. • He exhibits strong moral, work and business ethics.
Incubator organization	• The business has been directly developed from an incubator organization, the experience from which acted as a trigger for entrepreneurial action in its rejection, and as a strength to bring to bear on his business development.
Environmental factors	• He is a deviant from the social norm within his country. • The funding environment is not receptive to new, young and growth businesses. • Due to the constrained nature of the domestic market, he has developed an international approach to business development.

11

The 'Tree of Entrepreneurship'

Alison Morrison

Introduction

Each of the foregoing country-specific accounts presents its own unique mosaic of factors which are of import in the promotion and/or inhibition of entrepreneurial behaviour particular to their geographical and societal setting, and to individual entrepreneurs. In considering the most appropriate method of cross-country analysis, the author was cautious about applying any attempt which 'forced' the data to 'fit' a sanitized framework. It is believed that this may have devalued the richness and specificity of the content. Thus, this chapter commences with a general discussion as to what factors within environments and cultures contribute to the promotion and/or inhibition of entrepreneurship. This is followed by the adoption of a holistic approach recognizing a certain structure and associated key themes which compose the process of entrepreneurship, presented in the form of the 'tree of entrepreneurship' (Figure 11.1). It is rooted in society, supported by a trunk of social, economic, political and technological structures, has branches which hold the mobilizing factors required for entrepreneurship, and leaves which are the manifestation of entrepreneurial behaviour. Each of the tree's components is identified, discussed and illustrated, and the chapter culminates with some final thoughts on an international perspective of entrepreneurship.

Entrepreneurial culture

Haggett (1983) proposed that if we were searching for a single unit in man's organization of the world today, there would seem to be simple and persuasive reasons for using the country as this basic unit. This was exactly the thinking behind the country-by-country organization of this text. However, what has been evident in each of the country specific accounts is the diversity of entrepreneurial cultures that exist within each of these organizational units. In most cases multiple cultures exist under the one encompassing title of the host country. This leads us to question the extent to which it is true that any one society has one homogeneous culture. Within countries, factors such as social class, regional characteristics, ethnic grouping, and religion historically have and will continue to interact. This results in layers of subcultures. Clearly, culture as a researchable phenomenon is worthy of extensive research in itself, as evidenced by the seminal works of, for example, Hofstede (1980), Tayeb (1988), Trompenaars (1993), and Hampden-Turner and Trompenaars (1994). Thus, it is considered important to acknowledge that the following discussion on culture linked to entrepreneurship is cursory in nature. It does, however, play an important role in extending knowledge and understanding of the linkage between entrepreneurship and cultural specificity.

Currently, the term 'entrepreneurial culture' has become popular and widely accepted internationally. It can be described as one in which a positive social attitude towards personal enterprise is prevalent, enabling and supporting entrepreneurial activity. Culture is the pattern of taken-for-granted assumptions about how a given set of people should think, act and feel as they go about their daily affairs (Hall, 1959). The thematic country accounts have clearly illustrated the range and diversity of entrepreneurial cultures that exist, each of which enable and support entrepreneurial behaviour to varying degrees. In other words, there is no such thing as one identifiable entrepreneurial culture. According to Timmons (1994, p. 9), what is needed is a favourable environment which combines social, political and educational attributes. In particular it requires:

> A culture that prizes entrepreneurship, an imperative to educate our population so that our entrepreneurial potential is second to none; and a government that generously supports pure and applied science, fosters entrepreneurship with enlightened policies, and enables schools to produce the best educated students in the world.

Furthermore, as advocated by McClelland (1961, p. 388), it is important to recognize that culture is not a static, but a dynamic variable, which has the potential to be modified to the benefit of future generations.

> If man wants to control his destiny, he must learn to deal less in terms of the supposed reasonable consequences of historical events and more in terms of their often unintended or indirect effects on the motives and values of the next generation.

As evidenced in the majority of countries represented in this text, there has been an attempt by policy-makers to directly effect a change in the motives and values of next generations. In this way, they aim to establish a regime whereby the individual, rather than the state apparatus, can flourish in recognition of the value, qualities and contributions of entrepreneurs (Heelas and Morris, 1992). Thus, policy-makers have identified culture as a dynamic, changeable variable and have intervened accordingly in the 'cultural conditioning' of the populace with mixed degrees of success.

Hence, it is proposed that entrepreneurial behaviour is culture specific linked to the particular social structures of geographic regions, the historical background and traditions of populations, and has been impacted by the consequences of political intervention. Indeed, Hofstede (1980) supports such cultural specificity. He deepens our understanding of cultural issues in the provision of a framework for analysis that includes five dimensions. Each of these dimensions has been illustrated within the foregoing chapters.

- **Power distance**: the degree of inequality among the people which the population of a country considers normal.

> The 'Coloured' community of South Africa found itself in a socially marginalized position, both during the days of apartheid and subsequent to the democratic election of a new government. For the majority of the community this impacted negatively on entrepreneurial characteristics such as initiative and self-confidence. For others, with a strong desire to attain personal control, such oppression actually stimulated entrepreneurial behaviour.

- **Individualism**: the degree to which people in a country prefer to act as individuals rather than as members of groups.

Within Australia and North America, the high proportion of migrants in the populations has resulted in a history of individualism among settlers. This continues to be the case and significantly contributes to high levels of immigrant activity in the small business sector that makes a vital contribution to the nation's economic and social welfare.

- **Masculinity**: the degree to which such 'masculine' values, such as assertiveness, competition and success are emphasized, as opposed to such values as quality of life, warm personal relationships, service, etc.

Masculine values are clearly illustrated within the case study of the North American entrepreneur. These values included competitive spirit, aggressive selling skills, dogged determination, deviousness, symbolism of material wealth and resilience against considerable adversity.

- **Uncertainty avoidance**: the degree to which people in a country prefer structured over unstructured situations.

Singaporean society currently experiences a situation of near full employment with comfortable remuneration levels. In addition, the government-controlled Central Provident Fund saving scheme provides employees with a 'nest egg' for retirement. These two factors combine with a societal low tolerance for failure that results in a population that generally moved to avoid the uncertainty and lack of structure associated with entrepreneurial behaviour.

- **Long-term versus short-term orientation**: long-term orientation implies a stress on virtuous living in this world, with thrift and persistence as key virtues.

The Kenyan society as a whole does not prioritize the creation of savings for the future, being content to enjoy life as it is now. They remain a village, communal and rural person in their mentality with short-term planning horizons. This orientation is not particularly conducive for long-term financial investment and business development.

Thus, it is concluded that the attitude of a population towards entrepreneurship is a consequence of their cultural mind-set which is linked to their specific social, political and educational attributes. Furthermore, this culture is a dynamic variable subject to, and capable of, change over time.

The 'Tree of Entrepreneurship'

While frameworks such as Hofstede's are useful, it is apparent that no one universal, prescriptive model can be developed to accurately account for the process of entrepreneurship in every social setting. Consequently, in Figure 11.1 the author has utilized a metaphor – the 'tree of entrepreneurship' – to symbolize the process. It recognizes that entrepreneurship is 'rooted' in the prevailing culture and attitudes of society at one particular point of time. The culture spawns, shapes and makes entrepreneurs who then interact within the 'trunk' of social structure, branching out to support the inputs required to bear the fruit of entrepreneurial behaviour. Furthermore, the 'tree' recognizes the organic and dynamic nature of entrepreneurship, in that some 'leaves' may wither and die, representing failed attempts at entrepreneurship. This in turn could weaken the roots of the 'tree'. Other manifestations will flourish and flower providing 'seeds' for future entrepreneurship, falling onto fertile ground to re-root and strengthen the 'tree of entrepreneurship'. Each of these four elements of the 'tree' are now discussed and illustrated, in relation to the countries represented in this text.

The roots: formative role of the entrepreneur's social development

The tree has its 'roots' in the person and the social development to which the individual is subjected. This recognizes entrepreneurship as both a natural and a cultural process. Although people may be born with the innate spirit of enterprise intact, at some indeterminable point in time it may become promoted or inhibited through their individual, unique social development process. Specific formative aspects that have been identified are ideological practices; cultural attitudes, values and beliefs; personal motivations and characteristics; the formal education system; family background; regional history and characteristics; and intergenerational role models. Each is now discussed.

- **Ideological practices**: the ideological practices of a population refer to the pattern of thinking that is most characteristic. This has specifically been evidenced in relation to the manner in which failure is viewed, and the management of financial resources at an individual's disposal.

> Singaporeans, Slovenians, Finnish, and to a certain extent the Scottish, have a low tolerance to failure which tends to leave a durable stigma. However, in more open societies such as North America and Australia entrepreneurial behaviour is

applauded and failure has few associated negative connotations, with the significance and value of having applied personal initiative and enterprise, albeit unsuccessfully, viewed as positive. Furthermore, within some societies there is a culture of saving for the future, while within others the focus is on living and spending to enjoy the moment. This has an implication for the amount of personal funds that may be available for investment in business. At one extreme is Singapore with an obsession with saving for the future in the form of provision for retirement. Short-termism as a dominant characteristic was clearly evidenced in the Kenyan example, however, this was also tempered by a desire to provide for retirement. The remaining countries presented a varying degree of planning horizons, the majority bordering on the short term.

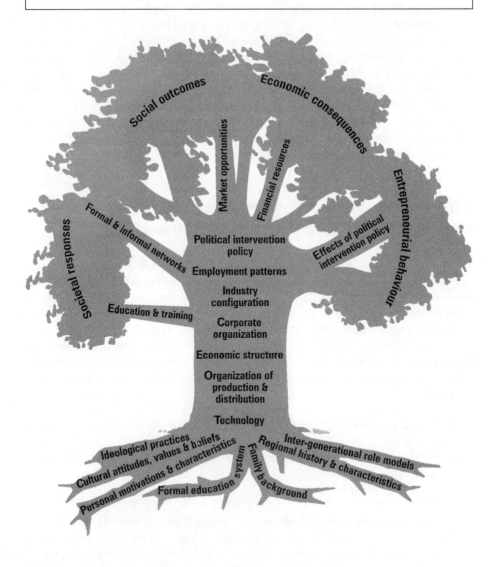

Figure 11.1 The 'Tree of Entrepreneurship'

- **Cultural attitudes, values and beliefs**: the dominant cultural attitudes, values and beliefs of a population at one particular point of time will result in a particular common mind-set relative to the degree to which entrepreneurship is supported by society.

> Societies that predominantly hold strong communal and collective values, such as Kenya, Slovenia, and South Africa, do not support individualistic wealth creation through entrepreneurship, while those with strong individualistic values such as North America and Australia generally do. Furthermore, in those countries where there is a moral obligation to provide for the community, the priority for income earned is kin as opposed to investment in private enterprise.

- **Personal motivations and characteristics**: each entrepreneur brings their own unique set of personal motivations and characteristics to interact with their specific host society and business environment, which is then translated into entrepreneurial activities and behaviour. However, it is possible to identify common themes and behaviours.

> All the entrepreneurs represented in the case studies exhibit the full range of themes as identified by Timmons in Chapter 1. However, in the cases of Finland, Australia and Kenya they are more of an implicit, 'low key' nature rather than aggressively explicit. The common key themes which emerged relative to all the entrepreneurs are that they bring intelligence and sound analytical skills to bear on risk management; they are all in some respect deviants from the social norms within their countries; to differing degrees they exhibit strong moral, work and business ethics; irrespective of industry sector a strong 'trader's' instinct is apparent; they are committed to life-long learning through both formal and informal mechanisms; and extensive use is made of both informal and formal networks.

- **Formal education system**: the manner in which the young are conditioned from an early age through the formal education system, and the fact that dominant approaches are frequently reinforced within family life, plays a significant role in the promotion or inhibition of characteristics generally associated with entrepreneurial behaviour.

> The formal education system has been recognized as a strong influence in the development of conformist, anti-entrepreneurial behaviour in Kenya, South Africa, Singapore, Finland and Slovenia. This has resulted in population masses ambivalent towards entrepreneurship as a consequence of their educational conditioning. Current examples of direct intervention within the formal education systems, designed to promote an entrepreneurial culture were presented in the cases of North America, Scotland and Mexico.

- **Family background:** it has been identified that a characteristic of entrepreneurship is that it tends to pervade family life, with the entrepreneur being unable to divorce business from social living. In this respect, family background plays a role in two ways. First, if an entrepreneur has previous experience of the effect of entrepreneurship from a family member they are more prepared for the consequences of their own activities. Second, family support of entrepreneurship can make a positive contribution to its sustenance.

> For all the entrepreneurs represented in the case studies positive immediate family support for their entrepreneurial behaviour had played an important part in its sustenance. What is also identified as of significance is the role of the extended family in enabling access to funds and markets to support individual entrepreneurs in the creation and development of their businesses. This was particularly emphasized in the accounts from Kenya, South Africa, Australia and North America.

- **Regional history and characteristics**: one of the reasons for the considerable variance in the responses of populations to entrepreneurship is a consequence of the history and resultant characteristics of their country. This is particularly relevant relative to the extent to which structures have historically been designed to enable individualism or communitarianism, and equality or hierarchy.

> In general, the historic political systems within Slovenia, South Africa, Kenya, and Finland have, to differing degrees, served to promote an anti-entrepreneurial culture due to the dependency on, or control of, the populace by the state which decreased the propensity for private enterprise. This has resulted in a significant power distance in society that has served to divide the population into the majority which are 'ruled', either formally or informally by an elite group. This serves to grow persons who are lacking in the personal attributes generally associated with entrepreneurs, in particular leadership, creativity, self-reliance and self-confidence. However, in the more egalitarian and democratic societies of North America and Australia these qualities are fostered, thus stimulating entrepreneurial behaviour.

- **Intergenerational role models**: the degree to which an entrepreneurial culture has been, and currently is, embedded in a country will result in the volume of practising and historic entrepreneurs who can be identified as role models for future generations.

From the case studies, no direct link to intergenerational role models was apparent. At one extreme, is Ann David the Kenyan entrepreneur, who is unique in her time and has few, if any, intergenerational role models to which to refer. At the other extreme, is Barry Potekin the North American, who has an abundance of role models. However, it would appear that the entrepreneurs represented within this text are less concerned with the existence of role models, and more interested in being entrepreneurial.

Thus, it is clear that the cultural context in which persons are rooted and socially developed plays an important influencing role in shaping and making entrepreneurs, and the degree to which they consider entrepreneurial behaviour to be desirable. From analysis entrepreneurship is recognized as both an intuitive response of members of society, and a result of cultural conditioning. Cultural dimensions significant to the extent to which entrepreneurial behaviour is supported by a society have been identified as communal versus individual; conformist versus divergent; and equal versus elitist. Furthermore, the role of the family, immediate and extended, is recognized as having the potential to make a positive contribution towards entrepreneurial behaviour through the provision of intergenerational role models, and as tangible and intangible support providers. Finally, the profile of an entrepreneur which emerges through the case studies is one who: is intelligent and analytical; is an effective risk manager and networker; possesses a strong set of moral, social and business ethics; exhibits a basic trader's instinct; and is dedicated to life-long learning in its many forms.

The trunk: promotion/inhibition of social structure

The tree 'trunk' represents the social, economic and institutional structure that hosts the socially developed entrepreneur. Within it, entrepreneurs may assess the degree to which it is sufficiently robust to support successful entrepreneurial behaviour. Kirzner (1980) proposes that an economically successful society is one whose members pursue the 'right' set of co-ordinated actions. Thus, it follows that the ideal economic organization for a society to promote entrepreneurship consists of the pattern of institutions and incentives that will promote the pursuit of entrepreneurship. This relates to social structural considerations of: political intervention policy; employment patterns; industry configuration; corporate organization; economic structure; organization, production and distribution; and technology. Each are now discussed and illustrated.

- **Political intervention policy**: governments throughout the globe have focused on identifying what form of interventionist policy will be most effective in the development of an entrepreneurial culture. This is designed to 'awaken' latent entrepreneurs within their respective populations. In particular, such policy has focused on education and training; the provision of a supportive environment and infrastructure; and specific measures aimed at supporting business innovation and development.

The accounts from Mexico and Scotland clearly illustrated the implications and effect of political intervention in the formal education systems, and public sector led life-long learning provision was evidenced in the cases of Kenya, Singapore, Australia, Finland and Slovenia. In addition, forms of public sector incentives, which are specifically targeted to stimulate innovative technology development, were seen to have been applied in Scotland, Mexico, Singapore and Finland. Each country communicated varying degrees of success achieved by the policy-makers.

- **Employment patterns**: in most countries internationally, the nature of work is changing, and the proportion of populations who have full-time and permanent work is falling. The concept of a job for life, with its planned career structure is rare. This has led policy-makers to focus on growing the number of persons who create new ventures, and/or enter into self-employment, as a means of bringing more members of the population into economic productivity. Furthermore, individuals have responded to these employment patterns by taking personal control of their own career through entrepreneurship. However, there are examples of countries which are exceptions to these general employment patterns, and who generate their distinct approaches to employment practices.

At one extreme we can identify Mexico, where heightened entrepreneurship as a means of creating employment opportunities, particularly for the young, is an explicit strategy within a country which is suffering from economic crisis, widespread poverty, low levels of educational attainment and high unemployment. In sharp contrast is Singapore that has experienced high and sustained economic growth in recent years, and has a situation of nearly full employment. These factors act as a deterrent for persons to enter into entrepreneurship in Singapore. An employment practice of particular interest was highlighted, linked to a strong tribal, clan or ethnic group identification, in a number of countries such as South Africa, Kenya and Australia. This leads to intergroup employment practices, favouring family and tribe which can result in protracted decision-making procedures, and diminishes the potential for positive business performance.

- **Industry configuration**: in the majority of countries represented in this text, the small firm is statistically dominant in the industry structure, in terms of operating units. This is particularly true relative to the service sector, where the SME makes up the majority of firms, often located at service points close to the customer. Increasingly, a strong indigenous small firm sector is being seen as a vehicle for regional economic development internationally.

Statistically, the small firm dominates the industry structure in Mexico, Scotland, Australia and Finland. Within the remaining countries the recognition of the social and economic significance of a strong indigenous small firm sector is constantly strengthening. This is particularly true in the case of Singapore where it represents a means of providing economic insulation from the volatile activities of multinational companies (MNCs).

- **Corporate organization**: current terminology associated with the strategies of large corporations includes downsizing, delayering, outsourcing, and re-engineering. This is a result of recognition of the importance of the ability to focus on core activities, adapting quickly and innovating within specific specialized markets. It has the potential to generate significant entrepreneurial opportunity, and is seen as a major contributor to new business growth within the small business sector.

Australia represents an example of one country where the workplace is undergoing major reform, as corporations streamline their operations and outsource non-core activities to effect savings and to achieve strategic goals. From such activity, the Australian, Scottish, Finnish and Slovenian entrepreneurs identified entrepreneurial opportunities in the form of acting as subcontractors to large corporations who had reached the decision to outsource a number of their activities. In contrast, the South African and Mexican entrepreneurs found themselves in a position where they contracted out a number of their activities, thus spreading the level of participation in entrepreneurial activity to self-employed craft persons. A further example of changes in corporate organization was provided by Singapore, where a partnership relation has developed between local enterprises and MNCs to assist small firm contractors to improve operating and process efficiency, and to widen their product ranges.

- **Economic structure**: in general, recognition of the distinctive contribution of the individual in the process of economic restructuring has ensured that entrepreneurship is supported by policy-makers internationally. The trigger of this recognition has usually been born out of adverse economic conditions, however, it has also been a response to a desire to enhance already strong economies.

Each of the countries in this text has experienced different degrees of volatility within their economies, and various causes of the problems faced. They are perhaps best depicted on a continuum moving from severe, transitional, moderate, to strong. First, at the severe end is Mexico, which has experienced profound economic recessionary problems with many persons living on an average of $1 a day.

Within this context entrepreneurship represents a means by which the economy, and the population, can be saved from yet further degeneration. Second, is Slovenia which has only evolved into an independent state, and been in a position to create an autonomous economic system, since 1991. Thus, economic restructuring is still in a transitional phase, within which the encouragement of entrepreneurship is of high importance. Third, Scotland and Finland have experienced moderate economic recession, and policy-makers have directed their efforts at expanding the pool of latent entrepreneurial talent to become agents in economic regeneration. Finally, Singapore has sustained high economic growth within which SMEs play a key role, benefiting the nation by their profusion and activity.

- **Organization, production and distribution**: changes in methods of organization, production and distribution have been intense, rapid, their nature complex, and implications for entrepreneurial success profound. Specific examples have been evidenced in the adoption of new political systems, and the privatization of previous public sector organizations. These activities have contributed to the creation of entrepreneurial opportunities.

Organization, production and distribution within industry have been particularly affected by changes in politics. Until recently, under apartheid and centralized political systems in South Africa and Slovenia, respectively, the majority of these populations have been deprived of the right to create and develop their own businesses. Furthermore, changes in political dogma in Australia, Finland and Scotland have resulted in the increasing privatization of traditionally public sector organized functions such as the railways, electricity supply and other such basic services. In Slovenia the privatisation process has been much more radical as central government released its hold on enterprise in general. These factors have contributed to entrepreneurship.

- **Technology**: society has undergone an enormous transformation, especially as regards computerization and this development is likely to continue. It has resulted in a rapid increase in information flow and has decreased distances in the world considerably as far as communication is concerned. It is no longer necessary for a company to conduct all of its business activities in the same place, the same country or even the same continent. Furthermore, from the policy-makers' perspective economic prosperity is seen to lie with those firms which are of an innovative, 'high-tech' nature.

In terms of technology as applied to business management, the Singaporean entrepreneur confidently manages businesses in his own country, Malaysia, Indonesia and Australia enabled by communications technology. The Scottish entrepreneur represents a 'high-tech' business which received considerable targeted support from a major government agency. This is the policy also adopted in Mexico, Singapore, Australia and Finland where the governments have deliberately targeted the stimulation of 'high-tech' businesses through their intervention policies. These are directed at promoting technological research and development, increasing the degree of technology applied to business management and development, and generally providing a supportive infrastructure.

These key features enable us to understand the manner in which entrepreneurship, culture, politics, society, the economy and business development and management are interwoven within the institutional structure of society. The pattern of institutions and incentives that promote entrepreneurship can be divided into those that exert a 'pull' function, those that combine a 'push/pull' function. Four 'pull' functions have been identified:

1 effective political intervention strategies which provide a supportive infrastructure;
2 industry configuration, structure and market which encourage SME development;
3 the streamlining of corporate organizations and the deregulation and privatization of former public sector organizations which generates market opportunities for entrepreneurship;
4 technological developments which extend the capabilities and scope of SMEs and contribute towards opportunities for innovative product/service development.

Two 'push/pull' functions have been identified:

1 employment patterns may push persons into entrepreneurship as an alternative to no job, alternatively the status accorded by society to entrepreneurial behaviour, and perceived economic benefits may pull persons into entrepreneurship;
2 adverse economic structures may push persons into entrepreneurship, or fortuitous economic structures may pull persons into entrepreneurship as they recognize the potential financial rewards.

The branches: mobilization of social action

The 'branches' extend from the 'trunk' to bear the elements that are designed to enable and mobilize latent entrepreneurial intent. The fertility will be influenced by the components of available resources and opportunities on one hand, and by the patterns of market demand on the other. Specifically, these elements include the effects of political intervention policy; access to necessary financial resources; availability of market opportunities; the existence and efficiency of formal and informal networks; and the provision of entrepreneurial education and training. These are now discussed and illustrated.

- **Effects of political intervention policy**: governments have directed policy towards supporting entrepreneurship. Outcomes resulting from such policy intervention can be identified as falling into four broad categories: financial assistance; education and training programmes; information, support and consultancy; and legislative changes. These are directed at mobilizing the latent pool of potential entrepreneurs into economic productivity.

The effects of political intervention have been mixed. Within a number of countries, e.g. Slovenia, it has been inconsistently applied which has resulted in limited impact on the level of entrepreneurial behaviour. In the case of Finland, an example of start-up funding was provided which was deemed to have been moderately successful in the stimulation of new venture creation. The approaches adopted in Mexico, North America and Scotland were evaluated as being relatively considered, strategic and effective. However, in Kenya early attempts at intervention led to a dependency culture. This brings into question the degree to which the state should intervene to contrive what is essentially a natural expression of personal enterprise, self-sufficiency and initiative.

- **Access to necessary financial resources**: no matter how supportive the prevalent culture and the environment factors are of entrepreneurship, if the entrepreneur cannot access necessary financial capital then it is unlikely that entrepreneurial intent will be translated into action. Internal sources of finance include the personal equity of the entrepreneur or that which is raised from family and friends. Principal sources of external finance are banks, equity from venture capitalists and informal investors, and public sector grants and loans.

The resources which entrepreneurs have to bring, or rather their scarcity, to the creation of ventures has been a recurring theme throughout this text. This has been discussed in relation to the commitment of private resources to kin before business in Kenya and South Africa; provision by the public sector of financial incentives for start-up in Finland, Scotland, Slovenia; the difficulties in raising funds for business start-up, expansion and growth in Singapore, Finland, and North America; and the need for entrepreneurs to commit personal securities such as the family home in order to raise capital as was the case of the Australian entrepreneurs. The whole issue of the financial resourcing of entrepreneurship was identified by the majority of authors as a prime area of concern.

- **Availability of market opportunities**: the entrepreneur is dependent upon either the creation of market opportunities, or the seizing of those which are emergent. The nature of the marketplace within which the entrepreneur is located will obviously determine their strategy. In some countries market opportunities have arisen from corporate restructuring, deregulation and privatizing of former public sector organizations and developments in technology. Furthermore, in certain geographic locations the domestic market could be fertile, in others is may be barren and the entrepreneur will require to develop the products or services and the capability to operate within an international arena.

> Within turbulent and/or dynamic societies, such as South Africa, Slovenia, Australia, and North America market opportunities tend to be plentiful. However, in more static societies with highly competitive, mature domestic markets such as Singapore, Finland and Scotland it can be more arduous for entrepreneurs to find fertile opportunities which can be translated into clearly differentiated, competitive, business propositions. Thus, the entrepreneurs located in these countries have developed the products, services and capabilities to successfully access and trade with the international marketplace. Furthermore, as illustrated in the case of the Mexican entrepreneur, and observed as characteristic of all the entrepreneurs represented in the case studies, they have a strong 'trader's' instinct relative to the manner in which they take their business concept to market.

- **Existence and efficiency of formal and informal networks**: the development and maintenance of effective informal and formal networks is recognized as a central feature of successful entrepreneurial activity. This is particularly true relative to those of an informal nature.

> Within the text examples of informal and formal entrepreneurial networks are numerous. For example, in Kenya the informal, tribal network provided support and facilitated market development in an urban setting; immigrants to Australia used the networks which evolved from their ethnic association to develop export markets; in Finland a strong national and local entrepreneurs' association network provided significant informal peer support, advice and motivation; the flea market traders in South Africa facilitated a valuable experiential learning network; and in Mexico the network established by the educational institute ITESM enabled 'entrepreneurs in training' to access support and advice from the business community and provided an international showcase for their products. With respect to formal networks, Australia operates within a highly formalized official environment that requires entrepreneurs to understand and learn to operate within this network in order to achieve business success.

- **Provision of entrepreneurial education and training**: it has been recognized that explicit provision of entrepreneurship education through the formal education system, training for pre start-up, survival of new start ups, and business development support thereafter can play a significant role in the birth rate of new ventures and their long-term survival. Furthermore, it has the potential to make a vital contribution towards the perpetuation of a culture that is positively inclined towards the process of entrepreneurship.

> The provision of entrepreneurship education through the formal system was most explicitly articulated in the cases of Mexico, North America and Scotland. Specific reference relative to the benefits of training throughout the life of the business was made in the contexts of Kenya and Australia, and has proliferated in

> many of the other countries to differing degrees. Such educational and training programmes are designed to raise awareness of entrepreneurship as a realistic career alternative, to equip existing and potential entrepreneurs with the skills and abilities necessary to succeed in business, and to reduce the probability of failure. In particular, it is seen as a means of creating a critical mass of entrepreneurial professionals by all of the countries, which indicates the profound significance of these programmes. This approach represents a long-term investment strategy.

Despite intensified interventions by policy-makers to strengthen the branches of the tree, to enable and mobilize entrepreneurial intent, it would appear that it has resulted in variable degrees of success. Specifically, it seems that any attempt at political intervention requires to achieve a balance between support directed at increasing self-sufficiency of entrepreneurs, while at the same time reducing dependency upon the state. This is particularly the case in addressing the important issues of financial resources scarcity, without entrepreneurs having to resort to a dependency upon the state as the main source. Market dimensions of significance to entrepreneurial behaviour were identified as static versus dynamic; regulated versus deregulated; and domestic versus international. Furthermore, it would appear that informal, rather than formal mechanisms have been more effective in mobilizing entrepreneurial behaviour, in respect to market management through the use of the entrepreneurs' trader's instinct. This is opposed to formal management techniques, and market development supported by the entrepreneurs' individual networks that provide market opportunities, support information dissemination, develops skills, and enable experiential learning. Finally, entrepreneurship education and training provision has been made available to potential and existing entrepreneurs with the commendable aim of creating a critical mass of professional entrepreneurs that will perpetuate a gradual change towards a sustainable entrepreneurial culture.

The leaves: outcomes of entrepreneurship

The 'leaves' are the manifestation of the outcomes resulting from the process of entrepreneurship. These outcomes have consequences for society and the economy of both a material and an immaterial nature. The response of society will serve to either perpetuate or smother future entrepreneurial behaviour, dependent upon the cultural attitudes and values of the host country at that particular time. Furthermore, a country's attitude towards success and failure will have a significant influence on the degree to which the entrepreneurial process is reinforced or weakened over time. Thus, the outcomes of entrepreneurship can be articulated relative to: societal responses; social outcomes; economic consequences; and entrepreneurial behaviour. Each is now discussed and illustrated.

- **Societal responses**: positive and negative economic consequences and social outcomes will combine to shape societal responses to entrepreneurship. Thus, each society will respond relative to their current interpretations in relation to ideological practices and cultural attitudes, values and beliefs.

In Slovenia the historical perspective was that entrepreneurship was intertwined with capitalist greed for material gains through the exploitation of others. In other countries, such as Scotland, Kenya and South Africa those members of society who deviated from the social norm of 'ordinary' employees to be successful entrepreneurs were frowned upon as being 'upstarts' daring to be successful. Whereas, entrepreneurship for material gain is recognized as socially legitimate in North America. As the outcomes of entrepreneurship become recognized as, on balance, positive societal responses are becoming gradually more pro-entrepreneurship, effecting incremental cultural change.

- **Social outcomes**: there is a belief that entrepreneurship has the potential to improve the fabric of society through the balancing of economic wealth creation with that of social responsibility to the community, sensitive to a country's cultural, historical and social values.

The importance of positive social outcomes was particularly emphasized in the accounts from Mexico, Finland and Australia. For example, the Mission Statement of ITESM, Mexico explicitly states that it wishes to form entrepreneurial professionals who are '… committed to the development of their communities, respect human dignity, and appreciate the cultural, historical and social values of their community'. It is proposed that societies will not permit entrepreneurship to be sustained if social amelioration is not one of the major objectives. The alternative is a society that destroys itself through capitalist greed and exploitation.

- **Economic consequences**: in Chapter 1 it was proposed that entrepreneurs were the first among equals in the process of wealth creation. This can be interpreted at an individual, community and national level. If successful, through the personal endeavour of individuals within society, economic consequences (as measured by the personal wealth of the entrepreneur, new job opportunities, and improved Gross Domestic Product) will be generated rippling out to the economic benefit of society as a whole.

Real economic benefits as a consequence of entrepreneurship have already been proved in Scotland, Australia and North America. In Finland, Mexico, South Africa and Slovenia the transition to an entrepreneurial culture is still in progress, as such the evidence is less conducive. However, in the case of Kenya there remains considerable doubt that the populace will ever be persuaded to participate in entrepreneurship, thus the economic consequences of the current low level of entrepreneurial behaviour are insignificant.

- **Entrepreneurial behaviour**: economic consequences, social outcomes and societal responses combine to either promote or inhibit future entrepreneurial behaviour.

Within North America, Australia and Scotland the positive impact experienced relative to entrepreneurship sows the seeds from which future entrepreneurial behaviour will be propagated. Conversely, the early examples of Slovenian entrepreneurship which exhibited negative features such as poor employment practices, high failure rates, and evidence of crude profiteering and general exploitation meant that the seeds of entrepreneurship fell on infertile ground. Thus, it is clear that the degree to which entrepreneurship takes root and flourishes will be influenced by the host society's evaluation of entrepreneurial behaviour evidenced as cultural acceptable, beneficial, or otherwise.

It is proposed that our 'tree of entrepreneurship' will grow and strengthen, or become diseased and die, dependent on the outcomes of entrepreneurship as evidenced and interpreted by the host society. In a number of the countries represented within this text, societal response towards entrepreneurship is exhibiting an incremental change, coming more into the mainstream of ideologies, cultural attitudes, values and beliefs. However, Hofstede (1994) reminds us that such changes are peripheral and do not affect the major dimensions of societies. The support of future entrepreneurial behaviour will be dependent on a society's interpretation of the peripheral worth of entrepreneurship as a tool in economic restructuring, and generator of both immaterial and material social outcomes. Entrepreneurship will not necessarily have the power to reach the innermost psyche of a society.

Entrepreneurship: an international perspective – final thoughts

It is considered that this cross-country collection has significantly enriched our understanding of entrepreneurship, and the factors that promote and/or inhibit entrepreneurial behaviour. If the 'discipline of entrepreneurship' is likened to a massive jigsaw puzzle, then we have managed to find and place some more of the pieces. The picture is becoming clearer and more complete. This has enabled us to identify the immense intricacy and complexity of human and entrepreneurial cultures, and that the relationship of entrepreneurs to their environment is not just a matter of demography and economics. A distinctive cross-country cultural variety has been highlighted, in which beliefs and dreams, traditions and taboos all have their place. Undoubtedly, few people have the capability to shake themselves free from deep-rooted and unconscious attitudes and values that come from being reared in a particular social and cultural setting. This far-reaching effect is emphasized by Haggett (1983 p. 458) in the following quote:

Humourists throughout the ages have warned us to choose our parents with care. Geographic humourists might remind us to choose our birthplaces with equal caution! Because it sums up so many economic and cultural considerations, our location in terms of nationality continues to be one of the prime determinants of our life.

However, despite our advances with the 'entrepreneurship jigsaw puzzle' many more pieces remain missing and a number of questions have emerged from this study which are, as yet, unanswered. These questions include:

- As many countries strive to create a communal entrepreneurial culture, does that limit the degree to which entrepreneurs can act individualistically?
- If a country's culture becomes predominately entrepreneurial, does this mean that the entrepreneur will move from being a social deviant to being accepted as the norm?
- If we develop an equal society where the majority of members are optimally functioning entrepreneurs, what then is the motivation for achievement and the scope for realization of entrepreneurial ambition?
- Educational systems, by their nature, encourage conformist behaviour whether it stimulates entrepreneurship or not, will this stifle non-conformist and socially deviant actions generally associated with entrepreneurs?
- Does providing a reasonable supply of entrepreneurs first require a society and environment congenial to creating potential entrepreneurs, or do entrepreneurs determine their own destiny independent of society and environment?

Certainly, these questions emphasize the complexity and intricacy of the subject area, which appears to be riddled with paradox. To be slightly controversial, we could take the above questions to an extreme. For example, if a country is successful in establishing an entrepreneurial culture then, in theory, the entrepreneur moves from being a social deviant on the periphery of society to social norm and a conforming member of the dominant community. In this scenario, our entrepreneur would not achieve 'hero' status, but would be subsumed as a normal member of society. This then may threaten accepted entrepreneurial characteristics such as individualism, and need for achievement, and indeed counteract entrepreneurial behaviour!

Finally, it is concluded that approaches to defining what makes and/or shapes an entrepreneur must work from a consolidation of understanding relative to a wide range of factors at work in society and the economy which influence entrepreneurial behaviour. They should not be driven by the prevailing attitudes of business monitors and governments at one particular point in time. Thus, it is proposed that entrepreneurship be recognized to represent an innovative value-adding social *and* economic activity. Fundamentally, it is a very basic human act, practised by ordinary, but at the same time exceptional, members of society, which can be applied to enhance human endeavour in all spheres of life: economic and material; social and immaterial.

References

Adam, H. and Moodley, K. (1993). *The Negotiated Revolution.* Johannesburg: Jonathan Ball.

Allardt, E. and Littunen, Y. (1972). *Sosiologia.* Neljäs, uudistettu laitos. Porvoo: Werner Söderström Osakeyhtiö.

Anderson, C. R. (1977). Locus of control, coping behaviors and performance in a stress setting: a longitudinal study. *Journal of Applied Psychology*, **62**, 446–451.

Anderson, C. R. and Schneider, C. E. (1978). Locus of control, leader behavior and leader performance among management students. *Academy of Management Journal*, **21**, 690–698.

Anderson, J. (1995). *Local Heroes.* Glasgow: Scottish Enterprise.

Ang, J. S. (1991). Small business uniqueness and the theory of financial management. *Journal of Small Business Finance*, **1**(1), 1–13.

Anon (1994). *Encyclopaedia of Slovenia*, **8**, 76.

Antonèiè, V. (1993). Distributive justice. *Teorija in praksa*, **30**(1–2), 46–53.

Asia Pacific Economic Co-operation (APEC). (1997). *Guidelines for PLG Project Design and Approval.* SME Policy Level Group.

Asian Development Bank (1995). *Asian Development Outlook 1995 and 1996.* Oxford: Oxford University Press.

Australian Bureau of Statistics (1988). *Small Business in Australia 1983–84 to 1986–87.* Canberra: Australian Publishing Services. Catalogue No. 1321:0.

Australian Bureau of Statistics. (1996). *Small Business in Australia.* Canberra: Australian Publishing Services. Catalogue No. 1321:0.

Bagby, R. D. (1988). Editorial: the winds of change. *Entrepreneurship, Theory and Practice*, Fall, 5–6.

Baty, G. (1990). *Entrepreneurship for the Nineties.* New Jersey: Prentice-Hall.

Beck, D. and Linscott, G. (1993). The African crucible: unity in diversity. In R. Christie, R. Lessem and L. Mbigi (eds) *African Management: Philosophies, Concepts and Applications*, 93–109, Johannesburg: Knowledge Resources.

Beddall. D. (1990). Small business in Australia: challenges, problems and opportunities – recommendations and main conclusions. *Report of the House of Representatives Standing Committee on Industry, Science and Technology*, January, Canberra: AGPS.

Begley, T. and Boyd, D. (1987). Psychological characteristics associated with performance in entrepreneurial firms and smaller businesses. *Journal of Business Venturing*, **2**, 79–93.

Berger, B. (ed.) (1991). Introduction. In *The Culture of Entrepreneurship*, 1–12. California: ICS Press.

Berger, B. (1994). A postscript on culture. *Development and Democracy*, **9**, 53–57.

Blommaert, J. (1988). *Intercultural Communication and Objects of Adaptation.* International Pragmatics Association, Working Document 3, 61–70.

Boime, A. (1976). Entrepreneurial patronage in nineteenth-century France. In E. Carter, R. Forster and J. Moody (eds) *Enterprise and Entrepreneurs in Nineteenth-*

and Twentieth-Century France. The Johns Hopkins University Press Ltd.

Brittain, J. W. and Freeman, J. H. (1980). Organizational proliferation and density dependent selection. In J. Kimberly and R. Miles (eds) *The Organizational Life Cycle. Issues in the Creation, Transformation, and the Decline of Organizations*, 291–338. Jossey Bass Publishers.

Brockhaus Sr, R. H. (1982). The psychology of the entrepreneur. In C. Kent, D. Sexton and K. Vesper (eds) *Encyclopedia of Entrepreneurship*. Englewood Cliffs: Prentice-Hall.

Brockhaus, R. and Horwitz, P. (1986). The psychology of the entrepreneur. In D. Sexton and R. Smilor (eds) *The Art and Science of Entrepreneurship*, 25–48. Cambridge: Ballinger Publishing Company.

Burns, P. (1991). *Small Business and Entrepreneurship*. London: Macmillian Education.

Busenitz, L. and Lau, C. -H. (1996). A cross-cultural cognitive model of new venture creation. *Entrepreneurship Theory and Practice*, 20(4).

Cannon, T. (1991). *Enterprise: Creation, Development and Growth*. Oxford: Butterworth-Heinemann.

Cantillon, R. (1755). *Essai sur la nature du commerce en general*. Imprint, 1931.

Carson, D., Cromie, S., McGowan, P. and Hill, J. (1995). *Marketing and Entrepreneurship in SMEs: An Innovative Approach*. London: Prentice-Hall.

Carter, S. and Cachon, J. (1988). *The Sociology of Entrepreneurship*. Stirling: Stirling University.

Chaganti, R. (1986). Management in women-owned enterprises. *Journal of Small Business Management*, **24**(4), 18–29.

Chan, K. B. and Chiang, C. (1994). *Stepping Out*. Singapore: Simon and Schuster (Asia).

Chell, E., Haworth, J. and Brearley, S. (1991). *The Entrepreneurial Personality*. London: Routledge.

Chew, R. (1996). Safety nets for entrepreneurship in Singapore. In A. M. Low and W. L. Tan (eds) *Entrepreneurs, Entrepreneurship and Enterprising Culture*, 224–253. Singapore: Addison-Wesley.

Coldwell, D. and Moerdyk, A. (1981). Paradigms apart: black managers in a white man's world. *South African Journal of Business Management*, **12**(3), 70–76.

Cole, A. H. (1971). *Business Enterprise in its Social Setting*. Harvard: Harvard University Press.

Collins, O. F. and Moore, D. G. (1964). *The Enterprising Man*. East Lansing: Michigan State University Press.

Commonwealth Department of Employment, Education and Training (1991). *Australia's Workforce in the Year 2001*. Canberra.

CommR (1980). *Teknologiakomitean mietintö*. Helsinki.

CommR (1983). *PKT–neuvottelukunnan raportti*. Helsinki.

CommR (1986). *Aluepolitiikkatoimikunnan mietintö*. Helsinki.

Cooper, A. (1966). *Small Business Management: A Casebook*. Homewood: Irwin.

Curran, J. and Burrows, R. (1986). The sociology of petit capitalism: a trend report. *Sociology*, **20**(2).

Dale, A. (1991). Self-employment and entrepreneurship. In R. Burrows (ed.) *Deciphering the Enterprise Culture*. London: Routledge.

Davis, C., Hills, G. E. and La Forge, R. W. (1985). The marketing/small enterprise paradox: a research agenda. *International Small Business Journal*, **3**, 66–73.

De Haas, M. (1990). Ethnicity in perspective. *Democracy in Action*, February.

de Tocqueville, A. (1990). *Democracy in America*. New York: Vintage Classics.

Deakins, D. (1996). *Entrepreneurs and Small Firms*. London: McGraw-Hill.

DEET (1991). *Australia's Workforce in the Year 2001*. Canberra: Commonwealth Department of Employment, Education and Training.

Doh, J. C. (1996). The strategy of SME development in Singapore. In A. M. Low and W. L. Tan (eds) *Entrepreneurs, Entrepreneurship and Enterprising Culture*, 235–243. Singapore: Addison-Wesley.

Drucker, P. (1986). *Innovation and Entrepreneurship*. London: Heinemann.

Fairlie, R. W. and Meyer, B. D. (1996). Ethnic and racial self-employment differences and possible explanation. *Journal of Human Resources*, **31**(4), 757–795.

Fass, M. and Scothorne, R. (1990). *The Vital Economy*. Edinburgh: Abbeystrand Publishing.

Financial Mail (1996). Stimulating a vital creator of employment: small business development. *Financial Mail*, South Africa, 19 April, 27–28.

Fock, S. T. (1995). *The Development and Continuity of Large and Successful Chinese Family Owned Entrepreneurships in Singapore*. Unpublished MSc (Management) Thesis, Singapore: National University of Singapore.

Frank, H., Plaschka, G. R., Roessl, D. and Welsch, H. (1989). Planning behavior in new ventures: a comparison between Chicago and Vienna entrepreneurs. Paper presented at the Babson Entrepreneurship Research Conference, St. Louis.

Garavan, T. N. and O'Cinneide, B (1994). Entrepreneurship education and training programmes: a review and evaluation, parts 1 and 2. *Journal of European Industrial Training*, **18**(8 and 9), 3–11, 13–21.

Gartner, W. B. (1989). Some suggestions for research on entrepreneurial traits and characteristics. *Entrepreneurship: Theory and Practice*, **14**(1), 27–37.

Gartner, W. B. Bird, B. J. and Starr, J. A. (1992). Acting as if: differentiating entrepreneurial from organizational behaviour. *Entrepreneurship Theory and Practice*, **16**(3), 13–32.

Gartner, W. B. and Vesper, K. H. (1994). Experiments in entrepreneurship education: success and failures. *Journal of Business Venturing*, **9**, 179–187.

Gibb, A. (1994). Do we really teach (approach) small business the way we should? *Journal of Small Business and Entrepreneurship*, **11**(1), 11–27.

Gibb, A. (1996). Entrepreneurship and small business management: can we afford to neglect them in the twenty-first century business school? *British Journal of Management*, **7**, 309–321.

Gilder, G. (1971). *The Spirit of Enterprise*. New York: Simon and Schuster.

Ginn, C. W. and Sexton, D. L., (1990). A comparison of the personality type dimensions of the 1987 Inc. 500 company founders/CEO's with those of slower growth firms. *Journal of Business Venturing*, **5**(5), 313–326.

Glas, M. (1997). (In press). *State of the Small Business in Slovenia*. Faculty of Economics: University of Ljubljana: Slovenia.

Glen, W. and Weerawardena, J. (1996). Strategic planning practices in small enterprises in Queensland. In *Changing Business Relationships: Small Business growth and Other Challenges. Proceedings of the joint SEAANZ and IIE Small Enterprise Conference*. Institute of Industrial Economics. University of Newcastle: New South Wales.

Godsell, G. (1991). Entrepreneurs embattled: barriers to entrepreneurship in South

Africa. In B. Berger (ed.) *The Culture of Entrepreneurship*, 85–98. California: ICS Press.

Goffee, R. and Scase, R. (1985). Proprietorial control in family firms: some functions of 'quasi-organic' management systems. *Journal of Management Studies*, **22**(1), 53–68.

Goffee, R. and Scase, R. (1995). *Corporate Realities: The Dynamics of Large and Small Organizations*. London: Routledge.

Goss, D. (1991). *Small Business and Society*. London: Routledge.

Government Gazette (1995). *White Paper on National Strategy for the Development and Promotion of Small Business in South Africa*. Cape Town: Notice No. 213 of 1995 of the Parliament of the Republic of South Africa.

Greenfield, S. M., Strickon, A., Aubey, R. T. and Rothstein, M. (1979). Studies in entrepreneurial behavior: a review and an introduction. In S. Greenfield, A. Strickon and R. Aubey (eds) *Entrepreneurs in Cultural Context*, 3–18. A School of American Research Book, University of New Mexico Press.

Haahti, A. J. (1987). *A Word on Theories of Entrepreneurship and Theories of Small Business Interface. A Few Comments*. Finland: Helsinki School of Economics, Working Papers F-170.

Haggett, P. (1983). *Geography, A Modern Synthesis*. New York: Harper Collins.

Hale, D. (1992). The Australian economy in the 1990s: can it adjust to free trade? *Economic Papers*, **11**(2).

Hall, E. (1959). *The Silent Language*. New York: Doubleday.

Hall, E. (1983). *The Dance of Life*. New York: Anchor Books.

Hammond, J. and Morrison, J. (1996). *The Stuff Americans are Made of*. New York: Macmillan.

Hampden-Turner, C. and Trompenaars, F. (1994). *The Seven Cultures of Capitalism*. New York: Doubleday.

Harisalo, R. (1988). *Uusi kapitalismi. Paikallinen yrittäjyyskulttuuri ja taloudellinen hyvinvointi*. Helsinki.

Heelas, P. and Morris, P. (1992). *The Values of the Enterprise Culture*. London: Routledge.

Heikkilä, K. (1979). *Freedom, Entrepreneurship, Future*. Suomen Yrittäjäin Keskusliitto r.y., Hämeenlinna, 129–36.

Hess, K. (1993). *Capitalism for Kids: Growing Up To Be Your Own Boss*. Chicago: Enterprise Publishing.

Hietala, K. (1987). *Yrittäjyyden edistäminen. Myyttejä, Mielikuvia, Asenneilmastoja*. Helsinki. Yliopistopaino.

Hills, G. E. (1988). Variations in university entrepreneurship education: an empirical study of an evolving field. *Journal of Business Venturing*, **3**(2), 109–122.

Hills, G. E. and Welsch, H. (1996). Entrepreneurial behavioral intentions and student independence, characteristics and experiences. *Frontiers of Entrepreneurship Research*. Wellesley, MA: Babson College Center for Entrepreneurial Studies.

Hine, D. and Kelly, S. (1996). Lapdogs or leaders? Small business role in the globalization of the Australian economy. In *Changing Business Relationships: Small Business growth and Other Challenges Proceedings of the joint SEAANZ and IIE Small Enterprise Conference*. Institute of Industrial Economics. University of Newcastle: New South Wales.

Hisrich, R. (1986). The woman entrepreneur: characteristics, skills, problems and prescriptions for success. In D. Sexton and R. Smilor (eds) *The Art and Science of Entrepreneurship*. Cambridge, MA: Ballinger Publishing Company.

Hofstede, G. (1980). *Culture's Consequences: International Differences in Work-related Values*. Beverley Hills: Sage Publications.

Hofstede, G. (1986). Cultural differences in teaching and learning. *International Journal of Intercultural Relations*, **10**, 301–320.

Hofstede, G. (1991). *Cultures and Organisations: Software of the Mind*. London: McGraw Hill.

Hofstede, G. (1994). Defining culture and its four dimensions. *European Forum for Management Development: Focus: Cross-cultural Management*. Forum 94/1: 4.

Hornaday, J. (1982). Research about living entrepreneurs. In C. Kent, A. Calvin, L. Donald, D. Sexton and K. Vesper (eds) *Encyclopaedia of Entrepreneurship*, 20–34. Englewood Cliffs: Prentice-Hall.

Hornaday, R. W. (1992). Thinking about entrepreneurship: a fuzzy set approach. *Journal of Small Business Management*, **30**(4), 12–23.

Hoselitz, B. F. (1951). The early history of entrepreneurial theory. *Explorations in Entrepreneurial Theory*, **3**, 193–220.

Human, L. (1984). *Freewheeling on the Fringes: The Chinese Community of South Africa*. Pretoria: UNISA Miscellanea.

Human, L. (1996). *Contemporary Conversations: Understanding and Managing Diversity in the Modern World*. Senegal: Goreè Institute.

Ilola, H. and Aho, S. (1988). *Lapin pienyritystoimintakokeilujen seurantatutkimus*. Oulun yliopisto. Pohjois-Suomen tutkimuslaitos. C 88. Oulu. Finland.

INEGI (1995). *Tomado del Periodico el Norte*. Datos del INEGI Mexico. 4 July, 13a.

Järvinen, K. (1948). *Entrepreneurial Mission Trough Times*. Jöderström OS akeyhtio, Turku.

Jennings, R., Cox, C. and Cooper, C. (1994). *Business Elites*. London: Routledge.

Johannisson, B. and Landström, H. (1996). University training for entrepreneurship. Paper presented at *IntEnt Conference*. 24–27 June. Arnhem.

Kao, R. W. (1994). From general management to entrepreneurship: the business ('B') school challenge. *Journal of Business Venturing,* Jan–Mar, 21–26.

Katila, S. (1991). *Maaseutuyrittäjien yrittäjyysmotivaatio*. Helsinki School of Economics Publications. M-52. Monisteita. Finland.

Kent, C. A. (ed.) (1984). The rediscovery of the entrepreneur. In *The Environment for Entrepreneurship*. Lexington: Lexington Books.

Kets de Vries, M. (1977). The entrepreneurial personality: a person at the crossroads, *Journal of Management Studies*, February, 34–37.

Kilby, P. (ed.) (1971). Hunting the heffalump. In *Entrepreneurship and Economic Development*, 1–40. New York: The Free Press.

Kirchhoff, B. A. (1991). Entrepreneurship's contribution to economics. *Entrepreneurship, Theory and Practice*, **16**(2), 93–112.

Kirzner, I. (1979). *Perception, Opportunity and Profit Studies in the Theory of Entrepreneurship*. Chicago: University of Chicago Press.

Kirzner, I. (1980). The primacy of entrepreneurial discovery. *The Prime Mover of Progress: The Entrepreneur in Capitalism and Socialism*. London: Institute of Economic Affairs.

Kolb, D., Rubn, I. and McIntyre, J (1984). *Organizational Psychology – An Experiential Approach*. Englewood Cliffs: Prentice-Hall.

Koopman, A. (1993). Transcultural management: in search of pragmatic humanism. In P. Christie, R. Lessem and L. Mbigi (eds) *African Management: Philosophies, Concepts and Applications*, 41–76. Johannesburg: Knowledge Resources.

Koskinen, A. (1986). *Starttiyrittäjät ja yritystoiminnan käynnistäminen*. Työvoimapoliittisia tutkimuksia Nr 66, Suunnitteluosasto, Työvoimaministeriö. Helsinki.

Koskinen, A. (1995). *Yrittäjyyden prosessin synty. Yrittäjien orientaatio ja uranvalinta*. Helsingin kauppakorkeakoulun Pienyrityskeskuksen julkaisuja M-73. Helsinki.

Koskinen, A. (1996). *Pienyritysten kehityskaaret ja areenat* Helsinki School of Economics Publications. A-116.

Kovaè, B. (1991). *Introduction to Entrepreneurship*. Ljubljana: University of Ljubljana.

Krueger, N. F. and Brazeal, D. V. (1994). Entrepreneurial potential and potential entrepreneurs. *Entrepreneurship: Theory and Practice*, **18**, 91–104.

Kuratko, D. F. and Welsch, H. (1994). *Entrepreneurial Strategy, Text and Cases*. Fort Worth: Dryden Press.

Law, L. G., Tan, L. A. and Wong, M. L. (1995). *How Small and Medium Enterprises Can Raise Finance*. Unpublished MBA Dissertation. Nanyang Business School, Nanyang Technological University: Singapore.

Lee, L. T. (1988). *Early Chinese Immigrant Societies: Case Studies from North America and British Southeast Asia*. Singapore: Heinemann (Asia).

Lee, T. Y. and Low, L. (1990). *Local Entrepreneurship in Singapore: Private and State*. Singapore: Singapore Institute of Policy Studies and Times Academic Press.

Lehmusto, M. (1987). *Aluepolitiikka ja teollisuusyritysten alueellinen liikkuvuus Suomessa*. Vaasan korkeakoulun julkaisuja. Tutkimuksia No 122. Maantiede 30. Vaasa.

Lessem, R. (1993). Four worlds: the Southern African business sphere. In P. Christie, R. Lessem and L. Mbigi (eds) *African Management: Philosophies, Concepts and Applications*, 17–40. Johannesburg: Knowledge Resources.

Maddi, S. R., Kobasa, S. C. and Hoover, M. (1979). An alienation text. *Journal of Humanistic Psychology*, **19**, 73–76.

Maddox, M. (1992). In the footsteps of MNCs. *Singapore Business*. July.

Mani, A. (1993). Indians in Singapore Society. In K. S. Sandhu and A. Mani (eds) *Indian Communities in Southeast Asia*. Singapore: Institute of Southeast Asian Studies.

McClelland, D. (1961). *The Achieving Society*. New York: Van Nostrand.

McClelland, D. (1987). Characteristics of successful entrepreneurs. *Journal of Creative Behavior*, **21**(3), 219–232.

McGrath, R. G., MacMillan, I. C., Yang, E. A. and Tsai, W. (1992). Does culture endure, or is it malleable? Issues for entrepreneurial economic development. *Journal of Business Venturing,* **7**(6), 441–458.

Mescon, T. S., Montanari, J. R., Tinker, T. (1981). The personalities of independent and franchise entrepreneurs: an empirical analysis of concepts. *Journal of Enterprise Management*, **3**(2), 149–162.

Ministry of Interior Affairs (1991a). *Aluepoliittisen selvitysmiehen väliraportti 21.3.1-991*. Sisäasiainministeriö. Kunta– ja aluekehitysosasto. Moniste 1.

Ministry of Interior Affairs (1991b). *Suomen alueellinen uusiutumisstrategia*. Aluepoliittinen selvitysmies Anssi Paasivirran ehdotus aluepolitiikan uudistamiseksi. Sisäasiainministeriö. Kunta– ja aluekehitysosasto. Moniste 18.

Ministry of Trade and Industry (1995). *Report of the Task Force on Institutional Reform for Productivity and Quality Improvements*. Singapore.

Monash University – SYNTEC Economic Services (1994). *Australian Economic Growth Forecasts*. Australia.

Morris, M. (1996). Dismissing myths, misunderstandings of entrepreneurship In *Business Day*, 22 April.

Morrison, A., Rimmington, M. and Williamson, C. (1998). *Entrepreneurship in the Hospitality, Tourism and Leisure Industries*. Oxford: Butterworth-Heinemann.

Musek, J. (1994). *Psychological Portrait of Slovenians*. Ljubljana: Centre for Science and Publicity.

Niittykangas, H. (1985). *Kehitysalueavustusten vaikutukset*. Jyväskylän yliopisto. Taloustieteen laitos. Keski–Suomen taloudellinen tutkimuskeskus. Julkaisuja 64/1985. Jyväskylä.

Niittykangas, H., Nenonen, T., Tervo, H. (1992). *Yritystoiminnan muuttuva toimintaympäristö ja 1990-luvun PK-politiikka*. Jyväskylän yliopisto. Keski-Suomen taloudellinen tutkimuskeskus. Julkaisuja 117. Jyväskylä.

Paasio, A. and Heinonen, J. (1993). *Perheyrittäjyys Suomessa*. Helsinki: SYKL, Tietosykli Oy.

Pearce, I. (1980) Reforms for entrepreneurs to serve public policy. In *The Prime Mover of Progress: The Entrepreneur in Capitalism and Socialism*. London: The Institute of Economic Affairs.

Plut, H. and Plut, T. (1995). *Entrepreneur and Entrepreneurship*. Ljubljana: Centre for Science and Publicity.

Pretorious, J. B. (1996). Perceptions and expectations on entrepreneurship courses – 1995. *Journal of Small Business and Entrepreneurship*, **13**(1), 72–78.

Rainnie, A. (1989). *Industrial Relations in Small Firms: Small Isn't Beautiful*. London: Routledge.

Ranasinghe, S. (1996). Entrepreneurship education and training in Sri Lanka: some reflections on past experience and future prospects. Paper presented at *IntEnt Conference*, 24–27 June, Arnhem.

Reid, G. and Jacobsen, L. (1988). *The Small Entrepreneurial Firm*. David Hume Institute. Aberdeen: University Press.

Reynolds, P. and Miller, B. (1992). New firm gestation: conception, birth, and implications for research. *Journal of Business Venturing*, **7**(5), 405–417.

Riehm, S. L. (1990). *Teenage Entrepreneur's Guide: 50 Money-making Business Ideas*. Surrey Books.

Rotter, J. B. (1966). Generalized expectancies for internal versus external control of reinforcement. *Psychological Monographs: General and Alied*, **80**(1), 1–12.

Ryan, C. (1996). Small business sceptical about new Act's effectiveness. In *Sunday Times Business Times*, 14 July, 11.

Sandhu, K. S. (1993). Indian immigration and settlement in Singapore. In K .S. Sandhu, and A. Mani (eds) *Indian Communities in Southeast Asia*. Singapore: Institute of Southeast Asian Studies.

Say, J. (1800). *A Treatise on Political Economy, or, the Production, Distribution and Consumption of Wealth*. Imprint 1964.

Scase, R. and Goffee, R. (1980). *The Real World of the Small Business Owner*. London: Croom Helm Ltd.

Schumpeter, J. A. (1934). The fundamental phenomenon of economic development. In P. Kilby (ed.) *Entrepreneurship and Economic Development* (1971), 43–70. New York: The Free Press.

Schumpeter, J. A. (1943). *Capitalism, Socialism and Democracy*, 6th edition (Counterpoint edition 1987). London: Unwin Paperbacks.

Schwartz, E. (1976). Entrepreneurship: a new female frontier. *Journal of Contemporary Business*, Winter, 47–76.

Scottish Enterprise National (1993). *Scotland's Business Birth Rate: A National Enquiry*. Glasgow: Scottish Enterprise.

Sexton, D. L. and Bowman-Upton, N. (1990). Female and male entrepreneurs: psychological characteristics and their role in gender-related discrimination. *Journal of Business Venturing*, **5**(1), 29–36.

Shapero, A. (1975). The displaced, uncomfortable entrepreneur. *Psychology Today*, 83–88.

Shapero, A. and Sokol, L. (1982). The social dimensions of entrepreneurship. In C. A. Kent, D. L. Sexton and K. H. Vesper (eds) *Encyclopaedia of Entrepreneurship*, 72–90. Englewood Cliffs: Prentice-Hall.

Shaver, K. G. and Scott, L. R. (1991). Person, process, choice: the psychology of new venture creation. *Entrepreneurship: Theory and Practice*, **16**(2), 23–45.

Singapore Economic Development Board (1989). *SME Master Plan*. Singapore.

Singapore Ministry of Trade and Industry (1986). *The Singapore Economy: New Directions*. Singapore.

Sit, V. F. S., Cremer, R. D. and Wong, S. L. (1991). *Entrepreneurs and Enterprises in Macau: A Study of Industrial Development*. Hong Kong: Hong Kong University Press and API Press.

Small Business Development Corporation. (1996). *Small Business in Western Australia – Fact Sheet December 1996*. Western Australia.

Small Business Development Corporation (1997). *Small Business in Western Australia – Information Sheet 1997*. Western Australia.

Smith, N. (1967). *The Entrepreneur and His Firm: The Relationship Between Type of Man and Type of Company*. Michigan: Michigan State University Press.

Stanworth, J. and Gray, C. (1991). *Bolton 20 Years On*. London: Paul Chapman.

Statistics Finland (1996). *Statistical Yearbook of Finland 1996*. Jyväskylä. Finland.

Statistics Finland (1997). *Enterprises 1996*. Finland.

Stevenson , H., Roberts, M. and Grousbeck, H. (1989). *New Business Ventures and the Entrepreneur*. Boston: Irwin.

Stincombe, A. (1965). Social Structure and organizations. In G. James (ed.) *Handbook of Organizations*, 153–193. Chicago: Rand McNally.

Supanov, J. (1970). Egalitarian rule and industrial attitudes. In *Naše teme*, **14**(2), 237–296.

Szczepanski. J. (1980). *Basic Concepts of Sociology*. Helsinki: Kansankulttuuri Oy.

Tan T. M., Tan W. L. and Young, J. E. (1994). A conceptualisation of the entrepreneurial infrastructure: the Case of Singapore. In *The Pursuit of Opportunity*, *Proceedings of the Fifth ENDEC World Conference on Entrepreneurship*, 76–84. Singapore.

Tan, T. M., Tan, W. L. and Young, J. E. (1997). The decision to participate in infrastructure networks: the Case of Singapore. In *Proceedings 42nd International*

Council for Small Business World Conference. June. San Francisco.

Tan, W. L. (1996). Assessing SME loan/financing proposals: academic prescriptions and practitioner approaches. In *Proceedings 41st International Council of Small Business Conference*. June. Stockholm.

Tan, W. L. and Begley, T. M. (1996). Entrepreneurship intention: a preliminary examination of the impact of cultural, economic and regulatory factors. In *Proceedings of the seventh ENDEC World Entrepreneurship Conference*. December. Singapore

Tan, W. L., Long, W. A. and Robinson, B. (1996). Entrepreneurship attitude orientation and the intention to start a business. *Journal of Small Business and Entrepreneurship*, **13**(4), 50–61.

Tan, W. L., Siew, L. K., Tan, W. H. and Wong, S. C. (1995). Entrepreneurial spirit among tertiary students in Singapore. *Journal of Enterprising Culture*, **3**(2), 211–227.

Tan, W. L., Zutshi, R., Allampalli, D. G. and Gibbons, P. (1997). Investment criteria of Singapore venture capitalists. In *Proceedings of the 42nd International Congress of Small Business World Conference*. June. San Francisco.

Tayeb, M. (1988). *Organizations and National Culture: A Comparative Analysis*. London: Sage.

Teo, S. and Lee, P. (1994). Awareness and utilisation of government assistance schemes among Singapore firms. In *Proceedings of the ENDEC World Conference on Entrepreneurship: The Pursuit of Opportunity*. Singapore. 172–182.

Tiihonen, J. and Virtanen, M. (1991). *Location decisions of firms using new technology*. Helsinki: Helsinki School of Economics and Business Administration. Discussion and Working Papers S-5.

Timmons, J. (1978). Characteristics and role demands of entrepreneurship. *American Journal of Small Business*, **3**(1), 5–17.

Timmons, J. (1994). *New Venture Creation*. Boston: Irwin.

Timmons, J., Smollen, L. E. and Dingee, A. L. (1990). *New Venture Creation*. Illinois: Homewood.

Trompenaars, F. (1993). *Riding the Waves of Culture*. London: The Economist Books.

Ukkonen, R. (1987). *Starttiyritysten seuranta. Starttiyritysten kehitys starttirahoituksen päättymisen jälkeen*. Mikkelin läänin työvoimapiirin julkaisu Nro 32. Mikkeli.

Vartiainen, H. J. (1982). *Uusien työpaikkojen luominen*. Työvoimaministeriö. Suunnitteluosasto. Työvoimapoliittisia tutkimuksia Nro 34. Helsinki.

Vesikansa, J. (1979). Sata vuotta yrittäjänvapautta. Markkinavoimat mursivat pykäläpadot. In *Vapaus, Yrittäjyys, Tulevaisuus*. Suomen Yrittäjäin Keskusliitto r.y., Hämeenlinna.

Vesper, K. H. (1993). *Entrepreneurship Education*. Washington: Washington Entrepreneurial Studies Center.

Vesper, K. H. and McMullan, W. E. (1988). Entrepreneurship: today courses, tomorrow degrees? *Entrepreneurship Theory and Practice*, **12**(3), 7–13.

Virtanen, M. (1991). *Regional Technology Policy Programs*. Helsinki: Helsinki School of Economics and Business Administration. Discussion and Working Papers S-1.

Virtanen, M. (1996). *Entrepreneurial Finance and Venture Capital Advantage*. Helsinki: Helsinki School of Economics Publications, A–113.

Weber, M. (1976). *The Protestant Ethic and the Spirit of Capitalism*. London: Allen and Unwin.

Welsch, H. and Gundry, L. (1993). Differences in familial influence in women-owned businesses. *Proceedings of the United States Association for Small Business and Entrepreneurship Conference*. Baltimore.

Wilken, P. (1979). *Entrepreneurship: A Comparative and Historical Study*. Norwood: Ablex.

Williams, O. (1992) *Identifying the Nature and Causes of Skill Deficiencies in Small Enterprises*. SEAANZ.

Wilmshurst, T. and Whitfield, D. (1996). Total quality management in small business: small business saviour? In *Changing Business Relationships: Small Business growth and Other Challenges Proceedings of the joint SEAANZ and IIE Small Enterprise Conference*. Institute of Industrial Economics. University of Newcastle: New South Wales.

Wiltshire, F. M., (1971). Report of the Committee on Small Business. *Parliamentary Papers*. **82**. Australia.

Wingham, D. (1997). *A Review of Business Perceptions in Start-up Business: A Single Industry Longitudinal Study Phase 1*. Unpublished.

Wingham, D. and Newby. R. (1993). Performance in small business terms: a conceptual schema. *38th World Conference: International Council for Small Business*. June. Las Vegas.

Wong, S. Y, Wong, C. L. Y., Kwan, R. Y. K. and Gansham, V. C. (1994). A conceptual model for depicting the relationship between entrepreneurship and the environmental factors in Singapore. *Journal of Enterprising Culture*, **1**(3 and 4), 449–472.

World Bank (1993). *The East Asian Miracle*. Washington: Oxford University Press.

Yu, T. F. L. (1995). *Adaptive Response: Entrepreneurship and Economic Development in Hong Kong*. Unpublished PhD thesis. University of New South Wales, Canberra, Australia.

Index